Dependence and Disillusionment

Dependence and Disillusionment

Emergence of National Consciousness in Later Nineteenth Century India

Second Edition

Sudhir Chandra

OXFORD
UNIVERSITY PRESS

OXFORD
UNIVERSITY PRESS

YMCA Library Building, Jai Singh Road, New Delhi 110 001

Oxford University Press is a department of the University of Oxford. It furthers the
University's objective of excellence in research, scholarship, and education
by publishing worldwide in

Oxford   New York
Auckland   Cape Town   Dar es Salaam   Hong Kong   Karachi   Kuala Lumpur   Madrid
Melbourne   Mexico City   Nairobi   New Delhi   Shanghai   Taipei   Toronto

With offices in
Argentina   Austria   Brazil   Chile   Czech Republic   France   Greece   Guatemala
Hungary   Italy   Japan   Poland   Portugal   Singapore   South Korea   Switzerland
Thailand   Turkey   Ukraine   Vietnam

Oxford is a registered trademark of Oxford University Press
in the UK and in certain other countries

Published in India
by Oxford University Press, New Delhi

First published in1975 by Manas Publications
This edition published by Oxford University Press 2011

ISBN-13: 978-0-19-807162-4
ISBN-10: 0-19-807162-0

Printed in India at Repro India Ltd., Navi Mumbai
Published by Oxford University Press
YMCA Library Building, Jai Singh Road, New Delhi 110 001

For
Professor V.N. Datta
My Guru

Preface to the Second Edition

Dependence and Disillusionment: Emergence of National Consciousness in Later Nineteenth Century India first came out in 1975. It was published by a dreamer, a poets' poet and a personal friend. He had an impulse to start a publishing house, and I was among the friends whose manuscripts he obtained for publication. His venture soon crashed for reasons beyond his control, and my maiden book simply faded out.

The Oxford University Press (OUP) has agreed to revive that still-born book. The readers will judge how relevant it still is to the growing historiography of Indian nationalism and to the fraught question of nationalism. But for some typos, the 1975 text has been left untouched.

The book owes much to two academic institutions. The first is the Indian Institute of Advanced Study, in the grand sylvan surroundings of which much of the book was written. The other is the Institut d'Etudes Avancees de Nantes, in France. Situated on the confluence of the majestic Loire and Erdre, the Nantes Institute has been an ideal place for preparing the 'Introduction' to the present edition. To both the distinguished institutions I wish to express my gratitude.

But for Geetanjali Shree's insistence, I would not have thought of a new lease of life for the book. Nor would I have so clearly grasped some of the things the 'Introduction' seeks to express. In writing the 'Introduction' I have received invaluable help from Constance Cournede, Pankhuree Dube, Raj Kumar Hans, and Sanjay Seth. To them I am beholden. I am also thankful to the editorial team at OUP for their unfailing courtesy and help.

Nantes   Sudhir Chandra
3 December 2010

Preface

This monograph seeks to outline the situation in which national consciousness emerged in India during the quarter of a century between 1858 and 1885. Producing a new kind of community orientation, this consciousness cut across traditional solidarities and loyalties even as it was influenced by them. Representing the coalescence of material interests, it was helped into being by a two-fold process: progressive realisation of a fundamental dichotomy between what came to be viewed as Indian and British interests; and rationalisation of narrow group interests as national interests. The situation thus carried within it a basic contradiction in so far as the very forces that facilitated the emergence of national consciousness also tended to discompose it.

Against the background of the multiple legacy of 1857, attention is focused on such significant issues as taxation and expenditure, famine, 'drain', *swadeshi*, racialism, employment of Indians and the freedom of expression in order to trace the interaction between official policies and Indian reactions. This is done because for understanding any group consciousness the image of reality on the minds of men is as important as the reality itself. This interaction not only reveals the continuing clash between the rulers and the ruled with their basically opposite aims and ways of thinking; it also accounts, in a large measure, for the division of interests and tussle for leadership within Indian society.

Those familiar with the historiography of the emergence of Indian nationalism would know that the two main approaches that have been adopted so far attempt to explain the phenomenon in terms of either caste or material interests. I think that they explain only a part of the reality. I have attempted a less constrictive approach in order to be able to account for a state of affairs where conservatism enabled Indians to change and yet stick to their traditions.

I have done this by taking into account the social motivation provided by perceived material self-interest on the one hand and, on the other, by the response pattern operating within the traditional social anastomosis. For studying the impact of traditional solidarities I have selected the religio-cultural units. How far I have succeeded is for the readers to judge.

While it has not been possible for me to stick to modern spellings in every case, even in cases where I have done so, the original spellings have been retained in footnotes. For example, Surendranath Banerji is invariably spelt as S. N. Banerjea when reference is made to his works. I have also dispensed with the formality of attaching a bibliography at the end of the book because those who care for references may see the foot-notes. All the private papers and official files referred to in the book were consulted at the National Archives of India.

This study is based chiefly on primary sources which I could consult through the kindness of the authorities and staff of the National Archives of India, and the Nehru Memorial Library, New Delhi, the National Library, the Indian Association and the British Indian Association, Calcutta, the Bombay Asiatic Society, the Cama Institute, and the Bombay Presidency Association, Bombay, and the Servants of India Society Library, Poona. To them I offer my thanks. I also thank the Kurukshetra University for permission to publish my doctoral dissertation of which this monograph is a revised version.

I am grateful to Prof. V. N. Datta, my supervisor, and to Prof. M. Mujeeb for their generous and valuable guidance. I am also grateful to Prof. N. R. Phatak, Shri B. N. Phatak, Prof. S. C. Dube and Rajendra Prasad for their suggestions and criticisms. Shri L. D. Ajmani, Q. A. Siddiqi and Sundaram extended ungrudging help for which I thank them. And a very special word of thanks to my friend L. Dewani; so also to Kamlesh, N. K. Dixit and Mrs. Seema Mukherjee.

As for my emotional debts, they are too precious to be mentioned. I shall ever cherish them. I know I can never repay them.

I am only too conscious of the defects of this work, not the least of which is the uncouthness of my style.

Sudhir Chandra

E-362 Greater Kailash I
New Delhi 110048

CONTENTS

Introduction
Understanding Indian Nationalism

More than eighty years ago Carlton J.H. Hayes began his *Essays on Nationalism* (1926) with the question: 'What is nationalism?' He admitted in answer:

> Peculiar difficulties confront the student who essays to deal with the impressive and vital phenomenon of nationalism. There has been, especially of late, a good deal of 'popular' writing on various aspects of it, and several scholarly treatises have recently dealt with its history among particular peoples, but no profound systematic treatment of the whole subject—the nature and history of patriotism, nationality and nationalism—exists in any language…. Small wonder that publicists have bungled and professors have been afraid! Lacking scientific investigation and scholarly analysis, the phenomenon appears vague, intangible and mysterious. There is no agreement as to precisely what it is or as to whether it is good or bad, transitory or eternal.[1]

Writing seventy years after Hayes—and an avalanche of writing on the question of nationalism that is unlikely to abate soon—Benedict Anderson needed to make a similar admission:

> Nation, nationality, nationalism—all have proved notoriously difficult to define, let alone to analyse. In contrast to the immense influence that nationalism has exerted on the modern world, plausible theory about it is conspicuously meager. Hugh Seton-Watson, author of far the best and most comprehensive English-language text on nationalism, and heir to a vast tradition of liberal historiography and social science, sadly observes: 'Thus I am *driven* to the conclusion that no "scientific definition" of the

1. Carlton J.H. Hayes, Essays on Nationalism, New York, 1926, p. 2.

nation can be devised; yet the phenomenon has existed and exists.'
Tom Nairn, author of the path-breaking *The Break-up of Britain,* and
heir to the scarcely less vast tradition of Marxist historiography and
social science, candidly remarks: 'The theory of nationalism represents
Marxism's great historical failure.'[2] (Emphasis in the original)

Meanwhile, including Anderson's own 'tentative suggestions' in his otherwise
path-breaking study, attempts have continued to be made to define nationalism
and fit the elusive and mercurial phenomenon into various theoretically, ideo-
logically or politically inspired procrustean moulds. Scholars inclined towards
order and clarity have laboured to provide their own meaning, framework or
typology to give nationalism some semantic stability, and distinguish it from
what is *not* nationalism. Besides unceasing scholarly interventions, specific
claims and contrary counter-claims have continued to be made by political
contestants over what is and what is *not* nationalism. And, invariably, both the
claims and the counter-claims are clothed in appropriate theoretical-ideological
terms. Indeed, given the intense passions that, more often than not, impregnate
the politics of nationalism in specific contexts, the distinction between professors and publicists gets blurred. Passions beguile even general, ostensibly
abstract, discussions of the subject.

　　Hayes' distinction between the publicist and the professor was not very
apt even when it was made. It is less so now. Publicists, of course, continue
to bungle as before, while some professors do retain the old healthy fear. But
many more professors are now busy bungling blissfully. Since nationalism still
is the primary principle of political arrangement, professors and publicists are
both born into nationalism. They, too, have their consciousness determined by
nationalism in ways of which they are not always and entirely conscious; even
those who consciously turn their backs upon it. Critiquing nationalism can be
as deeply rooted in personal passions as celebrating it.

　　All scholarship, ideally, should be self-reflexive. But, considering the near
certainty of one's personal affective involvement in the study of nationalism,
especially of the nationalism into which one is born, self-reflexivity is a sine
qua non for studying nationalism. One must keep examining one's mode of
examination. I do not remember having possessed such awareness when I
embarked as a young researcher on the project that eventuated in *Dependence
and Disillusionment.* That was during the early 1960s, just a decade and a
half into national freedom. Jawaharlal Nehru was alive, though the Chinese

2.　Benedict Anderson, *Imagined Communities: Reflections on the Origin and Spread of National-
　　ism,* 1983, revised edition, London, 1991, p. 3.

invasion had damaged his aura and hurt the nation's pride. My guiding impulse
was patriotism. Moving from the aftermath of 1857 on to the eve of the Indian
National Congress, the project was designed to understand the larger social
anastomosis in which national consciousness had emerged in India. However,
the book that ten years of research produced was not enthused by nationalism.
Not very characteristically for that time, but anticipating a change that would
soon gather momentum, it questioned the nationalist understanding of Indian
nationalism. Indeed, the word 'disillusionment' in the book's title intimates more
than the tragic later nineteenth century predicament which forced educated
Indians to depend on British rule even after they had lost faith in it. It intimates
also disenchantment with Indian nationalism and with nationalism in general.

It is worth recalling how this marked shift came about. In certain specific
details it may be autobiographical. But it also constitutes one narrative—there
can be others as well—of the changing historiography of Indian nationalism.
When the patriotically inspired project leading to the apatriotic *Dependence
and Disillusionment* commenced, the dominant Indian historiography of Indian
nationalism was nationalist. It was celebratory and it accepted as sacrosanct
the unity of India, which it explained variously in geographical, cultural and
historical terms. Indian nationalism, in that historiography, was but a modern
manifestation of that underlying unity. This historiography assumed and
promoted the pre-givenness of Indian unity. Its celebratory historiography
was not unique to Indian nationalism. All specific nationalisms develop, and
are sustained by, their own celebratory and unquestioning self-projection;
unquestioning in having their autonomous existence accepted as axiomatic
and inviolable by their followers. Thus, whatever the differences among the
believers about conceptualising it, Indian nationalism is *nationalism*. Pakistani
nationalism is *not*. That is Muslim *communalism/separatism*. Pakistan is
not—cannot in the Indian nationalist understanding be—the fruition of a rival
nationalism.

For nationalism to exist, there must exist a countervailing *other*(s).
Indian nationalism, as it took shape in the nineteenth century and later, viewed
itself as pitted against two prominent 'others': imperialism and 'communalism'.
However, there was a crucial difference in its mode of relating to those two
'others'. 'Communalism' was, and still is, a quintessential 'other'. It was, and
continues to be, clearly and categorically demonised. In fact, giving the word
a slant unknown to the English language, the Indian nationalist understanding
has invested communalism with an infallible pejorative connotation.

In relation to imperialism, ironically, Indian nationalism has always been
deeply ambivalent. The ambivalence lies in the recognition of the ruinously
exploitative aspect of British rule and at the same time appreciation of the gains

Understanding Indian Nationalism

that accrued from it. I was, of course, oblivious of this ambivalence within me at the time of undertaking my research project. It did not, then, seem odd that the patriotic impulse, which wished to recall the stirring but neglected nascence of Indian nationalism, accepted a valorised view of British rule. From a very early stage the beneficiaries of English education in India had had their consciousness impregnated with the belief that their country's all-round modernisation—from which arose nationalism—was in many ways a gift of British rule. So pervasive and naturally entertained was this belief that it was shared even by those who projected the idea of Indian nationalism back onto a deep past. If Indian nationalism took birth within such an ambivalent consciousness, so did the nationalist Indian historiography. It, too, tended to be similarly ambivalent. It was as one who had imbibed that historiography—including its differential attitudes towards 'communalism' and imperialism—that I began my research.

In keeping with its underlying ambivalence, the nationalist Indian histori-ography, like Indian nationalism from the outset, was unsparing in its economic critique of imperialism. However, it was fixated on a primary contradiction, the contradiction between what it saw as Indian/national and British/imperial in-terests. There was little appreciation of the problem of the relationship between supposedly national and a variety of other interests within the Indian society. A striking illustration of this is Bipan Chandra's *Rise and Growth of Economic Nationalism in India*.[3] Hailed as a tour de force when it came out and for years thereafter, this exhaustive study by a leading Marxist historian is actually a masterpiece of nationalist historiography. Carrying on in independent India the *expose* of the exploitative aspect of British rule which the pioneers of so-called economic nationalism had begun in the nineteenth century, Bipan Chandra refined and evidentially enriched R.C. Dutt's nationalist classic, *Economic History of India*.[4] There was no attempt to balance, let alone critique, the nation-alist perspective by analysing internal contradictions within the Indian society, something that a Marxist scholar should habitually have essayed.

Also, in consonance with the stereotypical nationalist understanding, Bipan Chandra looked upon 'communalism'—in contradistinction to Indian nationalism—as false consciousness. Three years after *Rise and Growth of Economic Nationalism*, he and two other Marxist historians—Romila Thapar and Harbans Mukhia—published *Communalism and the Writing of Indian History*.[5] Designed as a concerted historiographic intervention, this collection of three articles was meant to give a new direction to the writing of Indian history. However, having uncritically accepted the valorisation of Indian nationalism,

---

3.   Bipan Chandra, *Rise and Growth of Economic Nationalism in India*, Delhi, 1966.
4.   R.C. Dutt, *Economic History of India*, 2 vols, London, 1902 and 1904.
5.   Bipan Chandra, Romila Thapar and Harbans Mukhia, *Communalism and the Writing of Indian History*, Delhi, 1969.

the three historians could not even conceive of the possibility that Indian nationalism itself could, from a critical perspective, justifiably be described as false consciousness.

The most elaborate nationalist account of the early growth and development of Indian nationalism was S.R. Mehrotra's *The Emergence of the Indian National Congress*.[6] Gathering unprecedented wealth of details relating to various political associations, it charted the growth of nationalist politics in nineteenth-century India. It had little concern with the larger society within which the nationalist politics was unfolding, or with what kind of comprehensive changes that society was undergoing. This was, typically for those days, the case also with B.B. Majumdar's *Indian Political Associations and Reform of Legislature*, another important, though less comprehensive, nationalist account of organised Indian political activity during much the same period (and a little beyond) which had come out prior to Chandra and Mehrotra.[7]

Precisely when the nationalist historiography seemed to reign supreme within the Indian academia, a very different, unglamorous projection of Indian nationalism started emerging from England. Appearing with a bang through Anil Seal's *The Emergence of Indian Nationalism*, it severely damaged the self-image of Indian nationalism.[8] Seal's was not a solitary foray. He had equally gifted collaborators. The provisional result of their work was published in 1973 in a special issue of *Modern Asian Studies* and in book form the same year, from the Cambridge University Press. What this Cambridge historiography meant is summarized in Seal's imperious introductory declaration:

> Among the dominant themes of world history during the nineteenth and twentieth centuries have been the imperialism of the west and the nationalism of its colonial subjects. Nowhere were these theories developed more spectacularly than in South Asia; its history naturally came to be viewed as a gigantic clash between these two large forces....
>
> These assumptions were convenient, but historians of colony after colony have knocked them down. The emphasis has shifted from the elegant exchanges between London and colonial capitals to the *brutal clashes between colonial politicians* struggling at the more humdrum levels *where the pickings lay*.[9] (Emphases added.)

6. S.R. Mehrotra, *The Emergence of the Indian National Congress,* Delhi, 1971.
7. B.B. Majumdar, *Indian Political Associations and Reform of Legislature (1818-1917),* Calcutta, 1965.
8. Anil Seal, *The Emergence of Indian Nationalism: Competition and Collaboration in the Later Nineteenth Century,* Cambridge, 1968.
9. John Gallagher, Gordon Johnson and Anil Seal (eds), *Locality, Province and Nation: Essays on Indian Politics, 1870 to 1940,* Cambridge, 1973, p. 1.

The hubris of this language is revealing. There is no distanciation from the object of analysis. For, there is no distanciation from the self. The Cambridge group, whatever their internal differences in matters of details, shares a certain understanding of the relationship between the colonisers and the colonised. Of the exclusive veracity of that understanding they are convinced. This, noticeably, happens at a time when the process of decolonisation is still on. Even where decolonisation is formally over, like in the Indian subcontinent, serious historiographic enquiry has just about begun. Yet, the smug assertion is made that 'historians of colony after colony have knocked down' the old errors, and shown the truth.

A virtual semiotic war was, then, waging among rival historiographic certainties. Those were fecund and fractious years for the study of nationalism in the Indo-Pak subcontinent. Not surprisingly, those years saw also the first fruits of Pakistani scholars' efforts to create their own nationalist historiography. They needed to counter not just politically, which Pakistan in any case had done by coming into being, but academically Indian nationalism's suzerain claim to be the sole authentic nationalism for the entire Indo-Pak subcontinent.[10]

I

Those were exciting years. The nationalist Indian historiography dominated the academic scene in the country. But it was being shaken by competing historiographies. The challenge for an aspiring entrant into the warring discursive field was to grapple with all and refuse to be simply derivative or reactive. It was during those early years of my research, that my patriotic view of Indian nationalism started turning critical. The critical turn, though, was produced by more than being faced with warring viewpoints. It was set in motion as soon as I began delving into later nineteenth century newspapers, periodicals and records of political associations. The gradual discovery of what lay buried there revealed details that confirmed what my patriotic imagination had anticipated. But it also revealed ugly marks on the attractive visage of Indian nationalism that I had not apprehended.

The critical turn had, thus, begun a little before encountering historiographic rivalries. Once that encounter began, what proved personally most liberating was the nationalist Pakistani perspective. It acted like a revelation and the revelation came through Aziz. His declaratory sub-title, *A Study in Nationalism*, was followed by his inaugural sentence: 'This book deals with *Muslim nationalism* in Imperial India.' (Emphasis mine) The natural reaction

---

10.   Worth mentioning in this context is K.K. Aziz, *The Making of Pakistan: A Study in Nationalism,* London, 1967 and Khalid B. Sayeed, *The Political System of Pakistan,* London, 1967.

for one steeped in the Indian nationalist self-understanding, like I then was, would have been to reject Aziz's as a partisan attempt to academically bolster up the 'false' two-nation theory. Instead, as I read through the book, I discovered and in the act of discovery felt freed from an inherited blindness of which I had had no awareness.

It will, perhaps, make more sense if I conveyed, without further vitiating it with hindsight, an idea of what *The Making of Pakistan* did to me then. I shall do that by citing from an unsolicited review, my first ever, that I felt impelled to write of the book:

> Nationalism in its ultimate analysis is an abstract notion. It becomes an irresistible force with the help of various factors which gradually inject a sense of emotional unity among otherwise scattered individuals and groups. This transformation may appear artificial or genuine depending on the angle from which it is viewed. But the selection of an angle is a subjective process which is influenced mostly by the sub-conscious mind in spite of the volitional exercise of intellectual honesty. Thus, while for most of us in India the growth of Indian nationalism has been a noble and natural development, the emergence of a separate consciousness among the Muslims has been attributed to the machinations of a sinister imperialism and of self-seeking individuals. Pakistan, in other words, is not regarded as the consummation of an organic Muslim nationalism but as the outgrowth of communalism.
>
> *The Making of Pakistan* enables us to realise that our approach to the national movement in general and to Partition in particular has been wistful. It provides us with the essential dimension of empathy without which no historical understanding is possible. Itself biased to an extent, it nevertheless exposes our own bias.[11]

Cambridge historiography did nothing so dramatic. It alerted me, though, against reducing nationalism to politics, then explaining politics in terms of interests, and end up believing that nationalism, already reduced to politics, is ipso facto explained in terms of interests alone. It showed the excesses into which a narrow conceptualisation of complex phenomena like nationalism and politics can lead. The nationalist Indian historiography, too, had been engaged primarily with high nationalist politics. But, betraying a different kind of excess, it had overlooked interests, and seen in nationalist politics but the flowering of noble ideals.

11. 'The Partition in Perspective', *Economic and Political Weekly*, vol. 3, no. 22, 1 June 1968, pp. 837–38.

The critical turn in my understanding of Indian nationalism was not a result of reading alone. There also operated, as it invariably does, a kind of symbiosis between researching the past and experiencing the present. However, except by way of a generalised account of salient contemporary developments—a kind of sociology of historiography—academic discourse rarely records the individual's existential experience of those developments. But individual experience may diverge, in certain respects radically, from the general trend. Besides, if self-reflexivity is crucial for studying nationalism, academic discourse must allow room for personal experience.

Just when research was revealing warts on the fair face of nationalism, the Indo-Pakistan war of 1965 broke out. In an instant the country was seized by chauvinistic hysteria and illustrious pacifists like Vinoba Bhave and Jaya Prakash Narayan were blessing the Indian war effort. It is likely that, but for the incipient critical turn in my understanding of Indian nationalism, I would have been similarly seized. Instead, I was on a different trail. As a student of history I knew that contemporaries could never know the real causes of a war. Yet, it was difficult to avoid a particular suspicion. We in India had come to believe that the dictators in Pakistan tended to whip up anti-India hysteria whenever they needed to divert their people's attention from pressing domestic problems. This time even the Indian government under Lal Bahadur Shastri had been very shaky for a while. Could it not have been similarly tempted?

The *magic* of nationalism was gone. Its residual hold remained, ready for further erosion. That came with another war in 1971. This was the war that dismembered Pakistan and created Bangladesh. Other aspects of its euphoric reception apart, the war was seen in India as having belied the two-nation theory. History, it began to be argued, had in less than two and a half decades demonstrated the falsity of Pakistan's claim to be a nation. But no scepticism was expressed about Bangladesh's basis to be an independent nation. Nor was it realised that the birth of Bangladesh may have belied the two-nation theory, but it had not affirmed the rival claim that India was one nation. If anything, it was pointing to a multi-nation theory for the subcontinent. As a reminder against wishful readings of the present may be recalled the following argument put forward by so sober and balanced a scholar as Sayeed for the continuing unity of Pakistan. Even as he documented the widespread resentment felt in East Pakistan towards West Pakistan, he discerned in 'fear of India', 'hope for the unity of the country'.[12] Sayeed could not have imagined that he would within four years be witness to East Pakistan becoming an independent nation with help from the same dreaded India.

---

12. Sayeed, *The Political System of Pakistan*, pp. 208–09.

As a guide for the future, the present is like an oracle. Even as it predicts the future, every oracle carries signs that elude comprehension. Invariably it is a missed sign that brings in disaster. For all its bare visibility, the present keeps something of itself hidden. It is never, like the oracle, what humans take it to be.

These were valuable lessons. One such lesson came in 1968 with the Prague Spring and its promise of socialism with a human face. The Soviets crushed it brutally. One could reasonably have expected that, whatever political compulsions some people offered in defence of the Soviet action, they would at least recognise its brutality. That was naïve. Many intelligent and otherwise sensitive people saw no brutality and it could in no way be rendered visible for them. This experience was replicated right then at home. The Naxalite movement suddenly hit the headlines. The average middle-class Indian reacted to it with horror and the mainstream Marxists castigated it as adventurism. The Indian State came down upon the Naxalite youth with a ferocity that did not scruple to use extra-constitutional violence. Again, no argument was possible.

An abiding lesson followed. The image of reality is in human affairs more important than the reality. Indeed, the image is integral to the reality. Even where the two can be meaningfully separated, the historian's job is not so much to separate, as to illuminate the dynamic interaction between the image(s) and the reality.

None of the warring metanarratives—the Indian nationalist, the Cambridge neo-imperialist, and the Pakistani nationalist—was wrong. They each had their characteristic blind spots, a resistance to looking into themselves. They were fixated on their own particular image of nationalism. In the neo-imperialist reckoning, nationalism was about base material interests, about a 'brutal' scramble for the 'pickings'. In the nationalist saga it was all about idealism and sacrifice. How was the many-sided complexity of nationalism to be comprehended?

Intellectual-emotional deliverance from unselfconscious patriotism prompted an alternative understanding of nationalism. (One can never be certain if this deliverance is complete. It never, perhaps, is.) With a youthful overweeningness that now embarrasses, I broadcast the emerging alternative in the *Economic and Political Weekly*, the natural habitat then for academic debates. Declaring that nationalism was not sacrosanct, and the historian's supreme allegiance was not to the nation, but to knowing, the article asseverated:

Nationalism is essentially a subjective phenomenon which, aided by certain objective conditions, inspires an increasing number of people in a given society and progressively becomes a powerful force. It comes into existence through a complex working of the corporate consciousness at both the conscious and the unconscious planes, and represents the egotism of the more powerful and articulate sections in that society. The base whose material interests are served by nationalism is narrower than the base which is only emotionally stirred by it. But those standing at the latter base also tend to awaken gradually to their own interests. The ensuing tussle takes different forms, and proportionately as more and more sections get a better deal, the material base of nationalism enlarges. Meanwhile those who control the leverage and appropriate the fruits of nationalism try to contain, by emotionally charging, those who are aspiring for a better life within the nation state. The state so gears its system of education as to instill into young impressionable minds values that are calculated to facilitate the maintenance of the status quo. The chief of these values are respect for order, obedience to the authority of the state and patriotism. History performs none too insignificant a role in the exercise of power through a subtle manipulation of thought processes. It is utilised, as a discipline, to perpetuate a highly selective corporate memory aimed at producing a conservative bias.[13]

The asseveration, for all its anarchic drift, was formulaic. It carried unmistakable marks of disenchantment with nationalism. But the disenchantment was about what nationalism had grown to be. It was, in other words, a product primarily of the experience of nationalism in the present. It may, though, have also been vaguely influenced by the strong scholarly indictment of nationalism which, beginning with Hayes in 1926, had found its most forceful expression in Elie Kedourie's *Nationalism*.[14] Even after showing how nationalism, in history, had been a source of 'war or militarism or intolerance', Hayes had hesitated to pronounce an unqualified verdict of 'Evil'. Thinking of some unknowable future, he had conceded, 'Grant that there is a rampant, blatant nationalism which produces evil fruitage and which is a curse, and it will gladly be conceded that there may be a sweet amiable nationalism which will bring forth good fruit in abundance and will be to all men a solace and a blessing.'[15] But Kedourie was ready for no illusions. His was a sustained and unmitigated condemnation of nationalism.

However, the general intellectual climate in the West, from where came most of our theoretical generalizations, was not entirely hostile to the idea of nationalism. It was also, theoretically, presented as a positive force. A most influential defence of nationalism, portraying it as a positive manifestation of liberalism in the modern West, was Hans Kohn's *The Idea of Nationalism* (1944).[16]

---

13. Sudhir Chandra, 'History and Nationalism: A Personal Response to the Indian Situation', *Economic and Political Weekly*, 8 September 1973, vol, 8, no. 36, pp. 1623–25.
14. See Elie Kedourie, *Nationalism*, Oxford, 2000 (fourth, expanded edition).
15. Hayes, *Essays on Nationalism*, p. 246.
16. See Hans Kohn, *The Idea of Nationalism: A Study in its Origins and Background*, New Brunswick, New Jersey, 2008.

The projection of nationalism as a liberal force carried a special appeal for the Indian nationalist narrative. What further added to that appeal was the distinction made there between civic and ethnic nationalism. It came close to corresponding to the Indian nationalist contradistinction between nationalism and communalism. Even in relation to the larger understanding of nationalism as a historical phenomenon, then, the atmosphere was no less fractious. But that was Nehruvian India. There nationalism as an ideology had not lost its utopian appeal. That was certainly true of the intelligentsia north of the Vindhyas. Kohn, rather than Hayes, let alone Kedourie, was the one to resonate within them.

II

This, then, was the changing background to the making of Dependence and Disillusionment. This explains how, when finally done in 1975, the book could with nonchalant even-handedness detail the instrumental seamy aspects of early Indian nationalism and also its organic exhilarating aspects. It did that within a fairly wide perspective, offering a close but comprehensive social, economic and political view of the wider context in which Indian nationalism emerged. The book was not a triumphal portrayal of Indian nationalism, which it could not have been as the handiwork of a patriot-turned-sceptic. Nor was it an unqualified indictment, which it could easily have been in the wake of my trenchant piece on 'History and Nationalism'.[17]

Research had revealed both the beauty and the ugliness of nationalism. Its face had ugly warts. But it was beautiful too. The challenge was to show the warts and yet retain the beauty of the face. To realise that none of the diametrically opposed positions about nationalism—neither the nationalist nor the imperialist, neither Kohn nor Kedourie—was wrong. They were only misleading. Further, after experiencing the hideousness of nationalism in the present, the challenge was also to realise that a *beginning* need not be the same as its end. History, in any case, is a diachronic discipline. It studies process, movement, change, even as it recognises the reality of continuity. The very idea of change, and of evaluating change as good or bad, desirable or undesirable, necessary or unnecessary, is denied if every beginning is necessarily seen in the image of later developments. Seen that way, all diachrony would mean mere teleology, historical determinism.

That, moreover, implies a Manichean insistence on seeing things in either-or terms. Things, in that scheme, can only be either this or that. They cannot be both this and that. That is not life, which is the stuff of history. In life opposites operate in inextricable fusion. One of my preferred lessons in history-writing comes from Dostoyevsky, the master painter of the human condition.

17.   'History and Nationalism', *Economic and Political Weekly,* cited before.

In the opening pages of *The Brothers Karamazov*, Dostoyevsky describes the reaction of Fyodor Pavlovich Karamazov to the news of his estranged wife's death in the following way: '... the story is that he ran out into the street and began shouting with joy... but others say he wept without restraint like a child.... It is quite possible that both versions were true.' The possibility—near certainty—of mutually irreconcilable versions being true is what the historian should learn to discern and describe.

The nationalism *Dependence and Disillusionment* describes is a split phenomenon, and the world in which it takes birth is a world of fluid contrariety. It is a world that does not correspond to the neat binary sets of categories such as liberal/conservative, reformer/revivalist, secular/communal, nationalist/communalist, and so on, in terms of which most of us think and make sense of the world around us. The book, rather, seeks to depict the working out of that multi-faceted contrariety, paradox, in different spheres of life. Beginning with 'The Legacy of 1857', and focusing on both the rulers and the ruled, it shows how they felt pulled in opposite directions. In the very year with which this book begins, the contrariety of the situation was articulated with prophetic clarity by Lord Stanley, the then Secretary of State for India in the following words:

> We do, I believe, regard—and undoubtedly we ought to regard—the natives of India as persons towards whom it is our duty to feel goodwill, and for whose welfare it is our duty to labour; but that is not enough. It is not enough to regard them as objects upon whom it is our power to operate important changes for good. We must look upon them also as men with whom, and not against whom, we have to work—as men with feelings of their own—as men who, although politically subject to us, have a sense of their own independence—and as men who will be apt to be all the more tenacious of their intellectual independence and national customs, because of the political subjection in which they are held.... The position of a conquering and governing race confers many advantages as regards the influence which may be exercised over a conquered people; but that position carries with it this disadvantage—that a conquering race almost inevitably displays a certain sense of superiority—a certain arrogance ... a certain disregard of the feelings of others, which not being placed under such circumstances, it is hardly possible for us to understand.[18]

At the heart of nationalism, it can be argued, lies a constantly unfolding opposition. It was no different in India. Except that, inevitably, the working out

---

18. Quoted in The Reverend Lal Behari Day, *Searchings of Heart in Connection with Missions in Bengal*, Serampore, 1858, pp. 8–9.

of that opposition within Indian nationalism carried the marks of the specific circumstances of its birth and evolution. Encoding that opposition in its title, the study closely follows certain aspects of that unfolding in latter nineteenth century India. In that it combined dependence on and disillusionment with British rule, the emerging Indian nationalism contained a striving for freedom and also loyalty to British rule. It was, necessarily, rooted in the recognition of interests that were national and basically opposed to imperial interests. Without the pivotal idea of the 'national' and the attendant othering of the 'imperial' could not have been created and sustained the dream of unity and freedom. In their actual shaping, however, national interests carried their own ever-unfolding contradiction. The very condition of subjection created an objective dichotomy of the national and the imperial. But in the process of the discovery and articulation of that dichotomy, even sectional interests got perceived or projected as national interests. Consequently, even as national consciousness promoted unity, it produced immediate or potential fissures within the society. The unity nationalism envisaged was, by the very logic of its being, meant to supersede existing socio-cultural unities based around caste, sect, religion, language, and so on, and usher in a new overriding national cohesion, which would command total and supreme loyalty from its members. But nationalism also relied on, or otherwise strengthened, the very unities and loyalties that it was meant to supersede.

It was important, while dealing with the paradox at the heart of nationalism, to remember the fusion of image(s) and reality in experiential life and realise that sectional interests were not sectional for those who fought for them as national, nor for those others who shared that projection. The study inserts this analysis and also presents the idealism and solidarity that 'spurious' national interests produced as effectively as did 'genuine' national interests. It resists the temptation to ascribe the powerful role of sectional interests to the cunning, hypocrisy, deception, or bad faith that retrospective analysis unmistakably shows to have been in operation at a deeper level. Seeing through the magic of an idea or ideology is important to knowing. But recognising the efficacy and glory of that magic, while it lasted, is no less important.

Most works suggest more than what they set out to articulate, and resonate more than what they suggest. Even as it focuses on the larger socio-economic-political background within which national consciousness and nationalist politics emerged, *Dependence and Disillusionment* carries intimations of other historical and historiographic developments as well. It was designed to trace the making of a new pan-Indian consensus following the emergence of national consciousness. This implied the creation of an expanding public sphere which, in turn, rested on a fast-crystallising notion of citizenship, the subject Indians' citizenship dream, and got locked in a causal relationship with civil society.

Public sphere, civil society, and citizenship are post-1975 terms like which do not figure in the book. I am deliberately bringing them in here to indicate how the historical process described in the book could be better appreciated today.

The emerging public sphere and civil society implied various levels of conflict also. However, because its focus was on the emerging consensus, the book merely hinted at some of the conflicts. Also, some of those conflicts were in 1975 not so pronounced as they became in the following two decades. Read, for example, the following from the concluding pages of the book, 'While the projection of religious and sectional loyalties pertaining to the majority community would pass for culturally oriented national consciousness, that relating to the minority communities would be resented.' This was written in the pre-Hindutva era when the dominant self-image of Indian nationalism was secular. It was anathema to suggest, then, that Indian nationalism had since its inception carried traces of special concern for the majority community. That even the most explicitly 'civic' or 'political' Indian nationalism betrayed signs of 'ethnic' nationalism. But now when 'Hindu nationalism' openly claims to be Indian nationalism and, *aided by that claim,* has come to share the centre stage of national politics and reached out in areas till recently unreceptive to it, the above remark reads very differently.

As for the book's historiographic intimations, perhaps the most significant one comes right at the outset, in the 'Preface' to the text. Hinting at the divisive force that came to counter the unifying dynamics of nationalism as a consequence of the rationalisation of sectional as national interests, it states: 'The situation thus carried within it a basic contradiction in so far as the very forces that facilitated the emergence of national consciousness also tended to discompose it.' The text illustrates the transformation of narrow into national interests. Though it does not, in keeping with its primary function, elaborate the disturbance—discomposition— mentioned in the 'Preface'.

By thus insisting on the coevality of consensus and conflict as constituent elements of Indian nationalism, *Dependence and Disillusionment* gestures towards a radical historiographic departure. The nation always represents— indeed, the nation always *is*—certain dominant interests or elite groups. To borrow the sub-title of Disraeli's novel, *Sybil*—the nation always is 'Two Nations'. And, to borrow Subaltern historiography's perhaps most memorable phrase, the nation always represents—always is—the dominant fragment(s). Even in moments of euphoric triumphalism, the fragment is the nation. But—and this but is crucial—the larger triumphalism, too, represents the nation. As do the collective passions and frenzies that, as national responses to special contingencies, keep surfacing from time to time. This is what the already mentioned tussle between the narrower and the larger bases of nationalism is about.

Ceaseless historiographic interventions, focusing on various conflicts within the nationalist consensus, have since followed. We now know infinitely more about women, Dalits, peasants, labourers, Adivasis, and others. And we now have a larger number of competing ways of looking at the national consensus, including its rejection. We may, in this context, remember that way back in 1925, the great pioneer nationalist, Surendranath Banerjea, had the realism to call his autobiography *A Nation in Making*.[19] There still remains reason for that kind of realism, for us to be able to think of India as a nation in (un)making. This (un)making includes paradoxical possibilities, from dismemberment of the nation-state to its substitution by a supra-national political formation. Nationalism today is both waning and waxing, as would appear, among other signs, from the simultaneous scramble to join the European Union and the generally bloody nationalist splintering after the collapse of the Soviet System.

The historiographic scene is no less exciting, nor any less fractious, today. For *Dependence and Disillusionment* to reappear at this conjuncture is to be exposed to a difficult examination.

---

19.   Surendranath Banerjea, *A Nation in Making*, Kolkata, 1998.

1

The Legacy of
1857

INDIAN public opinion in the later 19th century was significantly affected by the great revolt of 1857. Its formation on a countrywide scale was rendered possible by the process of administrative unity and internal stability. To the extent, moreover, that it grew as a reaction to official policy and European attitudes towards Indians, the character of public opinion was largely determined by the pervasive and abiding effects of 1857 on the thinking of men. Because, besides producing certain shifts in official policy, the memory of those traumatic days left an impact not only on contemporaries but also on later generations. As Bartle Frere,[1] then a member of the governor-general's executive council, observed: 'a very great alteration had taken place in public feeling, which was shared even by many persons who were entitled to be classed amongst the most philanthropic well-wishers of India.'[2] John Lawrence, when viceroy, found the existing forces beyond human control, and admitted that the effects of the 'Mutiny' would be 'felt for generations'.[3] As late as 1883, another viceroy, Ripon, discovered that the distinguished administrator-historian Alfred Lyall's[4] recollections of 'that terrible time' were still very stinging.[5]

The conflict between Indians and non-official Europeans was aggravated in 1857. The arrogance of the latter, quite natural in a

1. Sir Henry Bartle Edward Frere (1815–84) was chief commissioner of Sindh, 1850-59; member of the supreme council, Dec. 1859 to Apr. 1862; governor of Bombay, 1862-67; member of the council of India, 1867-77.
2. *Proceedings of the Legislative Council of India*, vol. VI, pt. I, Calcutta, 1860, col. 48.
3. Lawrence to Cranborne, 16 Sep. 1866, *Lawrence Collection*, reel 2.
4. Sir Alfred Comyn Lyall (1835-1911) was secretary to the government of India in the home department, 1873-74, and foreign department, 1878-82; lieutenant-governor of N.W.P., 1882-87.
5. Ripon to Kimberley, 4 Mar. 1883, in L. Wolf, *Life of Lord Ripon*, London, 1921, vol. II, p. 134.

ruling community, took a violent turn. Mercy was spurned and retribution glorified in the hysteria that followed terror and anger, and
permitted no time for the schooling of mental reactions. 'Men who
have suffered as our countrymen have suffered', wrote the *Friend of
India*, 'who hear the blood of their wives, brothers, and friends
shrieking to them for vengeance, cannot stop to weigh words'.[6] The
agony of personal tragedy was not confined to a few; it was difficult
to find among the ruling community in Calcutta someone 'who had
not lost near relatives or dear friends'.[7] In such an emotionally charged atmosphere grew a new kind of literature which mirrored something of the contemporary Anglo-Indian and British mind, and sustained the passions generated by the outbreak. For instance, a song
in the *Punch*, pronounced 'worth five battalions' by the *Friend of
India*, exhorted Europeans to 'REMEMBER THE WOMEN AND
BABES WHOM THEY SLEW', and reminded the soldiers, 'THY
FOOT SHALL BE DIPPED IN THE BLOOD OF THY FOE, AND
THE TONGUE OF THY DOGS SHALL BY RED THROUGH THE
SAME'.[8]

The *Freeman*, to quote another example, evoked the 'laws of God
and of man' to demand that all the 'regiments of sepoys guilty of
these atrocities must be exterminated'.[9] The wrath was not confined
to the 'Pandys'; it attempted to implicate the English educated Indians
en masse. The *Times*, for example, described Nana Saheb as 'the
true barbaric ideal', the 'type of the revolt'. Represented as the symbol of 'Young Asia', he was said to have revealed 'what we are to expect from communicating European arts and accomplishments to
Hindoos without our religion or our manly character'.[10] The *Friend
of India* stamped this view with the approval of Indian experience:[11]

> There is the whole truth. The sleek, polished, educated native who speaks
> English like Englishmen, and quotes Milton and Shakespeare, is a savage,
> with a cruelty such as savages never feel. That, the conviction of the
> Anglo-Indians, is at last the conviction also of Great Britain.

Unhappy about Canning's supposed clemency, the *Friend* added ex-
pectantly: 'We can wait till the belief resolves itself to action'. Men
with such frenzied minds could scarcely distinguish between the rebel and the loyal Indian in their demand for retribution.

Revenge became an obsession with non-official Europeans. Such
in fact was the frenzy that even Christian divines in England lagged
behind none in crying for retribution. They conformed, though, to

6. *Friend of India*, 15 Oct. 1857.
7. O Cavenagh, *Reminiscences of an Indian Career*, London, 1884, p. 212.
8. *Friend of India*, 22 Oct. 1857.
9. *Ibid.*
10. *Ibid.*
11. *Ibid.*

the dignity of their profession by stressing that this would not be personal vengeance but 'just and due retribution' which was 'mercy as well as duty'.[12]

The *Bible* was utilised to put Europeans into a proper frame of mind. An 'Invitation to United Prayer' urged them to 'set apart the half hour from 1/2 past 7 to 8 o'clock in the morning daily, till the end of the month for special prayer'. 'Passages of Scripture suitable to the present crisis' were suggested to be 'profitably read and meditated upon'. It was believed that for the sake of 'His beloved people in this land', and for 'the sake of His cause in India He will preserve the British Dominion in India'.[13]

No less potent than faith in providential predetermination was the notion that a strong deterrent was necessary for the immediate and future safety of British rule and the European community in India. It was felt that 'the present opportunity' should be used to 'teach them a lesson for the benefit of intending mutineers for the future'.[14] But nothing short of capital retribution was expected to answer the purpose. The argument was devastatingly simple: 'For our religion, for our teaching and preaching, they have an utter contempt. Fortunately they understand what it is to be hung, and have a particular objection to it.'[15] It led to but one conclusion: 'What we have to teach the followers of Mahomet and the worshippers of Vishnu is that, whatever their creed or caste, we treat murderers as we do dogs, and in all moral respects rate them a great deal lower.'[16]

Self-righteously simulating to be offended by the revolt of an ungrateful race,[17] non-official Europeans swiftly perceived in the 'mutinies' an opportunity to realise the claims of a superior status advanced by them since the turn of the century.[18] They represented the crisis as the logical conclusion of an official policy which had been

---

12. *Friend of India*, 19 Nov. 1857. Stray exceptions could, indeed, be pointed out. For example, Rev. Dr Thomas Guthrie (1803-73), a Scottish Free Church preacher and philanthropist, said: 'Had I been an Indian, and had I been in India, I would have fought on the side of what you call mutineers. I would have fought for my country. I would have fought for all its liberties. I would have fought for my native land. I would have fought for my faith. The very reason why I honor Wallace and Bruce for repelling the foot of a foreign foe from Scotland would have led me, had I been there, to take the side of the natives... we have put down our sponge in the Ganges, and we have brought it home full of wealth, and then we have squeezed it out on this shore of ours, and that is the bottom of the mischief, at least of the miseries of India at this day.' Home Department, Public Proceedings, A, 25 Mar. 1859, No. 65.
13. *Bengal Hurkaru*, 12 Jun. 1857.
14. Letter by J. J. Cave, *Englishman*, 19 Jun. 1857.
15. *Times* quoted in *Friend of India*, 22 Oct. 1857.
16. *Ibid.*
17. *Calcutta Review*, vol. XXX, 1858, pp. 424 ff.
18. *Englishman*, 4 Jun. 1857.

'to *butter the Black and snub the Saxon*,' and demanded its replacement by a policy of sternness towards Indians and close co-operation with themselves. They argued that to treat Indians and Europeans as equals was 'exactly the same in principle as putting the cat with the rat'. For, the moment the 'native' ceased to fear the white man with the latter's 'hands tied as at present, he becomes the white man's master.'[19] Also, the sepoy having betrayed his unreliability in peace and more so in war, India could clearly 'be retained under English rule much more easily by the aid of a truly loyal adventurer class than through the imaginary affections of the natives'.[20] The country, 'won as it was, by the sword of the adventurer, can only be kept by the same sort of stuff.'[21]

To achieve this end, non-official Europeans had to be treated with dignity and organised into a 'Garde Nationale'. Besides, as an inducement to settle in India, they had to be 'allowed some voice in its government', instead of being 'shut out from the only places in the public service which are associated with profit and distinction'.[22]

From an immediate point of view, too, the outbreak was a blessing in disguise, a 'Providential visitation to compel the government to burn the Black Acts' which had been introduced early in the year to place resident Europeans on a footing of equality with Indians. But the events of 1857 had demonstrated the danger of investing Indian magistrates with the power to try Europeans in criminal cases. 'Had the Black Act been passed, we should one and all be made liable to fates quite as bad as those of the poor murdered victims of Meerut and Delhi. Only we should have met our fates under the color of pretended law.'[23]

1857 thus armed non-official Europeans with an argument that could be employed—as it really was—to oppose every move towards the advancement of Indians. They developed the idea of 'Saxon domination' which meant 'stringent laws for natives, and license for Europeans—exclusion of natives from all places of trust and authority—and a general and avowed postponement of their interests to the interests of Europeans.'[24]

The policy of inequality and force recommended by non-official Europeans was the only one they could conceive of in the context of the existing circumstances and mood. But it had a drawback. It was patently suited for rejection. Those who had to govern India could cherish no such illusions about the practicability of re-

19. *Bengal Hurkaru*, 25 Jun. 1857.
20. *Englishman*, 4 Jun. 1857.
21. *Ibid.*, 20 Jun. 1857.
22. *Bengal Hurkaru*, 27 May, 26 Jun. 1857.
23. *Ibid.*, 22 May 1857; *Englishman*, 19 Jun. 1857.
24. Canning to Granville, 24 Dec. 1857, in E. Fitzmaurice, *Life of Lord Granville*, London, 1906, vol. I, pp. 280-82.

tribution and revenge. Whatever the *Englishman* might have expected him to learn from the 'mutinies', Canning possessed sufficient practical-mindedness to know that it was impossible 'to hold and govern India without employing, and, to a great degree trusting natives, both in civil and military service'.[25] There existed sections of Indians whose interests were linked with British rule which derived a good deal of sustenance from their goodwill and collaboration.[26] Lawrence, Outram,[27] Grant[28] and other lieutenants of Canning in the task of restoring British supremacy and order saw eye to eye with him.

Canning's 'moderation' further inflamed non-official Europeans. Engaged in a struggle for survival, they had expected to be treated as a privileged community. But they were confronted with measures like the Press and the Arms Acts (1857) which recognised no legal distinction between them and Indians. Consequently, they denounced the Press Act for striking 'friend and foe alike'; indeed it struck 'friends much harder than foes'. They felt that it would have been 'an act of justice to those who have done their best to support the Government in this perilous crisis, if the Act had drawn a wide distinction between the English papers, and the vehicles of slander and treason'. It was 'simply ridiculous' in such a crisis 'when everything we possess, our fortunes, our lives and the lives of all who are dear to us, are staked upon the suppression of this revolt, to suspect any English Journalist of opposition or even lukewarmness to his own cause'. In reward for 'a fair and honest support to the Government' the Anglo-Indian Press had received 'A GAGGING ACT'.[29]

Their protest against the Arms Act was stronger because, as viewed by them, it had equated 'the loyal with murderers, mutineers, and rebels.' Their reaction was particularly sharp also because they looked upon licensing of arms not as a temporary device to deal with the exigency of 1857, but as the beginning of the disarmament of India. Since a continent could not be disarmed 'in a day, or a week, or a month, or six months', the idea behind the measure should have been to ensure that if the British were 'to meet another revolt it shall not be one of armed men'.[30]

25. Canning to Victoria, 25 Sep. 1857, *Letters of Queen Victoria*, London, 1908, vol. III, p. 251.
26. Canning to Granville, 11 Dec. 1857, in Fitzmaurice, *op. cit.*, vol. I, p. 274.
27. Sir James Outram (1803-63) was resident at Satara (1845), Baroda, 1847-54, and Oudh, 1854-56; first chief commissioner of Oudh; military member of supreme council, 1858-60.
28. Sir John Peter Grant (1807-93) was member of the supreme council, 1854-59; lieutenant-governor of Bengal, 1859-62.
29. *Englishman*, 15 Jun. 1857; *Bengal Hurkaru*, 15, 16, 27 Jun. 1857; *Friend of India*, 18 Jun. 1857; for attacks on Canning's policy see M. Maclagan, 'Clemency' *Canning*, London, 1962, pp. 132 ff.
30. *Friend of India*, 22 Oct. 1857.

The attack was renewed when a Bill was introduced before the expiry of the Arms Act of 1857 to perpetuate the powers assumed by the government. Speaking in the legislative council, Charles Jackson[31] harped on the experience of 1857 to stress the unwisdom of depriving 'the European Community of the means of self-defence'. It was absolutely necessary, he thought, that Europeans, 'a small class compared with the large native population, and many of them residing in isolated districts', 'should have the means of protecting themselves'.[32] Mordaunt Lawson Wells,[33] Jackson's successor in the legislative council, was even more emphatic. There could be, he asserted, no equality 'when Europeans had to defend their very lives against hordes of natives'.[34]

The argument of protection for Europeans had little justification. They could in actual practice possess arms without restriction. What really irked them was the intolerable equation with Indians. Even Jackson, while conjuring up visions of the horrors of 1857, admitted that the legal restrictions imposed on Europeans were not meant to exist in practice. That he still arraigned the measure as 'a specimen of double hypocrisy',[35] showed that considerations of prestige lay at the bottom of the irritation. The sense of belonging to the ruling race having been strengthened in 1857, special privileges began to be claimed on this ground, as also on the ground of ensuring the security of the dominant minority amidst alien millions.

The refusal of the government to toe the line suggested by non-official Europeans, besides perpetuating the protracted hostility between the civilian and the 'interloper', had the significant effect of adding to the fury of the latter against Indians. The indiscriminate and sweeping attacks on Indians as a race had made it necessary for loyal Indians, specially the rich and educated classes in Bengal and Bombay, to defend themselves and safeguard their interests. They naturally supported the policy enunciated by Canning. Some of them were even prompted to pay back the European traducers of Indian character in their own coin. As the *Indian Field* remarked, 'the worm will turn when trodden on; and so will the Bengalee.'[36] By its sustained advocacy of Indian interests the *Hindoo Patriot* became the focal point of Anglo-Indian ire in Bengal, as did the *Rast Goftar*, though to a less extent, in Bombay. And the one individual who cut

---

31. Sir C. R. M. Jackson was puisne judge of the Calcutta supreme court, 1855-62; member of the governor-general's legislative council; retired in 1863.
32. *Proceedings of the Legislative Council of India*, vol. V, Calcutta, 1859, cols. 649-50.
33. Sir Mordaunt Wells (1817-85) was puisne judge of the Calcutta supreme court, 1859-62, and of the high court, 1862-63; member of the supreme legislative council, 1860.
34. *Proceedings of the Legislative Council of India*, vol. VI, pt. I, cols. 608-09.
35. *Ibid.*, vol. V., cols. 649-50.
36. *Indian Field*, 29 May 1858.

non-official Europeans to the quick by describing them as the 'sweepings' of the West was Rajendralal Mitra, the scholar-leader.[37]

But the 'adventurers' were determined not to 'submit to be bespattered by whitewashed barbarians, even though they be Bengalis by birth, and cowards by instinct'. The *Friend of India* echoed the sentiments of an overwhelming proportion of its countrymen in India when it wrote with brutal frankness: '... when the Baboos clamour for political freedom we only reply, not to have been kicked is gain; not to have been cudgelled is for you a ground for endless gratitude.'[38] The *Friend*, it is interesting, claimed to represent moderate as against extremist opinion,[39] and was regarded by Indians as 'the ablest spokesman' of non-official Europeans.[40] The sheer rabidity of anti-Indian European opinion is further reflected in the petition of 694 Europeans, including some uncovenanted civilians, against the Arms Act:[41]

> That your petitioners are living in the midst of a native population at least one thousand times more numerous than themselves; some of whom are lawless and rapacious, some cruel and blood-thirsty, many reckless and unprincipled and very many actuated by a profound hatred of all Europeans and descendants of Europeans, and of all Christians, and that many of the said natives are said to be in possession of concealed arms... That your petitioners are convinced that to deprive them of the right to possess Arms would be to expose them, their lives, famillies, and property without protection to the fury and rapacity of the abovenamed lawless, blood-thirsty and unprincipled persons.

That many responsible local officers shared similar views is clear from the communications on disarmament sent by a number of them in the North Western Provinces. These were so strongly worded and contained such severe recommendations as to oblige the governor-general in council to condemn their tone and spirit 'in terms of great severity'.[42]

But censure from the highest quarters could not assuage European mistrust of Indians. More than ever conscious of his numerical inferiority, the resident European now tended to be haunted by the dread of a catastrophe similar to that of 1857. Even a baseless alarm could now cause him a 'disgraceful panic'.[43] The aggressivity pro-

37. Raja Rajendralal Mitra (1824-91) was scholar, antiquarian and statesman; for long a member of the British Indian Association, he rose to be its president; wrote for the *Hindoo Patriot*.
38. *Friend of India*, 29 May 1858.
39. *Ibid.*, 15 Oct. 1857.
40. *Rast Goftar*, 3 Jan. 1858; *Bengal Hurkaru*, 25 May 1857, however, thought that the *Friend* was writing wildly.
41. Home Department, Public Proceedings, A, 15 Oct. 1860, Nos. 82-4.
42. *Ibid.*, 3 Aug. 1860, No. 7: see T.R. Metcalf, *The Aftermath of Revolt*, Princeton, 1965, pp. 307-08.
43. Mayo to Argyll, 9 Sep. 1870, *Argyll Papers*, reel 313.

duced by persisting fear became characteristic of European menta-
lity in India; for the proneness to get panicky was 'the natural legacy
of the Mutiny'.[44]

The British clung to the memories of 1857 with a pathological
persistence, and transmitted to the succeeding generations a partisan
and emotionally evocative account of those times. The popular por-
traiture presented the British as heroically humane and forgiving in
the face of unbelievable cruelties perpetrated on white men, women
and children by the dastardly rebels.[45] Kanpur supplied the theme
for a tragic epic; and G. O. Trevelyan,[46] moved by 'the memory of
fruitless valour and unutterable woe', performed the solemn task.[47]
Pilgrimage to Kanpur became a dismal duty and revived for every
Briton who came to India the sombre recollections of those dreadful
days. Thus H. M. Kisch,[48] standing on the threshold of his career
as a civilian, recorded the melancholy impressions of his visit to the
memorial at Kanpur and the Residency at Lucknow;[49] and Grant
Duff,[50] visiting Kanpur on 16 December 1874, renewed his recollections of those sad days through Trevelyan's 'eloquent book'.[51]

The government was in a quandary. It had to attempt the impossible role of reconciling the expectations of both non-official Europeans who, having fought and won its war, insisted on being treated
as a privileged class, and of the rich and educated Indians who looked
upon it as the dispenser of equal justice. The conditioning circumstances of the British rule in India necessitated certain special concessions to Europeans behind the facade of equality. This, naturally,
agitated Indians. At the same time, political exigencies obliged the
government to repose confidence in at least some sections of Indians.
And this was so much 'gall and wormwood to the dominant white
race'.[52]

II

In official policy there occurred, after 1857, significant shifts in

44. Mayo to Argyll, 9 Sep., 9 Nov. 1870, and enclosures for examples of such
    panic, *Argyll Papers*, reel 313.
45. H. Beveridge, *A Comprehensive History of India*, London, 1862, vol. III,
    pp. 685-709.
46. George Otto Trevelyan (1838-1928), M.P., was the son of Charles Trevelyan;
    he was interested in Indian affairs, and visited the country in 1863.
47. G. O. Trevelyan, *Cawnpore*, London, 1894; first published in 1865.
48. H. M. Kisch (1850-1942), I.C.S., first came to the country of his service in
    1873.
49. Ethel A. Waley Cohen, ed., *A Young Victorian in India Letters of H. M.
    Kisch*, London, 1957, pp. 182-83.
50. Sir Mountstuart Elphinstone Grant Duff (1829-1906) was under secretary
    of state for India, 1868-74, and governor of Madras, 1881-86.
51. M. E. Grant Duff, *Notes of an Indian Diary*, London, 1876, pp. 54, 56.
52. *Homeward Mail*, in *Bombay Times*, 20 Oct. 1860.

emphasis which, being typical of the British approach to imperial problems, created a good many anomalies. Revenge as a basis of policy being impracticable, a *modus vivendi* between reliance on the goodwill, if not affection, of the ruled, and dependence on force had to be evolved. The state of unpreparedness in which the outbreak had caught the British in spite of isolated and somewhat vague warnings had brought home the conviction that without 'some barometer and safety-valve combined in the shape of a deliberative council', the government would be 'always liable to very unlooked-for and dangerous explosions'.[53] Indians also had warned that the events of 1857 had 'raised the questions of the advisability of introducing the independent element into the Legislative Council'.[54] Attributing the revolt to the evils arising from the inaccessibility to Indians of the legislative council, Syed Ahmad Khan, the emerging Muslim leader, opined that their inclusion in it was 'not only advisable but absolutely necessary'.[55]

But 1857 had also emphasised the need for a strong executive. The status of the supreme legislative council, which had since 1853 attempted to act as a miniature parliament, was consequently lowered. Nomination by the executive was jealously retained; and the principle of representation was denied to both Europeans and Indians: the secretary of state even forbidding the authorities in India to nominate 'natives who are in any sense the exponents of active opinion or who could take any part in the deliberations'.[56] When a later secretary of state, Northcote, suggested for the legislative council 'somewhat more of a representative character than at present without going the length of an elective assembly',[57] Lawrence replied that 'anything like an approach to representative Members would not answer'. He echoed Wood in stressing the usefulness of Indian members of rank who seldom took 'any real interest in their duty', and always looked up to the viceroy with a desire 'to be in his good graces'.[58] Later, when a viceroy, Ripon, proposed the introduction of a representative element, Hartington, the secretary of state, put his foot down.[59] Throughout 1858-85 the endeavour was to obtain the advantage of the association of Indians without incurring the implied risks.

The policy of seeking the co-operation of Indians was qualified

53. Frere to Wood, 10 Apr. 1861, in J. Martineau, *Life of Sir Bartle Frere*, London, 1895, vol. I, p. 340.
54. *Hindoo Patriot*, 21 May 1859.
55. C. H. Philips, ed., *The Evolution of India and Pakistan 1858-1947*, London, 1962, p. 30.
56. Wood to Frere, 18 Feb. 1861, in Martineau, *op. cit.*, vol. I, p. 336.
57. Northcote to Lawrence, 30 Apr. 1868, *Lawrence Collection*, reel 2.
58. Lawrence to Northcote, 1 Jun. 1868, *ibid.*, reel 3.
59. See H. L. Singh, *Problems and Policies of the British in India 1885-1898*, Bombay, 1963, pp. 86-7.

by the decision to align the princes and upper classes to British rule. Both the participation of many Indian States in the revolt of 1857 and the crucial assistance rendered to the British by many others in crushing it alike pointed to the desirability of such a change in policy as would remove elements of friction and link the interests of the States with British rule. The princes were, therefore, assured that the British would not only eschew further territorial expansion, but also honour existing treaties and engagements.[60]

The policy of reliance on the aristocratic classes was strengthened by the British experience in Oudh which exposed the futility of enlisting the lower classes. Though the East India Company had benefited the village occupants at the cost of the *talukdars*, the former had fought for the latter during 1857. The logical moral, as expressed by Canning, was: 'Property and superior station will carry influence with them, do what we will.'[61] The viceroy, therefore, wished the superior proprietors to know that the government intended 'practically to recognize their claim to authority and respect, and to strengthen itself by their active support'. They had only to be reminded that property had its duties besides its rights.[62]

Among the viceroys, Lytton was the best exponent of the policy of alignment with the aristocracy. He dismissed as a 'fundamental political mistake' the belief that India could be held by good government, 'that is to say, by improving the conditions of the Ryots, strictly administering justice, and spending immense sums on irrigation works & c.' Politically the Indian peasantry was an inert mass which would move, if at all, in obedience 'not to its British benefactors, but to its native chiefs and princes, however tyrannical they may be'. The baboos, whom the British had 'taught to write semi-seditious articles in the native press', represented 'nothing but the social anomaly of their position'. The vital need in such circumstances was to 'secure completely, and efficiently utilise, the Indian Aristocracy' without investing it with 'any increased political power independent of our own'.[63]

The like-minded secretary of state, Salisbury, delighted the viceroy with his exposition of the policy towards different classes. The masses, he thought, 'must never be counted upon to resist their real

---

60. 'Proclamation by the Queen to the Princes, Chiefs, and the People of India', A. B. Keith, ed., *Speeches & Documents on Indian Policy.* Oxford, 1922, vol. I, pp. 383-84.

61. Home Department, Judicial Proceedings, A, 18 Dec. 1860, Nos. 10-4; *Friend of India*, 4 Feb. 1858, wrote: 'The self-interest even of all peasantry was against the Talookdars; but self-interest after all is not the moving spring of human affairs.'

62. Home Department, Judicial Proceedings, A, 18 Dec. 1860, Nos. 10-4; see J. Raj, *The Mutiny and British Land Policy in North India 1856-1868*, Bombay, 1965, pp. 12-40.

63. Lytton to Salisbury, 11 May 1876, *Salisbury Papers*, reel 814.

enemies, or sustain their real friends, at the right moment'. The baboos, 'a deadly legacy from Metcalfe and Macaulay', could be nothing 'else than opposition in quiet times, rebels in times of trouble'. The aristocracy alone was really worth having the loyalty of, because then 'we can hardly be upset'.[64]

This policy and the decision to have effete legislative councillors affected the nominations to the supreme legislative council. That is why the first batch of three Indians was connected with the Indian States.[65] Subsequently nomination was extended to the upper classes in British India, like the zemindars. But till 1885 not a single Indian who could be called a representative of the educated middle classes, with the possible exception of V. N. Mandlik,[66] was nominated to the council; though in the presidency councils men like Dadabhai Naoroji (1825-1917) and Badruddin Tyabji[67] had begun to be appointed. Kristo Das Pal,[68] a middle class Bengali, was certainly nominated by Ripon, but as the accredited spokesman of the zemindars to advocate their case vis-a-vis the ryots during the debates on the Bengal Rent Bill. Mandlik's position was rather ambivalent, for he was also a landlord and seemed more an upper class man at the time of his nomination.[69]

The situation contained elements of sharp conflict between the government and the educated middle classes. In the circumstances obtaining immediately after 1857 the only sensible course perhaps was the one followed by the authorities. The masses being politically non-existent, no value could be attached to them as allies. Yet they were not ignored altogether. Measures were introduced from time to time with a view to improving their condition. The nascent middle classes, not possessing the confidence to stand alone, were then playing the second fiddle to the affluent elite in Bombay and Bengal.[70] The authorities could hardly be expected to have the om-

---

64. Salisbury to Lytton, 9 Jun. 1876, *Ibid.*, reel 822.
65. The Maharaja of Patiala, Raja of Benares and Sir Dinkar Rao (1819-95). Rao was the chief minister of the Gwalior State during the revolt and had helped the British.
66. V. N. Mandlik (1833-89) was a governmnt servant till 1862 when he joined the Bombay bar; government pleader in 1884; member of the Bombay legislative council, 1874-82; nominated to the supreme council in 1884; a leading member of the Bombay and the Bombay Presidency Associations.
67. Badruddin Tyabji (1844-1906), bar-at-law; judge of the Bombay high court; president of the third Indian National Congress (1887); till his elevation to the bench took part in various political movements and was one of the founders of the Bombay Presidency Association.
68. Kristo Das Pal (1838-84) was the paid assistant secretary and later on secretary of the British Indian Association; edited the *Hindoo Patriot* from 1861 till his death; member of the Bengal legislative council in 1872, and of the supreme council, 1883-84.
69. *Indu Prakash*, 25 Feb. 1884.
70. See chapter 2.

niscience to visualise the power the middle classes became, particularly in Bengal, during the 1870s and 1880s.[71] There seemed no alternative to alignment with Indian princes and upper classes. Meanwhile, as the authorities felt secure in the loyalty of these sections, a tussle for leadership was going on between the upper and the middle classes. Gradually the balance tilted in favour of the middle classes, though for long the outcome remained uncertain. But modifications in official policy could not synchronise, in point of time, with every change in the relative strength of the two classes in society. The fluid uncertainty of the situation and the rigidity of official thinking both explain why Lytton and Salisbury contemptuously dismissed the baboo as the barking dog who could be silenced with a few loaves and fishes. The first serious attempt to deal with the middle classes was made by Ripon who recognised in them the emergence of a new force in Indian society and politics. He failed in the face of vested interests, and the conflict with the middle classes weighed with increasing pressure on his successors.

Besides inducing the adoption of a liberal exterior, evidenced by the royal proclamation of 1858 and the formal association of Indians in legislation, 1857 strengthened the British faith in armed force as the basis of empire. More than ever 'Cantonments and arsenals, field batteries and breaching batteries, seemed more essential to the government of the country than courts of law, normal schools, and agricultural exhibitions.'[72] Without subscribing to the current fashion of advocating dependence on brute force alone, Bartle Frere admitted that the conviction of British military superiority must be produced on the Indian mind.[73] Characteristic of the military reorganisation after 1857 was the lack of faith in Indian sepoys with its corollary of trusting the 'Little White faced Men'.[74] European troops in India began to be viewed as 'the bullion deposit on which the security of the Indian Empire' depended.[75] The 1857 ratio of 1 to 7½ between European and Indian troops was made 1 to 2 in a quick overhaul.[76] The change might appear excessive; but, as Lawrence argued, it was necessary in view of the changes following

71. Criticising the policy of alignment with the traditional ruling classes, P. Spear maintains that the revolt of 1857 discredited them and induced the people to follow the English educated middle classes. *India: A Modern History*, Ann Arbor, 1961, pp. 279-81. This view seems fallacious because the importance of the middle classes increased in Bengal and Bombay, precisely the areas where the revolt had not spread, while in the regions most affected by it the influence of the traditional ruling classes remained more or less unimpaired.

72. G. O. Trevelyan, *The Competition Wallah*, London, 1866, p. 259.

73. Frere to Durand, 16 Jan. 1859, Martineau, *op. cit.*, vol. I, p. 271.

74. Mayo to Argyll, 9 Sep. 1869, *Argyll Papers*, reel 312.

75. Mansfield to Lawrence, 21 Jan. 1867, *Lawrence Collection*, reel 6.

76. Lawrence to Cranborne, 4 Jan. 1867, *ibid.*, reel 3.

1857.[77] Even Mayo, in spite of his anxiety to produce financial equilibrium, begged of Argyll,[78] the secretary of state, not to consent to
'the removal of a single British Bayonet or Sabre in India'.[79] The relative efficacy of Indian troops was further damaged by removing
them from arsenals and artillery, and by equipping them with weapons that were inferior to the weapons of European troops. Though
'purely military considerations', admitted the secretary of state, were
'decisive against withholding the best available weapons from any
portion of our troops', political calculations pointed 'the other way'.[80]
Disarmament and exclusion of Indians from commissioned ranks
were also aspects of the increased British fear and distrust of Indians.

Here again were elements that would provide Indians not only
with material grievances but also with what they felt was a stigma
on their national character. Even as the altered British policy was
in the process of being implemented, the *Hindoo Patriot* warned the
rulers against the difficulties that would accrue from the supersession of 'blind faith in the loyalty of the sepoys which brought about
the mutinies of 1857-58 ... by an equally blind distrust in the people
at large.'[81]

By sharpening the dichotomy between generous promises and the
maintenance of a rigid, vigilant autocracy, the experience of 1857
made it more difficult for the British to resolve the contradiction between profession and practice that always characterised their rule.
This had a marked effect on political development in India during
1858-85.[82]

One of the most difficult problems bequeathed by 1857 threatened, according to Wilson,[83] to corrode 'the very heart of our political existence.'[84] This was the creation of a huge deficit and the consequent inevitability of increased taxation. The three years following
the May outbreak had shown deficits of £ 7,864,222, £ 13,393,137, and
£ 9,290,129 respectively. In round numbers this meant a liability of
30 millions on an annual income of 37 millions.[85] Meanwhile, the
Indian debt had almost doubled. On 30 April 1857, 'the capital of the
Public Debt in India was £ 55,546,652, and in England it was £ 3,894,
400, and the interest payable upon the whole was £ 2,525,375.' In
1860 these figures had risen to £ 71,202,807 in India and £ 26,649,000

---

77. *Ibid.*
78. Duke of Argyll (1823-1900) was secretary of state for India, 1868-74.
79. Mayo to Argyll, 9 Sep. 1869, *Argyll Papers*, reel 312.
80. Secretary of State's Despatch, Military, No. 51, 25 Feb. 1869, *ibid.*, reel 315.
81. *Hindoo Patriot*, 12 Sept. 1861.
82. See chapter 4.
83. James Wilson (1805-60) came to India in 1859 as the first finance member of the governor-general's council.
84. *Proceedings of the Legislative Council of India*, vol. VI, pt. I, col. 87.
85. *Ibid.*, cols. 89-92.

in England, the annual charge on the total of £ 97,851,807 being
£ 4,461,029. The aggregate increase for the three years, £ 38,410,755,
had saddled India with an annual increase of interest to the tune of
£ 1,935,654.[86] In plain words, said the finance member, 1857 had cost
the people of India 'in a direct public charge, independent of all other
losses and sacrifices, the sum of £ 38,410,755', besides entailing an
annual charge 'of no less than £1,935,654 for...many years to come.'[87]
The crisis, he added, was 'infinitely worse...than any similar occasion
which we have recorded in India, or than the most pressing modern
crisis in England.'[88]

The situation was fraught with future troubles. Of the two possible alternatives to meet the financial crisis, economy in expenditure
was ruled out by the prevailing circumstances,[89] and the unavoidable
enhancement of taxation was a source of 'much trouble and some
danger'.[90] This was bound to stimulate the growth of national consciousness.[91]

III

Indians were affected by 1857 largely in relation to its effect on
Europeans. Zemindars, merchants and the educated middle classes,
having their interests connected with British rule, were charged of
disloyalty by the Anglo-Indian Press. Not only was Nana Saheb represented as 'the most favorable specimen of the Europeanised native
that India could produce';[92] specific charges of conspiracy were made
against men like Jagannath Sankerseth,[93] president of the Bombay
Association, who had nothing to gain and everything to lose with the
overthrow of the British. Assuring its readers that it had taken particular pains to ascertain facts, the Bombay Standard wrote that 'political discussion has for many months past been rife throughout the
Presidency and the state of public feeling thereby evinced is in the
last degree unsatisfactory—nearly the most disloyal being the young
men of our colleges.'[94]

Having 'suffered in character from the effect of these mutinies',[95]
these Indians had to accept the onus of proving their loyalty. This the

86. *Proceedings of the Legislative Council of India*, vol. VI, pt. I, col. 94.
87. *Ibid.*
88. *Ibid.*, col. 99.
89. See chapter 3.
90. Mayo to Argyll, 1 Sep. 1871, *Argyll Papers*, reel 314.
91. See chapter 3.
92. *Bombay Standard*, 2 Mar. 1858.
93. Jagannath Sankerseth (1802-65), business magnate; conservative Hindu; one of the founders of associational politics in Bombay; promoted education; nominated to the Bombay legislative council.
94. Quoted in *Rast Goftar*, 28 Feb. 1858.
95. *Hindoo Patriot*, 31 Dec. 1857.

Hindoo Patriot did with that characteristic forthrightness which had brought upon it the opprobrious description of 'the organ of the sepoys'.[96] Certain grievances, wrote the *Patriot*, were endemic in foreign rule. But the realisation of 'substantial benefits' resulting from British rule had made Indians desire its continuance.[97] The *Rast Goftar* even asserted that it was English education that had 'led the majority of the people of this country to stand by the British in their hour of trouble'. It quoted Dr Wilson[99] to the effect that 'it remains to be proved that the educated natives have either assisted in or sympathised with the deplorable rebellion which has occurred in the North West Provinces. They know as much of the power and resources of Britain and the advantages to be derived from its benign administration in India...as makes them desire the continuance and prosperity of that administration.'[100]

English educated Indians felt that the revolt of 1857 was 'a war of anarchy against established Government'.[101] It is a measure of the changing character of the effect of 1857 on the Indian mind that by 1885 Lakshmi Bai, Nana Saheb and the others had not become national heroes. Rather, the shade of Deo Narain Singh[102] was invoked 'to bear witness to his trials and sufferings, his gigantic exertions to crush out the seeds of rebellion and restore peace and order.'[103] This was natural in a period characterised by the coexistence of national consciousness and loyalty to British rule.[104]

Mere profession of loyalty, however, was not enough in the frenzied atmosphere of 1857-58. The wild allegations of the Anglo-Indian Press had to be countered. The *Hindoo Patriot* attempted to knock the bottom out of these charges by arguing that while the atrocities attributed to the rebels were either gross exaggerations or 'unreal creation of morbid imaginations, the retributive excesses were sad

96. *Friend of India*, 21 Nov. 1857.
97. *Hindoo Patriot*, 21 May 1857.
98. *Rast Goftar*, 17 Jan. 1858.
99. Rev. John Wilson (1804-75) studied surgery and medicine before coming to India as an ordained missionary; worked for the promotion of female and higher education in Bombay; studied and wrote about Indian society; highly respected among Indians.
100. *Rast Goftar*, 31 Jan. 1858.
101. R.J. Mitter, ed., *Speeches by Rajendralala Mitra,* Calcutta, 1892, p. 7.
102. Raja Sir Deo Narain Singh (1820-70) belonged to the family that had owned the *jagir* of Saiyidpur Bhitari till its resumption in 1828 when a perpetual pension of over Rs. 36,000 a year was granted to it; helped the British during 1857 and was responsible for the maintenance of order; received an additional annual grant of Rs. 25,000; was nominated to the supreme legislative council.
103. Speech by Surendranath Banerji, *Report of the Proceedings of a Public Meeting on the Vernacular Press Act, etc.,* Calcutta, 1878, col. i, p. 6.
104. S. Chandra, 'The Loyalty of Educated Indians to the British Rule (1858-1885)', *Journal of Indian History,* vol. XLIV, pt. II, No. 131, pp. 417-28.

realities'.[105] About the accusation that Indian character was 'surchar-
ged with vileness and exceptionally and unapproachably depraved',
the *Patriot* insisted that an entire race could not be calumniated 'on
the basis of the acts of some of the sepoys'.[106] The *Rast Goftar* even
tried to turn the tables on non-official Europeans who, it wrote, had
done 'all that lay in them to convert the present   Military, into a
national revolt'.[107] It asserted that 'but for the staunch firmness and
consummate Statesmanship of those at present at the helm of State',
the British might 'have had to regain possession of their Indian Empire from the decks of their men of war.'[108] As a warning to Europeans, who wanted Indians to become 'hewers of wood and drawers of
water' in their own land, the *Rast Goftar* referred to Burke's dictum
'*that subjects will be rebels from principle when rulers are tyrants
from policy*.'[109]

The *Hindoo Patriot* tried to belittle the 'Saxon domination' party
by claiming that the entire hue and cry had been engineered by a
cabal of non-official Europeans. Anxious to 'create for themselves a
position they were by no means entitled to', they were exploiting the
crisis to advance their undue claims by 'finding fault with the authorities and abusing the native of the soil'.[110]

This further inflamed non-official Europeans. Their irritation
was particularly aggravated by an address presented on behalf of
5,000 Indians from Bengal, Bihar and Orissa to the governor-general
in council. Conceived as a 'national protest' against the faction of
Europeans who had 'ventured to carry their misstatements to the foot
of the Throne', strong terms were used in the address to defend the
official policy and Indians:[111]

> It has become notorious throughout this land that your Lordship's admin-
> istration has been assailed by faction, and assailed because your Lordship.
> in Council has refused compliance with capricious demands, and to treat
> the loyal portion of the Indian population as rebels, because your Lord-
> ship has directed that punishment for offences against the State should be
> dealt out with discrimination, because your Lordship having regard for the
> future has not pursued a policy of universal irritation and unreasoning vio-
> lence, and finally because your Lordship has confined coercion and punish-
> ment within necessary and politic limits.

This made the Anglo-Indian Press frantic. The framers of the address, 'a parcel of natives who would shriek at a drawn sword or

105. *Hindoo Patriot*, 6 May, 19 Aug. 1858.
106. *Ibid.*, 8 Jul. 1858.
107. *Rast Goftar*, 31 Jan. 1858.
108. *Ibid.*
109. *Ibid.*, 3 Jan. 1858.
110. *Hindoo Patriot*, 19 Aug. 1858.
111. *Friend of India*, 24 Dec. 1857.

faint at a pistol',[112] were condemned for composing 'wilful and scandalous falsehoods' on the principle of 'God bless all those who've anything to give'.[113] Even Bruce Norton,[114] otherwise sympathetic to Indians, attacked the Bengalis for their lip loyalty and Canning for not thinking it 'unbecoming' to record his cordial thanks for a petition in which the Bengalis had 'insulted the English inhabitants of Calcutta as a faction'.[115]

Relations between Indians and Europeans, which had been deteriorating for some decades, were irrevocably damaged during 1857-58. Realisation of self-interest and their relatively weak position initially impelled Indians to seek a rapprochement with Europeans. The crisis over, some sensible Europeans in Calcutta having business relations with Indians were ready to respond favourably. Taking advantage of the assumption of Indian government by the Crown, they hastily arranged a meeting at the Calcutta Chamber of Commerce to offer thanks to the Queen and to convey to her the loyalty of all sections of people.[116] But the rancour was too deep rooted to be ejected by demonstrations of loyalty in the form of meetings and professions. The acrimonious debates on the Arms Bill, the overbearing disposition of Europeans in opposing trial by Indian magistrates, the insulting charges of Mordaunt Wells to the jury, and numerous similar occurrences convinced Indians that Europeans were not inclined to treat them on an equal footing.[117] The determined refusal of Europeans to forget 1857 created an insuperable psychological barrier between them and Indians. Raja Amir Husain Khan of Mahmudabad (1849-1902), who had managed to efface the past when 12 of his brothers and cousins were murdered by the British in 1857, complained that the latter refused to do so and left 'their ruins standing to perpetuate the memory of bloodshed'. He wished he could persuade the lieutenant-governor 'to have them razed or rebuilt'.[118] The growing racialism of Europeans, naturally resented by Indians, became a powerful factor in the growth of national consciousness in India.

While the shadow dividing Indians and non-official Europeans lengthened, the faith of Indians in the government gained fresh strength and justification, albeit for the time being, as a result of their experience of 1857. They felt grateful for the contrast between non-

112. *Ibid.*
113. *Englishman*, 16 Dec. 1857.
114. John Bruce Norton (1815-83) barrister-at-law, came to India, 1842; sheriff of Madras, 1843-45; clerk of the Crown, 1845-62; government pleader; advocate-general, 1863-71; member of the Madras legislative council; fellow and law lecturer of the Madras University; patron of Pachaiyappa's school at Madras; wrote mainly on Indian law.
115. A Hindu, *Native Fidelity during the Mutiny*, Calcutta, 1905, p. 329.
116. *Hindoo Patriot*, 11 Nov. 1858.
117. See chapter 2.
118. W.S. Blunt, *India under Ripon : A Private Diary*, London, 1909, p. 152.

official Europeans, who had 'allowed their judgment to run away with their feelings', and 'those at the helm of the state', who, 'in the teeth of philippics', had striven 'to sow the seeds of amity and goodwill among their subjects'.[119] Particular gratitude was expressed for Canning who had 'by his wise acts, his humane policy and his discriminating sense of justice, made the people of India more attached to the British rule than they ever were before.'[120]

But Canning's policy could succeed only with backing from England where also people had become 'rabid with desire of indiscriminate vengeance'.[121] Macaulay (1800-59) observed that the 'cruelties of the sepoys have inflamed the nation to a degree unprecedented within my memory'.[122]   The appearance of moderation and coolness in England, therefore, gave relief and hope to Indians.[123]   The normal supposition would have been that in view of the events in India 'anything like justice or fair play was quite out of the question'. That the members of parliament had evinced not a 'feeling of irritation' but 'a degree of self-criticism of their own kith and kin' gave evidence of 'the moral stamina of a nation which could thus subordinate the common emotions of human nature to the requirements of justice and equity'.[124] Since the Tories—because of the fortuitous circumstance that they then happened to form the opposition—were the first to show sanity and moderation, they were specially favoured by Indians.[125] It was late in the 1870s that preference for the Liberals began. This faith in parliament sustained the loyalty of Indians even after they had ceased to trust the authorities in India, and delayed the advent of extremist thinking in Indian politics.

The royal proclamation of 1858, however, created a situation in which faith in the authorities in India could not survive long. Its immediate effect on Indians was to set their minds at rest. After the suspense and horror of 18 months they felt assured that instead of being treated as members of a vanquished race, they had been promised equality, peace and fair prospects. The proclamation was pronounced 'a Charter of the Civil and Religious rights and liberties of the people of India'.[126] The sincerity of the sovereign and of her people in Britain was not questioned. The point was whether and how far the royal command would be executed in India.[127] This meant that the blame for non-fulfilment of promises—unavoidable in certain

119. *Rast Goftar*, 2, 9 May 1858.
120. *Ibid*, 13 Feb. 1859.
121. Granville to Canning, 9 Sep. 1857, in Fitzmaurice, *op. cit.*, vol. I, p. 259.
122. G.O. Trevelyan, *Life and Letters of Lord Macaulay*, Oxford, 1961, vol. II, p. 359.
123. *Hindoo Patriot*, 7 Jan. 1858.
124. *Rast Goftar*, 29 Aug. 1858.
125. *Hindoo Patriot*, 18 Feb., 1 Jul. 1858.
126. *Rast Goftar*, 7 Nov. 1858.
127. *Hindoo Patriot*, 4 Nov. 1858.

respects because of the circumstances bequeathed by 1857 and on the whole because of the logic of imperialism—would be thrown initially on the authorities in India.

Besides being grateful to the authorities in India, Indians also realised the necessity of combination. They could not view 'with apathy or indifference' the disappearance of the court of directors, 'that powerful barrier between the ignorance of the British public and the interests of British India'. This was sure to enhance, to the detriment of Indian interests, the influence of public opinion in Britain and of non-official European opinion in India.[128] The European 'adventurers', who had agitated for the removal of the East India Company as a ruling power, were expected to interpret the change 'in the light of concession to their clamour'. They might even 'assume to take law into their own hands and assert a political superiority over their native fellow-subjects'; and experience showed that the authorities had not always been impervious to 'the attractions of newspaper popularity' offered by non-official Europeans.[129] To counter-check the threat of growing non-official European influence it was incumbent on Indians to organise their opinion on an institutional basis.

The triumphant emergence of the British from the trials of 1857 and the crushing defeat of their adversaries plainly indicated that British might was invulnerable. Further contest on these lines was impracticable. But the constitutional mode of agitation, which had gathered momentum on the eve of the renewal of the charter of the East India Company in 1853, was given a temporary setback at the same time as the wisdom of reliance on it was highlighted. This was because of two reasons: the authorities had become chary of making real concessions; and those Indians who linked the advancement of their country with British rule were put on the defensive.

In spite of the jolt received by constitutional political activities, the nascent associational politics progressed in Bengal where the British Indian Association remained during the subsequent decades an active and influential political organisation. But in Bombay political activity was paralysed, with the Bombay Association being forced into hibernation. In its sixth report the managing committee of the Association admitted that the 'revolt' had thrown it into 'inaction'. The Association became extinct soon after. The need for renewed political activity, however, continued to be felt.[130]

The difference in the personnel of the British Indian and Bombay Associations can perhaps account for the varied effect on politics in the two presidencies. Most of the members of the British Indian Association, whether zemindars or educated middle class men, realised

128. *Hindoo Patriot*, 25 Feb. 1858.
129. *Ibid.*, 8 Apr. 1858.
130. *Rast Goftar*, 29 Jan. 1860.

that their interests lay with the government and in antagonism to non-official Europeans. Moreover, the preservation of their interests demanded the continuation of political activity through an established association—particularly in view of the Rent Bill and the indigo disturbances. The interests of the Bombay Association leaders, on the contrary, were largely linked with those of European merchants and bankers. They could not profitably carry on politics that threatened to alienate them from non-official Europeans. Also, the suspicion cast on their president must have suggested caution to the canny merchant princes who dominated the Bombay Association. This, however, was a temporary effect. In course of time the dynamics of the Indian scene compelled the revival of political associations in Bombay too.[131]

IV

Victory in 1857 changed the British 'from an aggressive and advancing power to a stationary one',[132] and completed India's transition, through an era of turbulence and war, into 'a compact whole to be legislated for'.[133] The strategic importance of a countrywide network of transport and communication having been stressed, India became an administrative and political unit following the development of the railways, roads and the postal and telegraph systems. Laws were codified and the same civil, criminal and penal codes introduced in the country. Education advanced with the opening of universities.

Consequently, as Surendranath Banerji (1848-1925) picturesquely put it, the diverse peoples of India were 'welded together into a compact and homogeneous mass'. Direct contact with the West sowed 'the seeds of a civilization containing the germs of India's future greatness, of her political, moral and intellectual regeneration'. The spread of higher education quickened the process which had been providing the educated classes with a common medium of communication, and elevating them to 'a common platform of thoughts, feelings and aspirations'. The railways further weakened divisive prejudices and enabled the 'patriot' to view 'in the distant horizon the faint streaks of that dawn which are to usher in the day of his country's regeneration and union'.[134]

1857 thus brought about changes in the minds of men and in official policy that had a notable effect on the growth of national consciousness, and facilitated such objective conditions as were essential to its manifestation.

131. See chapter 2.
132. Frere to Wood, 10 Apr. 1861, in Martineau, *op. cit.*, vol. I, p. 337.
133. *Minute by the Hon'ble Mr Stephen on the Administration of Justice in India*, p. 134, Stephen to Argyll, 12 Oct. 1871, enclosure, *Argyll Papers*, reel 320.
134. Address to the Students' Association, Calcutta, 16 Mar. 1878, *Speeches of Surendranath Banerji*, Madras, not dated, pp. 215-21.

S IGNIFICANT structural changes in Indian society had, by the middle of the 19th century, altered the equation of social power. Old elites either withered away or managed to retain a semblance of their former power. The new elites that emerged, however, comprised classes that often clashed with each other in spite of collaboration at times. The circumstances of the emergence of these classes and their internal relationships as well as their responses to the traditional culture and to the British impact influenced the character of Indian nationalism.

The introduction of a new economy and English education produced the classes that aspired to social and political leadership. The social reconstruction following the Permanent Settlement in Bengal gave status of a high order to a class of adventurers who had igratiated themselves with the traders from the West by the offer of their money as *banias* and of their services as *duboshes*. The wealth thus acquired was invested in zemindaries.[1]

Some of the most important families of Bengal thus rose to be the leaders of society. The two branches of the Shobha Bazar Deb family, which owed its prosperity to the association of Nava Krishna (1732-97) with the East India Company, for decades retained hold on social and political leadership. Radhakant Deb (1784-1867) remained until his death the first president of the British Indian Association; he also led for more than 50 years the orthodox phalanx of Hindu society, besides being one of the champions of education. After his death the leadership of the orthodoxy devolved on his cousin, Kali Krishna (1808-74), whose brother, Narendra Krishna (1822-1903), was one of the important leaders and presidents of the British Indian Association.[2]

1. See B. B. Misra, *The Indian Middle Classes*, London, 1961.
2. C.E. Buckland, *Bengal under the Lieutenant-Governors*, Calcutta, 1901. vol. II, pp. 1022-23, 1067-68; *Raja Kali Krishna Bahadur*, undated memorial volume; *Calcutta Review*; vol. XLV, 1867, pp. 317-26.

The greatness of the Tagore family was similarly laid.[3] The two branches of this family, represented by such men as Dwarakanath (1794-1846), Prasanna Kumar (1801-68), Ramanath (1800-77), Debendranath (1817-1905) and Satyendranath, made rich contributions to all spheres of life. In a sense, the history of this family could well be a study, in microcosm, of modern Bengal.

Initially these emerging families viewed themselves as the 'middling class' who would be the harbingers of 'the dawn of a new era'. Attaching great value to land and to *laissez faire* in trade, they rejoiced in the increasing value of land which had risen within 30 years since 1800 from Rs. 15 to Rs. 300 in Calcutta.[4] Slowly and imperceptibly, however, the important zemindar families came to acquire the status of an aristocracy.

In view of the heavy stakes they had in the maintenance of law and order, and in the preservation of their rights and privileges as an important class, the zemindars were the first to conduct politics on an institutional basis. They were aided by an initial identity of interests with independent European traders. The proceedings of the government to resume *lakhiraj* land induced the zemindars to unite for political purposes. Prasanna Kumar and Ramanath Tagore started the *Reformer* in 1831. In April 1838 the Landholders' Society was established.[5]

The zemindars kept up this lead through the British Indian Association, which remained for years the premier political organisation in the country. They were helped by the constant recruitment to their ranks following the circumscription of the flow of capital in Bengal. By making the ownership of land a status symbol *par excellence*, and offering the certainty of a fair and perpetual return, the Permanent Settlement became an effective disincetive to investment in new and risky ventures. Profits of business and professional savings were sunk in zemindaries.[6] The great commercial magnate, Mati Lal Seal (1791-1854), possessed many zemindaries.[7] So did Durga Charan Law (c. 1823-1904) who rose from humble origins to be a president of the British Indian Association.[8] The classic example, perhaps, of rise from middle class *bania* life to the new aristocracy was that of Joy Kishen Mukerji (1808-88), the founder of the Uttarpara Mukerji family.[9]

The creation of new classes initialy followed a similar pattern

3. See J. W. Furrel, *The Tagore Family*, Calcutta, 1892.
4. *Bengal Herald*, 13 Jun. 1829.
5. Furrel, *op. cit.*, pp. 90-6.
6. See *Hindoo Patriot*, 27 Feb. 1858, 'A Voice for the Commerce and Manufacture of India', *Mookerjee's Magazine*, vol. III, Nos. XXI-XXII, pp. 335-61.
7. L. N. Ghose, *Indian Chiefs, Rajas, Zamindars &c.*, Calcutta, 1881, pt. II, pp. 49-50.
8. *Ibid.*, pp. 25-6.
9. Buckland, *op. cit.*, vol. II, pp. 1050-51.

in Bombay which, replacing Surat as the hub of commercial activities in western India, attracted four Parsi families to seek their fortunes under the aegis of the East India Company. [10] While the scions of these families retained their monopoly as brokers, the patriarchs invested the profits thus earned in independent business. [11] To offer a few illustrations, Cowasji Jehangir Readymoney (1812-78), the merchant prince and philanthropist, and his brother, Hirji (1808-1901), were brokers to Cardwell, Parsons & Co., and Lyon Bros. Only in 1846 did Cowasji start as an independent merchant. The Petits, who became the foremost industrialists before J. N. Tata (1839-1904), were brokers to Rennie, Scovell & Co and Dirgoin, Hunter & Co. The Kamas, the founders of the first Indian firm in England, were brokers to Leckie & Co. [12]

Parsis had a hand in virtually all the imports from and exports to Europe. Their eastern trade was direct and extensive. While cotton was an important item of trade, the fortunes of the Readymoneys, Dediseths, Banajis, Kamas, Petits, Jijibhais and others were made in opium. [13] However, after 1840, Parsis began to be displaced by Jews in the China trade, [14] and in Bombay Hindus and Muslims started entering new avenues both in collaboration and in competition with Parsis.

Looking for fresh pastures, the more adventurous among these traders turned to industrial manufacture. The lead came from K. N. Davar (1814-73), and the success of his joint-stock company in its first year (1854) induced M. N. Petit (1803-59) and M. F. Pandey (1812-76) to launch, in 1855, what came to be known as the Oriental Spinning and Weaving Company. [15] The cotton boom produced by the American Civil War temporarily arrested the progress of the industry which, however, took rapid strides thereafter in spite of artificial impediments. [16] Even Hindu banking houses got over their natural diffidence and stepped beyond their traditional avocation to invest in the cotton textile industry. Thus Mangaldas Nathubhai (1832-90) and Varjivandas Madhowdas hailing from established mercantile families, [17] became manufacturers. So did Vinayakrao Jagannath Sankersett (1831-73), Morarji Goculdas (1833-80), Abdulla Dharamsi and other non-Parsi traders.

Becoming a zemindar in Bengal and an industrial manufacturer in Bombay, the former Indian broker to the foreign traders formed

10. These were: Banaji, Wadia, Seth and Modi or Wachghandi. D. E. Wacha, *Shells from the Sands of Bombay*, Bombay, 1920, pp. 279-80.
11. *Ibid.*, p. 98.
12. *Ibid.*, pp. 626-28.
13. D. F. Karaka, *History of the Parsis*, London, 1884. vol. II, p. 245.
14. *Ibid.*, pp. 257-58.
15. *Ibid.*, pp. 247-48.
16. See chapter 3.
17. Wacha, *op. cit.*, p. 104.

a new elite and wrested the leadership of society. Like the British Indian Association in Bengal, the Bombay Association was dominated by such lumaniraries of the upper classes as Jagannath Sankersett, Cowasji Jehangir Readymoney, Varjivandas Madhowdas, Manakji Nasarwanji Petit and Framji Nasarwanji Patel (1804-92).[18]

The oligarchic leadership, which had crystallised in Bengal and Bombay by 1858, depended on the co-operation of the educated middle classes. The two needed each other. A creation of new professions and of English education, which also gave them a rather amorphous unity of outlook, the middle classes were yet seeking the group consciousness and strength necessary for group assertion. Nor had the upper classes so far betrayed such exclusive or selfish spirit as to make a parting of the ways imperative. Rather, they were anxious to enlist educated middle class men who alone could provide the sustained intellectual effort that elevated the level of political discussion and improved the chances of its success. To the middle classes such an association offered a means of acquiring recognition and influence. Gifted men like Girish Chandra Ghosh (1829-69), Harish Chandra Mukerji (1824-61), Peary Chand Mitra (1814-83), Kissory Chand Mitra (1822-73) and others thus actively associated themselves with the British Indian Association.[19] Not always did they see eye to eye with the zemindars. Girish Chandra Ghosh, for instance, assailed the Permanent Settlement. Bengal had prospered, he told a public meeting organised by the British Indian Association, not because but in spite of the permanent zemindary system. If the principle of the Permanent Settlement was correct, there could be no justification 'for depriving the industrious poor of its benefit whilst the lazy non-resident proprietor of mismanaged acres is indulged with every facility for luxurious dissipaton.[20] This provided in course of time a major issue on which the zemindars and the middle classes tried their respective strength.

The dependence of the Bengal upper classes on the middle class talent is highlighted by the editorship of their organ, the *Hindoo Patriot*. After Harish Mukerji's death, Kristo Das Pal became not only its editor, but also, along with Digambar Mitra (1817-77), the master mind of the British Indian Association.[21] When the controversial Rent Bill was being discussed in the legislative council, the zemindar leaders of the Association nominated Pal rather than one

18. *Minutes of Proceedings of the Bombay Association,* vols. I, II.
19. Ghosh and Mukerji were clerks in the office of the Military Auditor-General. Ghosh edited the *Bengalee* and Mukerji the *Hindoo Patriot* Peary Chand was a middling merchant, writer and theosophist. His younger brother, Kissory Chand was writer and social reformer.
20. *Bengalee,* 20 Jan. 1863.
21. R. G. Sanyal, *The Life of the Hon'ble Rai Kristo Das Pal Bahadur,* Calcutta, 1887; Bholanauth Chunder, *Raja Digambar Mitra,* Calcutta, 1893. Belonging to a petty middle class family, Mitra rose to be a large landowner.

of their own class to fight their case.

Unlike Bengal, where some zemindar families had a continuing tradition of learning, including English education, the upper classes in Bombay were educationally ill-equipped. Bombay presented for long the spectacle of men of status having little education, and educated men possessing a social position of not much consequence. Illustrative of this is the fact that three of the first five Indian members of the Bombay legislative council did not know English; and the other two were inadequately educated. [22] It was perhaps his experience in western India that made a contemporary educationist generalise that in Asia it was 'indeed the privilege of the wealthy to be ignorant'.[23] The Poona Sarvajanik Sabha admitted that not many educated people in the presidency possessed 'wealth, rank, position, and influence'.[24] The anomaly caused by the divorce of status and education continued till the 1870s when English educated persons started carving out for themselves, through rise in government service and independent professions, places of honour in society.

The Bombay middle classes were handicapped by the late start of English education which, beginning after the overthrow of the Marathas in 1818, produced its first beneficiaries towards the 1840s. They included persons like Naoroji Fardunji (1817-85), Dadoba Pandurang (1814-82), Vinayak Vasudev, Dadabhai Naoroji, Dr Bhau Daji (1821-85), and Narayan Dinanathji (? -1870); all of whom were to leave a mark on the public life of the presidency, and some on that of the country.[25]

It was natural for the captains of Bombay business, shrewd enough to realise the advantages of political combination, to appreciate the need to have educated middle class men for the formulation of various demands. Thus while all the higher offices of the Bombay Association were distributed among the *shetyas* in accordance with their affluence, Dr Bhau Daji and Naoroji Fardunji were appointed its first secretaries. It was also natural that the Association's maiden petition to British parliament should be the handiwork of the two secretaries and of Narayan Dinanathji.[26]

The circumstantial equilibrium between the upper and the middle classes was being disturbed, however, by a growing incompatibility of interests, and by the natural conflict of generations. This

22. *Times of India*, 25 Jan. 1862.
23. Edwin Arnold, *Education in India*, London, 1860, quoted in *Bombay Times and Standard*, 1 Dec. 1860.
24. Petition to governor of Bombay, *Native Opinion*, 28 Jul. 1872.
25. *Ibid.*, 22 May 1870. Fardunji and Dinanathji were interpreters in Bombay high court; Panduranga, a noted Marathi grammarian, teacher and reformer; Vasudev oriental translator to the Bombay government and Marathi scholar who became the sheriff of Bombay; Daji a leading medical practitioner and indologist.
26. *Ibid.*

first became clear in Bengal, where a whole generation of men like Radhakant Deb and Prasanna Kumar Tagore had been overawed by the territorial revolution the East India Company had wrought in India. More important, the phenomenal rise of their families had been due to co-operation with the alien rulers. To bask in official favour and to obtain titles and private entry to the government house constituted the acme of their aspirations in public life. Not that their politics was sheer selfishness masquerading as public spirit. Experience and egotism had so framed their psychology as to render them incapable of believing 'that any good object could be gained in opposing the powers that be'.[27]

Vested interests checked the escalation of political aspirations among the generations of zemindars that followed. But among the educated middle classes, their minds imbued with ideas of freedom, equality and democracy, every new generation revealed a larger conception of rights and aspirations. The difference between the approaches and attitudes of Kristo Das Pal, the cautious, provincial statesman, and Surendranath Banerji, the orator-politician whose jurisdiction extended over the whole of India, represents the enlargement of middle class aspirations between 1858 and 1885.[28]

This and the material circumstances of the two classes worked towards a conflict. As against the recognition and privileges enjoyed by the upper classes, the middle classes possessed no privileges, and they had to earn bread and recognition the hard way. Most of them aspired to 'get a Government situation';[29] the rest flocked to 'the bar and law'. Both of these being over-stocked, educated and discontented men emerged in increasing numbers, incapacitated by their education to follow alternative vocations. For, higher education in India attended too much to philosophy, metaphysics, perhaps even to literature, and too little to practical science'.[30] Liberal education was in fashion. In one year, history, language, logic, moral philosophy and political economy were offered as voluntary subjects by five times as many B.A. students of the Bombay university as had opted for chemistry, mechanics, astronomy, optics and other branches of natural science; botany, geology and physical geography, it may be added, were chosen by none.[31]

Frustration followed the failure of educated men to 'obtain employment worthy of their talents and acquirements'.[32] An M.A.

27. *National Paper*, 15 Apr. 1874, in *Raja Kali Krishna Bahadur*, p. 8.
28. Cf R. C. Palit, ed., *Speeches and Minutes of Kristo Pal*, Calcutta, 1882; *Speeches of Surendra Nath Banerji*, 2 vols., Calcutta, 1894.
29. M. Carpenter, *Six Months in India*, London, 1868. vol. I, p. 56.
30. Temple to Salisbury, 26 Feb. 1875, *Salisbury Papers*, reel 818.
31. *Rast Goftar*, 2 Feb. 1873.
32. Temple, *Men and Events of My Time in India*, London, 1882, p. 15. Henceforth referred to as *Men and Events*.

or B.A. could be found accepting jobs worth Rs. 50 or 60 a month, and, though rarely, an Indian barrister returning home to be a munsif.[33] These men, 'thrown adrift on society', were 'in most cases the hopes of their families'. Educated by their parents after sacrificing 'the comforts and even the conveniences of life', they represented so many false foci of 'long-cherished dreams of riches and elevation in the social scale'.[34] The impulsion 'to demand increased privileges' rather than 'acquiesce in their present status'[35] brought the middle classes into conflict with both the upper classes and the government.

The expanding energies and the growing problems of the middle classes needed something more than the cramped, exclusive British Indian Association. Early in the 1860s, Ishwar Chandra Vidyasagar (1820-91), educationist and social reformer, and Dwarkanath Mitter (1833-74), a lawyer elevated to the bench in 1867, conceived of an alternative association that would act as 'the voice and the organ of the middle classes'. The idea miscarried because of inadequate support.[36] Abortive attempts were also made simultaneously to convert the British Indian Association into a more representative institution by having its membership fee reduced from Rs. 50 to Rs. 5 a year. In 1868, the *Amrita Bazar Patrika*, a pioneer of that fervent nationalism that was to become a force towards the end of the 19th century, dismissed the British Indian Association as 'a small section of the vast community of this vast country'. The paper also floated the idea of an all-India organisation in which Bombay, Calcutta, Madras, Oudh and the Panjab would be represented, and where the wants of India and the best modes of meeting them would be discussed. This would not be an ordinary association; it was intended to be a parallel government for the country. The *Patrika* brushed aside the objection that the time was not ripe for such a body, and philosophised: 'On certain occasions man may be subject to time, but generally time is subservient to man.'[37] Despite its rhetoric, the *Patrika* was serious about replacing the British Indian Association.[38] It was at this juncture that the *Native Opinion* reported from the western metropolis of India that the graduates of the Calcutta university had started a new association, and exhorted the Bombay graduates to bestir themselves like-

33. *Bharat Mihir*, 21 Nov. 1878, *Report on Native Press, Bengal*, 30 Nov. 1878, p 9.
34. *Selections from the Writings and Speeches of Raja Peary Mohan Mukerjee*, published by T. N. Mukerjee, Calcutta, 1924, pp. 29-30.
35. Temple, *Men and Events*, p. 431.
36. S. N. Banerjea, *A Nation in Making*, London, 1925, p. 41.
37. *Amrita Bazar Patrika*, 16 Apr. 1868, *Report on the Native Press, Bengal*. 29 Jan. 1878, pp. 12-3.
38. This discussion is based, often *verbatim*, on S. Chandra, 'The Indian League and the Western India Association', *The Indian Economic and Social History Review*, vol. VIII, No. 1, 1971, pp. 73-98, though some of the details have been omitted here.

wise.[39] The appeal went unheeded, and the report proved unfounded.

Dissatisfaction was meanwhile mounting against the 'scandal of the British Indian Association' which had been 'tolerated long enough'. It was said to be 'high time for the native community to resent this impertinent representation, or more properly speaking, misrepresentation'.[40] Once again the *Amrita Bazar Patrika* took the lead. A public notice was issued in the first week of August 1875 announcing that an association was being planned to fulfil five objectives; these were to 'represent the views of the people on all public questions bearing on their material and political advancement'· to 'promote the general good' and disseminate 'political education amongst the people'; to 'maintain by all legitimate means the rights of the different classes of the community'; to create 'by all legitimate means a feeling of nationality in the minds of the people'; and to 'initiate measures for the development of the resources of the country'.[41] Pursuant to this notice, a public meeting, duly advertised in newspapers, was held on 25 September 1875.[42] On that day began the brief existence of the controversial Indian League.

Intended though it was to represent the middle class which had been resenting the upper class domination of the British Indian Association, the Indian League had to face serious opposition throughout the ten months that elapsed between its foundation and the establishment of a rival middle class association. Considerations of personal prestige might have contributed marginally to dissensions among the middle class leaders. But it was uneven conceptions of nationalism, which in turn produced differences in the understanding of national interests and in the modes of serving them, which seem to have created a feeling among the educated leadership of Calcutta that the interests of the country were not in safe keeping with the *Patrika* group. Not only pride, which did engender clash of personalities, but prudence, which counselled caution as against romanticism in nationalism, brought about the suppression of the League. The *Patrika's* conception of nationalism, with its extremist inclination, must have been a red rag for most of the educated people who treated nationalism and loyalty to the British as compatible categories. Even before Lytton came to India and decided to curb the freedom of the vernacular Press, the *Patrika*, it is significant, had obliged the authorities to discuss the desirability of modifying the existing law on the subject.[43] Co-operation with the coterie conducting such a newspaper had obvious risks which most of the educated leaders were loath to incur. Yet, the Indian League initiated the process of

39. *Native Opinion*, 10 May 1868.
40. Letter by A Poor Native, *Indian Daily News*, 14 Sep. 1875.
41. *National Paper*, quoted ibid., 6 Aug. 1875.
42. *Ibid.*, 25 Sept. 1875.
43. Home Department, Judicial Proceedings, A, Apr. 1878, Nos. 203 and 206.

self-assertion by the Bengali middle classes. The Indian Association consummated it.

The inauguration of the Indian Association was resolutely resisted by the League. After the first resolution had been proposed at the public meeting held to organise the new association, the need for another middle class association was denied in a cogent but futile speech by Kalicharan Banerji (1847-1907), a leading advocate of the Calcutta high court. Surendranath Banerji replied that neither the British Indian Association, which represented 'only a section of the people', nor the Indian League, which represented 'no portion of the community whatever', possessed the 'organisation to keep up or stimulate political life among the people'. When Hemant Kumar (?-1892), the eldest of the Ghosh brothers who managed the *Patrika*, retorted, 'that's a lie', Surendranath demanded his expulsion. During the brief pandemonium that followed, several invitees, reporters and the Leaguers left the meeting. The remaining resolutions having been passed on the resumption of proceedings, the Indian Association was formally established.[44]

The Indian Association soon managed to be accepted as the undisputed organisation of the Bengali middle classes. Almost imperceptibly the Indian League was consigned to oblivion; its president, Rev. K. M. Banerji (1813-85), became the head of the Indian Association, and even Kalicharan Banerji decided to own the infant he had attempted to strangle at its birth. In far-off Bombay also the emergence of the Association was welcomed.[45]

The founders of the Indian League were men of enthusiasm and idealism whose self-righteousness had made them ostentatiously assertive. In the first flush of success they had lacked the balance to appreciate differences of opinion and the sense to recognise the need for compromise. There was, therefore, no love lost between the League and the British Indian Association. It was too late by the time the League awoke to the shock of opposition from all around and attempted reconciliation. But the projectors of the Indian Association, led by Surendranath Banerji and Ananda Mohan Bose (1847-1906), barrister-at-law, were men of practical prudence. Instead of sharpening division on class lines, as the League had done, they sought to conserve their energies by trying to work, whenever possible, in conjunction with the British Indian Association. This explains why the *Hindoo Patriot,* which had contemptuously ignored the League at the time of its creation, blessed the Indian Association with the expectation that its young members would 'both deserve and command success' by conducting 'their operations with judgment and moderation'.[46]

44. *Hindoo Patriot*, 31 Jul. 1876; *Supplement to Bengalee*, 5 Aug. 1876.
45. *Native Opinion*, 20 Aug. 1876.
46. *Hindoo Patriot*, 31 Jul. 1876.

Both the British Indian Association and the Indian Association were in fact anxious to avoid a clash. Realising that the circumstances of the two interests—one distinct and defined, and the other inchoate and struggling for an identity—demanded representation through separate organisations, they accepted the existence of two associations. The two united to convene a public meeting against the licence tax; they were joined by the dying Indian League in a strong petition on the civil service question.[47] The secretary of the Indian Association even acknowledged the assistance proffered by the leading lights of the elder association, particularly Maharaja Narendra Krishna Deb Bahadur and K. D. Pal.[48] But co-operation became increasingly difficult as the British Indian Association betrayed its timidity and selfishness in matters like the Vernacular Press Act.[49]

Despite the will to maintain mutual understanding, there appeared presages of the coming conflict. When Temple decided to frame rules for enhancing the rates paid by the occupancy ryots, the Indian Association felt obliged to appoint a sub-committee and undertake preliminary enquiries in the mofussil in order to protect the agricultural community, 'the basis and the foundation of the whole social fabric'.[50] This source of friction, however, remained dormant as the question was shelved by the government for the time being.

The forcing of the issue was deferred only temporarily. The Indian Association being anxious to prove worthy of its name, instead of being recognised as a body of the middle classes in but one presidency, the peasantry were uppermost in its designs of broadening its base. Ripon's Rent Bill to grant some relief to the Bengal ryots brought the two associations into collision. While the British Indian Association fought the battle of the zemindars, the Indian Association organised monster meetings and rallies all over Bengal to awaken and organise the cultivators.[51] The British Indian Association became unquestionably a partisan body representing only the zemindars,[52] as sympathy for the cultivators spread as far as western India.[53]

This was in the 1880s and it marked the emergence of the middle classes in Bengal as the leaders of society, especially in politics. Seizing their newly won popularity, they started agitating for representation in legislative councils. Speaking in the name of people, they denied the claim of the upper classes to represent the people. The

47. *Sadharani*, 23 Jun. 1878, *Report on the Native Press, Bengal*, 29 Jun. 1878, p.3.
48. *The First Annual Report of the Indian Association*, Calcutta, 1877, pp. ii-iii.
49. See Chapter 4.
50. *The First Annual Report of the Indian Association*, p. 52. Sir Richard Temple (1826-1902) was the lieutenant-governor of Bengal from 1874 to 1877.
51. Home Department, Public Proceedings, B, Jun. 1882, No. 159, p. 3.
52. *Ibid.*, B, Jun. 1885, Nos. 269-72.
53. *Voice of India*, 15 Mar. 1884, vol. 2, No. 5, p. 160.

performance of the upper class nominees in the legislative councils lent credibility to the assertion, for, barring occasional exceptions, they voted and spoke 'according to official desires'. The authorities naturally preferred men who could 'pose as representatives of the people' while 'echoing back the official voice, and swelling the official chorus'. The middle class leaders decided to struggle for representation 'without the co-operation of the rich and the privileged classes whose selfish interest might induce them to hold aloof'. They even thought that the middle classes alone possessed patriotic fervour and constituted 'the main strength and the future hope of Hindustan'.[54]

Despite their admiration for their counterparts in Bengal and desire to emulate their performance, the middle classes in Bombay failed to destroy the pre-eminence of the mercantile aristocracy. In the metropolis of Bombay, the emergence of the middle classes as leaders of society was delayed by the comparatively slow diffusion of higher education and a certain lack of idealism. Bengal was way ahead of the rest of India in respect of higher education. Its lead began at the First Arts level and increased progressively, reaching the highest at the M.A. standard. Between 1864 and 1885, Bengal produced 5,252 F.A.s, 2,153 B.A.s and 491 M.A.s, as against 1,568 F.A.s, 933 B.A.s and 79 M.A.s in Bombay. In fact the number of M.A.s produced by Bengal was double the aggregate of M.A.s in the rest of the country.[55]

While the late beginning of English education in Bombay was the major factor in operation, a certain lack of idealism may be said to have played a minor role in delaying the emergence of the middle classes in Bombay as the leaders of society. The essentially commercial character of the city, its heterogeneous population and the absence of commonly shared stirring historical traditions were hardly conducive to idealism. In a sense Bombay was more alive than any other part of the country. People and everything around them moved on relentlessly. They had vitality, life, energy and enterprise. But in the absence of a past to think of, tradition to recount or bygone glory to bask in,[56] they lacked that sentimental cohesion which could act as a catalyst to the awareness and assertion of group identity through the consciousness of material grievances.

Pherozeshah Mehta (1845-1915) and Badruddin Tyabji, two prominent middle class leaders, exemplify this. Mehta, a successful lawyer and man of business, openly confessed to his lack of idealism.[57]

54. Speech on the repeal of the Vernacular Press Act, Feb. 1882, A. Banerji, ed., *Speeches of Lal Mohan Ghose*, Calcutta, 1883, pp. 112-14.
55. *Report of the Indian Education Commission*, Calcutta, 1883, p. 28.
56. R. L. Mitra's speech on 'The Parsis of Bombay', 26 Feb. 1880, Mitter, ed., *op. cit.,* p. 105.
57. J.R.B. Jeejeebhoy, *Some Unpublished and Later Speeches and Writings of the Hon. Sir Pherozeshah Mehta*, Bombay, 1918, p. 29.

After the death of Sir Jamsetji Jijibhai (1811-77), the second Parsi baronet, Mehta, who had studied in England during the heyday of liberalism, baffled many contemporaries by his successful support to the unprecedented move of having the young third baronet elected the head of the Parsi community,[58] even though the latter possessed no qualifications except his family name. Also, when a group of self-seeking Parsi and Hindu *seths* broke away from the Bombay Association, Mehta sided with them.[59]

Politics for Tyabji was a means to raise his status in society, and to better the prospects of his community. Conducted with moderation, politics in those days often facilitated elevation to the bench or nomination to the legislative councils. When Temple left Bombay to seek a place in British parliament, Tyabji supported a memorial to the departing governor in the name of the public. This was widely condemned as a betrayal of 'Gladstone, Bright and Fawcett' and as the erection of 'a statue of repression and time-serving'.[60] In this 'Temple-worship'[61] Tyabji 'went into ecstasies, because Sir R. Temple promised him the assistance of government to found a Mahomedan school'.[62]

An established barrister belonging to the largest minority community, Tyabji seemed the best man to provide a secular image to political movements. Thus, before maturing their plan to organise 'a political association of active character', P. M. Mehta, a Parsi, and K. T. Telang (1850-93), a Hindu, thought it prudent to approach Tyabji and seek his co-operation 'as the representative of the third community to which he belonged'.[63] Tyabji agreed and took a prominent part in the inauguration of the Bombay Presidency Association on 31 January 1885. He also became the chairman of the council of the Association; but he attended its meeting for the first time on 4 January 1886.[64] He again disappeared thereafter. Such experiences[65] led Mehta, after Tyabji's death, to refuse to have anything to do with a memorial to the deceased leader. Mehta maintained that Tyabji's services had been 'more in the interests of the Mahomedan

---

58. Mehta's letter to *Times of India*, 23 Jul. 1877.

59. Discussed below.

60. *Native Opinion*, 28 Mar. 1880; *Subodh Patrika, Rast Goftar, Bombay Samachar, Dnyan Prakash* and *Indu Prakash* also condemned the memorial; *ibid* Temple was governor of Bombay from 1877 to 1880.

61. *Ibid.*, 21 Mar. 1880.

62. Mehta's letter to *Bombay Gazette*, 14 Mar. 1880.

63. Jeejeebhoy, ed., *op. cit.*, p. 185. Telang was a lawyer, politician, social reformer and writer; elevated to the Bombay bench.

64. *Manuscript Minute Book of Council Meetings* (Bombay Presidency Association), vol. I, p. 51.

65. See S. Chandra, 'Badruddin Tyabji: A Study of Personal and Group Interests in Indian Nationalism', *Bengal Past and Present*, Jul.-Dec. 1968, pp. 190-98.

community than of the country at large'.[66]

Moreover, upper class leadership in Bombay was more oligarchal than in Bengal, and the transmission of hereditary assets included political leadership also. The most remarkable, in this regard, was the position of the Parsi baronet family. Whether it was the Bombay Association, the Bombay Branch of the East India Association or the Bombay Presidency Association, the patronage of the existing Sir Jamsetji Jijibhai was considered indispensable.

The Bombay Association which, in spite of its chequered existence, continued till 1884 to be the chief political organisation in the city, was particularly dominated by the business magnates. At one stage, for example, Jagannath Sankersett and his son, Vinayakrao J. Sankersett, were its president and secretary respectively. After it had become defunct, the meeting that led to its revival was held on 27 April 1867 at Vinayakrao J. Sankersett's residence.[67] It was actually revived at a meeting held on 14 December at the house of its new president, Mangaldas Nathubhai.[68] It is an index of the latter's hold on the Bombay Association that till his resignation in 1875 most of its annual meetings continued to be held at his place. After Nathubhai, another merchant prince, Dinshaw M. Petit (1823-1901), was elected president on 6 April 1876.[69]

Scrupulous regard was shown to social status in the apportionment of offices. Thus while Jamsetji Jijibhai became, as a matter of course, the honorary president of the revivified Bombay Association, and Nathubhai its president, no less than four vice-presidents were appointed in order to accommodate Framji Nasserwanji Patel, Cowasji J. Readymoney, Byramji Jijibhai (1822-90) and V. J. Sankersett, all of them commercial magnates. But the formidable scholarship of Dr Bhau Daji and his services to the Bombay Association since its inception could get him only a place on the managing committee. Commoners were not permitted to vie with aristocrats. Even the managing committee, in fact, had many aspirants, and 'an unwieldy corpus of 40 members' was created to satisfy their concern for 'unreal personal glory'. This was done in spite of the example of the British Indian Association, which had 'a small workable and working body' as its managing committee.[70]

Even though the Bombay Association was revived, petty jealousies and selfishness of a rather inferior order kept politics at a low ebb in Bombay. Indiscriminatingly voted addresses to every departing dignitary and actions in the legislatve council created an impression that, 'basking in the sunshine of official favour and dazzled by

66. Husain B. Tyabji, *Badruddin Tyabji*, Bombay, 1952, p. 375.
67. *Native Opinion*, 28 Apr. 1867.
68. *Ibid.*, 15 Dec. 1867.
69. *Ibid.*, 9 Apr. 1876.
70. *Ibid.*, 22 Dec. 1867.

the light of the "stars" ', these upper class people were 'utterly unfit for the position they affect and are taken in some quarters to occupy as the leaders or representatives of the people'.[71]

Heated discussion on municipal affairs further exposed the selfishness of the upper class leaders. For example, in order to obtain relief at the cost of the middle and lower classes, a group of merchants headed by V. J. Sankersett attempted to have 'the occupiers' rates, and perhaps the house-tax too' substituted by 'the municipal income tax and license taxes'.[72] At a meeting held on 7 September 1872 at Sankersett's place in Girgaum with the host in the chair, a petition to this effect was proposed.[73] Though the meeting was confined to invitees, the petition was opposed on the first day by Dr Atmaram Pandurang (1823-93), R. G. Bhandarkar (1837-1925), B. M. Wagle (1838-87), Janardan S. Gadgil, N. R. Ranina (1833-1900), V. N. Mandlik, Naoroji Fardunji and others;[74] all of them, it may be noted, middle class men. The division, however, was not strictly on class lines. The secretaries of the project were Pherozeshah Mehta and Shantaram Narayan, both high court pleaders. Mangaldas Nathubhai, the rich president of the Bombay Association, on the other hand, kept aloof.

Also alarming was the contention of Narayan Vasudev (?-1874), a rich self-made merchant, that although some rate-payers might be dissatisfied with the degree of representation granted by the government, 'the majority of the people belonging to the old school are of opinion that Bombay is not fitted for representation yet'.[75]

The selfish opportunism of the initiators of this move was highlighted by the fact that most of them were acting contrary to their earlier professions. Some of them, viz., Sankersett, Kesowji Naik, a prominent mill-owner and cotton merchant, Narayan Vasudev, Nanabhai Byramji Jijibhai (1841-1914), son of Byramji Jijibhai,. and Raghunath Narayan Khote (1821-91), a merchant interested in insurance business, had only 28 months earlier, on 2 May 1870, assembled in the Town Hall to protest against the income tax. Now they were pressing for the same measure in order to get rid of the occupiers' rate.[76] And Shantaram Narayan had only a few months earlier, at

71. *Native Opinion*, 5 May 1872.
72. *Ibid.*, 13 Oct. 1872.
73. *Ibid.*, 20 Oct. 1872.
74. *Ibid.* Dr Pandurang was a medical practitioner and reformer; Bhandarkar a noted Sanskrit scholar and reformer; Wagle a legal practitioner and reformer; Gadgil for some time, till 1875, editor and proprietor of the *Indu Prakash*, an Anglo-Marathi weekly of progressive social and political views; Ranina a solicitor and reformer.
75. *Ibid.*, 27 Oct. 1872. It is interesting that Vasudev's nomination to the Bombay legislative council was attributed to his advocacy of Crawford, the prodigal municipal commissioner. *Ibid.*, 11 Aug. 1872.
76. *Ibid.*, 20 Oct. 1872.

a rate-payers' meeting on 21 May 1872, gone beyond the Bombay Association in demanding representation.[77]

A contrast to the Girgaum meeting was provided by non-official Europeans who, in collaboration with many Indian rate-payers, demanded representation unfettered by official interference. On 5 November 1872 a meeting was held in the Framji Cowasji Hall under the chairmanship of A. J. Macdonald of the Sir Charles Forbes & Co. to vote a petition to the viceroy against the Bombay Municipality Bill. Speaking at it, K. N. Kabraji (1842-1904), editor of the *Rast Goftar*, ridiculed the Girgaum memorial and criticised the Bombay government for treating it as representative of the feelings of the people. He even alleged that some of the 40 signatories to the petition had protested to the governor that they had signed it under a 'false impression'.[78]

The Girgaum faction added to its unpopularity by attempting to ruin the Bombay Association. Failing to oust Naoroji Fardunji, the secretary of the Association, in order to acquire control over it, V. J. Sankersett, Narayan Vasudev, Raghunath Narayan Khote, Byramji Jijibhai and Nanabhai B. Jijibhai seceded 'without the slightest public occasion for the step', and organised the Western India Association. Other prominent persons who left the Bombay Association to become founder members of the new Association were Shantaram Narayan, Pherozeshah Mehta, Ardaseer B. Kapadia, barrister-at-law, Maneckji Cursetji (afterwards Sir Jamsetji Jijibhai, third baronet, 1877) and Ahmedbhoy Habibbhoy, a prominent landowner of Thana.[79]

The move, as is clear, was not confined to 'mere capitalists with ignorant minds who subordinate every public consideration to their self-worship and mistaken ideas of greatness', but had 'aiders and abettors among some who have received a liberal education and whose minds thus polished have breathed the invigorating atmosphere of English life and witnessed instances of public spirit and citizenlike conduct'.[80]

The contumely that greeted the Western India Association proved fatal. *The Times of India* pronounced that the Association would consist of the 'plutocracy of Bombay on its sordid and selfish side', a few 'clever time-servers who have personal ends of their own to serve in connection with the Executive Government', and 'a few more' who represented 'that very small feeling of personal animosity to the Secretary of the old Association which his somewhat uncompromising manner may have stirred up'.[81] To this list were added by the *Native*

77. *Times of India*, 23 May 1872.
78. *Native Opinion*, 10 Nov. 1872.
79. *Ibid.*, 13, 27 Apr. 1873.
80. *Times of India*, 7 Apr. 1873 quoted this passage from *Native Opinion of* 6 Apr. and shared the disappointment.
81. *Ibid.*, 23 Apr. 1873.

Opinion 'one or two innocent simpletons with inherited position who probably do not fathom the intention of their astute colleagues and have no idea as to where they would go or lead them'.[82]   The *Indu Prakash* condemned the new Association as having been got up at 'a secretly packed up meeting',[83] while the *Rast Goftar* warned the public against the 'Sunkersett House Schemers' who had allowed Bombay to go to pieces by supporting Crawford, advocating the income tax and opposing representation.[84] Denying them the right to represent the people of western India, the *Gujarat Mitra* angrily admonished 'these illiterate fools to spend some time in the study of the English in the Elphinstone High School rather than rudely set themselves up as interpreters of native thought, and as expounders of political wisdom to Mr. Tucker, the Morning Star of Municipal misgovernment in Bombay'.[85] The *Dnyan Chakshu* took them to task for their 'undignified and idiotic notions of creating an anti-public body'.[86] The *Argus*, edited by a European, quietly advised the 'Sankersettonians' to act in harmony with the Bombay Association.[87]

Even Pherozeshah Mehta's exposition, in the Anglo-Indian newspaper *Bombay Gazette*, of the defectors' point of view failed to create an impression. For one thing, it admitted a tussle of personalities. The seceders, Mehta wrote, had found it impossible to work with a president who was 'wise in his own conceit', and a secretary 'who made a personal matter of every disagreement on a public question, who once had the sulks for six months together with us, because we ventured to suggest that a petition which he had drawn up might be somewhat improved by a few alterations'.[88] To this the *Bombay Gazette* quipped: '...if the president and the secretary were as they were, why did the offended members not manfully strive to turn them out?' Making fun of Mehta's allusions to European history in his communication, the *Gazette* observed that the writer sadly lacked the sense or knowledge to read the story of the Kilkenny cats in relation to the history of his own country.[89]

Nor did Mehta inspire credence by his claim that 'the principal reason' for the creation of 'the new association was that there were certain higher and nobler aims that still remained to be undertaken than those included in the programme of the old association'.[90] These

82. *Rast Goftar*, 20 Apr. 1873.
83. *Native Opinion*, 13, 27 Apr. 1873.
84. *Indu Prakash*, 21 Apr. 1873, quoted in *Native Opinion*, 27 Apr. 1873.
    Gujarat Mitra, 20 Apr. 1873, quoted *ibid*.
85. Henry Pendock St. George Tucker (1823-1905) was a member of the Bombay council.
86. *Dnyan Chakshu*, 23 Apr. 1873, quoted *ibid*.
87. *Ibid*.
88. Letter by Mehta to *Bombay Gazette*, 14 May 1873.
89. *Ibid*.
90. *Ibid*.

higher and nobler aims envisaged a contraction of the principle of popular representation by arrogating to 'the merest handful of people' political knowledge and, therefore, the prerogative to speak on public questions. It was this 'object', claimed the ideologue of the Western India Association, 'which distinguishes the old from the new association'.[91]

Mehta might have appraised correctly the social situation in India; but neither his principles nor his principals could be acceptable to those whose complaint against the Bombay Association had been that it was not representative of the people. More, not less, representation was the spirit of the age with which the middle classes were getting imbued. And, in any case, the unscrupulousness of men like Sankersett, Khote and Byramji Jijibhai being public knowledge, it seemed a daring travesty to talk of nobler and higher aims in relation to them.

Never since its revival had the Bombay Association enlisted popular support. Viewed as a body that served 'the ends of a few interested and forward people', it had failed to provide the desideratum of a representative association.[92] But the split of 1873 unexpectedly created widespread sympathy for it. Nothing, however, came of it. Lack of harmony among its members and a supreme unconcern for public affairs continued as before, occasioning the complaint that they had 'ample time to devote to their money-making pursuits, but no moment left to spend for their country's cause'. A dozen of them had time to sit on a committee, 'the all engrossing and important question before which is as to what sort and kind of people should receive invitations at Government House Entertainments'. Not one was 'willing enough to lead and guide a Representative Association'. Nor would the *shetyas* permit the infusion of new blood by reducing the rate of subscription, much less adopt the principle of representation as had been done by the Sarvajanik Sabha, the 'single olive branch' in the presidency.[93]

Even the performance of the Bombay Branch of the East India Association was no better. Though it had a larger middle class element than the Bombay Association, the top leadership of the two associations was to a great extent identical. Having among its members those who had formed the ill-fated Western India Association, the Bombay Branch of the East India Association also was afflicted with dissensions, and it remained more or less inactive. In three years it held only one annual meeting, in 1876.[94] In vain did Dadabhai Naoroji plead with Mehta to reform the Branch by persuading the members to let 'bygones be bygones'.[95]

91. *Ibid.*
92. *Rast Goftar*, 17 Sep. 1871.
93. *Native Opinion*, 23 May 1880.
94. *Ibid.*, 2 Apr. 1876.
95. Naoroji to Mehta, 26 Jan. 1883, *Mehta Papers*, reel 1.

Feeling against intermittent political animation and its utilisation for personal ends crystallised early in 1885 in the form of the Bombay Presidency Association. It seemed uncertain till the last moment whether another lease of life would be given to the Bombay Association or a new organisation be created. B.M. Malabari (1853-1912), editor of the *Indian Spectator* and one whose advice was sought and heeded, reported as late as 25 January 1885 that a public meeting could be expected any time during the week for the revival of the Bombay Association, as Mehta, Telang and Tyabji had been 'at it a good while'.[96] But the public meeting that followed gave birth to a new association. Perhaps the promoters were convinced of the necessity of beginning *de novo* if bygones were really to be bygones. With the old association were ineffaceably associated certain memories which, if at all, could be buried by erasing the old name.

To this extent the new organisation was a triumph of the middle class leadership. But this was a qualified triumph.   In Bengal the middle classes had successfully rebelled against the zemindar leadership a decade earlier, in 1875. In Bombay they lacked, even in 1885— the year of the Indian National Congress—the confidence to go alone. They had to court the co-operation of those very *shetyas* whom they had all along assailed for selfishness. Jamsetji Jijibhai was requested to be the president of the Bombay Presidency Association.   Among others, Mangaldas Nathubhai, Varjivandas Madhowdas, Byramji Jijibhai and Naoroji Fardunji, the men who had been the centre of public attack and counter-attack during the schism of 1873, were made vice-presidents.   Even when Sir Jamsetji resigned on an issue on which the public verdict went against him,[97] the middle class leaders felt obliged to have another aristocrat, Dinshaw M. Petit, as the new president.

The realisation was there that the wealthy self-seeking *shetyas* could not be trusted with the leadership of society; it found frequent expression in the form of pious, but ineffectual, exhortations in leading journals like the *Native Opinion, Rast Goftar* and the *Indu Prakash*.   But mainly because of its late development in Bombay, the middle class lacked the strength to challenge the business and industrial magnates of the metropolis. The effort, however, continued. It is instructive that while Mandlik's paper, the *Native Opinion*, harped on the necessity of a representative association, and suggested the wisdom of modifying the Bombay Association accordingly, Mandlik himself worked from within to hold the Association together in spite of internal dissensions and public criticism. Obviously, what he wrote and encouraged to be written, he himself found difficult to turn into reality.

96. *Indian Spectator*, 25 Jan. 1885.
97. *Indu Prakash*, 12 Oct. 1885; *Indian Spectator*, 18 Oct. 1885.

Nor were the *shetyas* as powerful as the zemindars. Unlike the British Indian Association, which represented a solid front of the landlord class even if in reality it was dominated by a select band of individuals, the Bombay Association, with the possible exception of its first five years, always remained a tottering house. Almost dead during the 1860s till its revival in 1867, when also it led a perilous existence, it was badly shaken by the Western India Association.[98] That it was against this mercantile aristocracy that the educated middle class of Bombay failed to stand is a commentary on the state of its development.

There were differences within the Bengal leadership also. But whereas these were more often than not the result of honest divergence of opinion about matters of communal concern, or of clashing class interests, in Bombay the differences were the upshot of vanity and self-seeking.

In Poona the middle classes were more powerful than in Bombay, despite the late introduction of English education. In the absence of a new aristocracy, there emerged no tussle for leadership between the upper and middle classes. The old Maratha *sardars*, who had been left in enjoyment of landed estates without their former powers, were too effete to offer a challenge to the emerging middle classes; and the latter's respect for the departed glory of the Maratha power found a focal point in these *sardars* who were its only living reminders. Moreover, the association of the Maratha aristocracy also ensured the prestige and financial stability of a movement or organisation. So, in spite of its creation by the middle class leaders, the Poona Sarvajanik Sabha had as its president H.H. Shrinivas Rao Parsharam Pandit *alias* Rao Sahab Pant Pratinidhi, Chief of Oundha. Its vice-presidents, with the exception of Madhaorao Ballal, were also H.H.s—the chiefs of Sangli, Jamkhindi, Vinchoor, Akulkote, Jat, Phalton and Kurundwad. But, unlike the top leadership of the Bombay Association, they were ornamental heads, and the Sabha was actually run by middle class leaders, particularly Ganesh Wasudeo Joshi (1828-80), Krishnaji Luxuman Noolkar, S. H. Chiplunkar (1824-78), M. G. Ranade (1842-1901) and S.H. Sathe (1836-1912).

Though the Sabha betrayed a pronounced inclination towards the aristocracy and the middle classes, as was evidenced by its obsessive pining for a permanent settlement of the Bengal type, it was based on a rather archaic system of representation and included members 'of all the other classes of the community'.[99] Despite its class bias, however, the Sabha evinced greater solicitude for the masses than did

98. *Minutes of Proceedings of the Annual General Meeting of the Bombay Association*, Bombay, 1875, pp. 5-7.
99. 'Annual Report of the Managing Committee of the Poona Sarvajanik Sabha for 1872-73', *Native Opinion*, 11 May 1873.

any other contemporary political association. The pains taken by it during the Deccan famine at the cost of inviting official hostility illustrate this.[100]

True to its claim of being the leader of the *mofussil*, the Sabha established a network of branches throughout the presidency. It wrote off Bombay, representing commercial interest, as an island, geographically, historically, commercially and intellectually isolated from 'the great interior', and preserving 'its separate and peculiar character'.[101] Never looking to Bombay for inspiration, the Sabha came to be respected by those who chafed under the selfish domination of the aristocratic Bombay leadership. They welcomed the news that a Sarvajanik Sabha, similar in its constitution and objects to the Poona Sabha, was likely to be established in Bombay.[102]

There also emerged in Poona, during the 1880s, a group of middle class idealists who thought in terms of making sacrifices for the regeneration of the country. Led by Vishnu Krishna Chiplunkar (1850-82), the fiery author of the *Nibandhamala* who had resigned as a teacher from government service, young and gifted men like B.G. Tilak (1856-1920), M.B. Namjoshi, G.G. Agarkar (1857-95)—despite the poverty of his family—and N.K. Dharap, who, too, had resigned from government service, devoted themselves to the promotion of education as the first step in this momentous process. The early history of the Deccan Education Society[103] which they founded represents the emergence of a new generation of self-denying public workers. They also provided Indian journalism with a novel fervour and boldness through the *Nibandhamala*, *Kiran*, *Deccan Star*, *Kesari* and the *Mahratta*.

Both in Bengal and Bombay the middle classes thus obtained remarkable influence and power between 1858 and 1885. By the latter date they had become supreme in Bengal and Poona; in Bombay they were hovering on the threshold of supremacy.

II

Besides political associations, the Press, dominated mainly by the educated middle classes, also represented the emergence of 'a new mental force'.[104] It not only reflected but also accelerated 'the many-sided intellectual energy'[105] and awakening that characterised the later 19th century Indian society. Even the authorities viewed it as

100. See *Quarterly Journal of the Poona Sarvajanik Sabha* for 1876-77.
101. Petition of the Poona Sarvajanik Sabha to the governor of Bombay, 28 Jul. 1872, *Native Opinion*, 18 Aug. 1872.
102. *Rast Goftar*, 17 Sep. 1871.
103. See P.M. Limaye, *Deccan Education Society*, Poona, 1935.
104. Temple to Salisbury, 28 Jan. 1878, *Salisbury Papers*, reel 818.
105. *Saturday Review*, 2 Nov. 1872, in *Native Opinion*, 8 Dec. 1872.

a valuable means' of 'ascertaining facts of social condition and political sentiment'.[106]

Ever since the days of Rammohan Roy, Indians had discerned the potentialities of the Press for the promotion of social and political activities. Thus the British Indian Association acquired the *Hindoo Patriot* and the Indian Association the *Bengalee*. The Poona Sarvajanik Sabha started its *Quarterly Journal* and the *Shivaji*, besides exercising influence over the *Dnyan Prakash*. Religious and social associations or reformers also had their journals. The *Din Bandhu* of Jyotiba Govind Phuley (1827-90), *Indian Spectator* of B.M. Malabari, *Subodh Patrika* of the Bombay Prarthana Samaj, and the *Indian Mirror*, *National Paper* and the *Sulabh Samachar* of different groups of the Brahmo Samaj were some such journals.

Whatever their origin, most of these papers discussed matters of general public interest. The advantage of anonymity made for greater candidness of expression than was possible on the platform or in the council room. This even occasioned from official quarters the suggestion that all articles in newspapers, at any rate in those conducted by Indians, should be signed with the real name of the writer under penalty of forfeiture of licence.[107]

So important became the Press that few leaders failed to make use of it. Ram Gopal Ghosh (1815-68), Girish Chandra Ghosh, Kissori Chand Mitra, Dr Rajendralal Mitra, Dwarkanath Mitter, Joy Kishen Mukerji and others wrote for the *Hindoo Patriot*. Surendranath Banerji owned, for a few years, and edited the *Bengalee*. Dwarkanath Vidyabhushan (1819-86) edited the *Som Prakash*, which owed its birth to Ishwarchandra Vidyasagar also.[108] Bankim Chandra Chatterji (1838-94) wrote for the *Sadharani*, which was edited by Akshay Kumar Sarkar (1846-1917), a distinguished Bengali writer and leader of the Indian Association. The famous Ghosh brothers conducted the *Amrita Bazar Patrika*.

In Bombay, M.G. Ranade (1842-1901), perhaps the most prolific writer among Indian leaders, contributed the bulk of the *Quarterly Journal* of the Poona Sarvajanik Sabha, besides writing frequently for the *Indu Prakash* and *Kasht Vilasini*.[109] The *Indu Prakash* was edited by such men as Janardan Sakharam Gadgil, Vishnu Parashuram Shastri (1827-76), hailed as the Vidyasagar of Bombay, and N.G. Chandavarkar (1855-1923), social reformer, political leader and lawyer who was elevated to the Bombay bench. D.E. Wacha (1844-1936), the Parsi merchant and politician, also wrote for it.[110] Gopalrao Hari

106. Secretary of State for India to Governor-General of India in Council, 31 May 1878. Home Department, Judicial Proceedings, A, Jul. 1878, No. 131.
107. *Native Press*, official publication, 1875, p. 44.
108. A.K. Roy, *Vidyasagar*, Calcutta, 1921, p. 69.
109. *Native Press*, pp. 40, 43.
110. *Contents of Papers sent to Delhi* (M.S.C. for a History of Freedom Movement in India, Bombay Office).

Deshmukh (1823-92), judge, social reformer and one of the earliest leaders of western India, wrote for the *Hitechchhu*. M.M. Kunte, scholar, teacher and, like Deshmukh, one of the earliest exponents of *Swadeshi*, wrote for the *Kasht Vilasini*.[111] A whole galaxy of leaders and scholars was associated with the *Rast Goftar*, its editors being men like Dadabhai Naoroji, S.S. Bengali (1831-93) and K.N. Kabraji. Naoroji Fardunji and A.F. Moos (1827-95), for a while a secretary of the Bombay Association, and the great scholar K.R. Cama (1831-1909) also wrote for it.[112]

The growth of the Press and the change in its character during 1858-85 present a graph of growing public consciousness. Before 1858 the important papers were the *Hinodo Patriot, Rast Goftar, Bombay Samachar, Jame Jamsed, Prabhakar* and the *Dnyan Prakash*. Between 1858 and 1885 were started prominent papers like the *Som Prakash, Bengalee, Indian Mirror, Sahachar, Sadharani, Navavibhakar, Bharat Mihir, Amrita Bazar Parika, Ananda Bazar Patrika. Bharat Sanskarak* and the *Dacca Prakash* in Bengal; and the *Indu Prakash, Native Opinion, Mitrodaya, Survodaya, Kiran, Shivaji, Maharashtra Mitra, Bodh Sudhakar, Belgaum Samachar, Nasik Vritta, Gujarat Mitra, Lok Mitra, Hitechchhu, Kesari, Indian Spectator* and the *Mahratta* in Bombay.

More important were the changing tone and wider scope of the Indian Press. Till the mid 1860s, barring papers with an essentially all-India outlook like the *Hindoo Patriot, Bengali, Som Prakash, Native Opinion* and *Indu Prakash,* the tendency was to dwell mainly on topics of local interest. There also existed a marked fear of the authorities. But progressively thereafter almost the entire Indian Press started discussing questions of wider importance with courage and independence. It started claiming greater rights and concessions for Indians, and some papers even discussed the question: 'When shall the Natives recover their country?'[113]

The Press had the momentous effect of carrying public consciousness to the smaller towns as a result of the discussion by local papers of problems that were agitating educated Indians in politically articulate cities like Calcutta, Bombay and Poona. Thus began to be created a growing body of educated persons with more or less similar views on certain common issues. For example, the *Nagpore Observer,* started in 1868, declared:[114]

> To reflect the views and express the aspirations of the more thoughtful class of natives, as well as to express the wishes and wants of the Native community at large, the *Nagpore Observer* has been started. Patriotic in

111. *Native Press,* pp. 40-1.
112. Wacha, *op. cit.,* pp. 767-68.
113. *Native Press,* p. 43.
114. Quoted in *Native Opinion,* 5 Apr. 1868.

principle, it will be ever national in tone, and will labour assiduously to promote among the various sections of the Native community that unity and harmony of sentiment, without which India will never be anything but what she now is—a mere appendage of the British Empire.

Similarly, the *Lahore Courant* was motivated by a desire 'to unite the educated natives of other Provinces with those of this Province in mutual bond of sympathy and co-operation'. It aimed at enabling the educated Panjabis to know about and discuss important national and provincial matters.[115]

In certain cases the mofussil papers proved more progressive and less patient than their counterparts and leaders in the prominent cities. Dissatisfied with the inactivity of the Bombay Association, the *Arunodaya* of Thana exhorted the Bombay editors to 'form another association' so that 'the others will be shamed into activity'.[116] Not satisfied with words, it campaigned vigorously, in its own limited sphere, for the establishment of a people's association.[117] Eventually the Thana Zilla Association was founded on 8 February 1868.[118]

In view of acute political consciousness among Indian journalists, it was no accident that the first attempt towards an all-India organisation came from them in the form of the Indian Press Association in 1878.

The educated men who conducted the Press and the political associations constituted a new phenomenon in Indian society. The caste system and the monarchical form of government having assigned the business of the state to a particular class, India had evolved no tradition of public participation in politics. Knowledge of the western democratic system and the proximity of non-official Europeans, with whom he waged his first political battles, made the common educated Indian realise that he too could claim a voice in the government of the land. Official policy of seeking Indian views on matters of public importance, specially in the presidencies, accelerated the awareness of political rights. This marked a veritable revolution in thinking and hastened the emergence of public life on democratic lines in India.

III

While the middle classes constituted a new force that quickened public life, they also represented a tension within Indian society. A different kind of stress which cut across class lines and lent a potential bias to national consciousness was generated by the multiplicity,

115. *Ibid.*, 5, 12 Mar. 1871.
116. *Arunodaya*, quoted *ibid.*, 25 Aug. 1867.
117. *Ibid.*, 27 Oct., 8 Dec. 1867. Govind Babaji Joshi toured the whole Thana district for the purpose.
118. *Ibid.*, 23 Feb. 1868.

and also the underlying unity of the Indian responses to the western impact. Representing a variety of attitudes from abhorrence to fasci_ nation, these were complex responses in each one of which rejection and acceptance of the West coexisted to varying degrees. Reacting to the impossibility of avoiding change and the urgency of preserving their communal moorings, Indians endeavoured to evolve rationally defensible and practically effective *via media*. In the event, Indian society changed and yet stuck to its traditions. What made this persistence possible was the instinctive conservatism of the people. Even the most ardent admirers of the West remained emotionally anchored to traditional values and norms. Thus was created, besides a recurring ambivalence, a belief, real or simulated, in the superiority of Indian culture which provided a defence mechanism against the western cultural onslaught.

The instinct to survive made the educated Indian discover 'many reasons', though not always convincing, to accord 'his preference to the system in which he was born and bred and not that with which circumstances have brought him in contact'.[119] No nation, he knew, could shine in borrowed feathers; it had to 'stick to its own nationality for ever and ever'.[120] At the same time, 'intelligent love for the welfare and advancement' of the country required the rejection of 'everything' that hindered progress and adaptation of whatever was 'calculated to raise her in the scale of nations'.[121]

The delicacy of conception necessary for a balance between preservation and adaptation often gave way to cultural chauvinism. For example, co-operation, claimed as the chief characteristic of Hindu, 'the most distinct of Asiatic civilizations',[122] was inordinately rationalised to justify not the idealised Hindu way of life but the existing Hindu institutions. Joint family was upheld in spite of the concomitant evils of the *zenana*, infant marriage and idleness.[123] Infant marriage was even denied to have been an evil; and with nostalgic regret for what had since happened, it was suggested that Radhakant Deb's 'memorable letter' to Bentinck in defence of *sati* had remained 'unanswered and unrebutted'.[124] Defence of caste, the ideal superstructure raised on the foundation of co-operation, was for such persons mere child's play.

As against this, Europeans were represented as having so confounded civilisation with material prosperity as to have become incapable of appreciating an order that did not comprise 'railroads, meat

119. *Hindoo Patriot*, 13 Apr. 1857.
120. K.C. Sen, *Lectures in England*, Calcutta, 1938, p. 412.
121. R.L. Mitra, 'Vernacular Education', 27 Feb. 1868, Mitter, ed., *op. cit.*, p. 30.
122. *Hindoo Patriot*, 13 Apr. 1857.
123. J.C. Ghosh in *Calcutta Review*, vol. LXXIII, 1881, pp. 275-300.
124. A paper read in 1869, *Selections from the Writings and Speeches of Raja Peary Mohan Mukerjee*, p. 1.

rations and universal suffrage'. Thus the distinguishing feature of English, 'a fair specimen of European civilisation' was competition. If the two civilisations were compared morally, aesthetically, intel-lectually and spiritually, Munro's verdict would be justified that in a cultural exchange between England and India the former would be a gainer.[125]

Revivalism was the logical corollary. Along with theology, phi-losophy and art, which did afford some ground for claims of greatness, the 'wisdom and excellence' of the ancient Hindus in politics and science were hailed as 'unparalleled'. Separation of powers was claim-ed to have been the order of the day in ancient India:[126]

> Even in those early times people were so keen about political rights that the question whether legislative powers should be united in the same per-son or body of persons who exercised executive powers was put in issue in some deadly battles in which Poroosram, the son of Jamadagni was at the head of the liberal party and the king on the opposite side. The result was that the legislative power was withdrawn from the hands of the execu-tive and entrusted to Brahmin counsellors.

Such glorified history, 'the strongest incentive to the loftiest pat_riotism', was utilised to inspire the upcoming generations by even in-tellectually westernised men like Surendranath Banerji:[127]

> ...what Hindoo is there, who does not feel himself a nobler being altoge-ther, as he recalls to mind the proud list of his illustrious countrymen, graced by thrice-immortal names of a Valmiki and a Vyasa, a Panini and a Patanjali, a Gautama and a Sankaracharya? For ours was a most glorious past.

Without subscribing to indiscriminate worship of the past, even cold, calculating educated Hindus felt inspired by their ancient glory. Speaking before Europeans, Kristo Das Pal, the phlegmatic politician, could go into ecstasy about India, the elder sister of Britain and 'the mother of the world's ancient civilization, literature and arts'.[128]

The nostalgia thus produced imparted an acuteness to the reali-sation of the existing degradation:[129]

> We Hindus have borne, and do still bear the hardships and misery which follow the downfall of the prestige of a nation. In every bone, vein, and pore of our bodies, this sense of national degradation works as a slow con-suming fire. God forbid that even our deadliest enemies should suffer as

125. *Hindoo Patriot*, 13 Apr. 1857.
126. *Selections from Peary Mohan Mukerjee*, pp. 1-2.
127. Speech before Young Men's Association, Calcutta, 24 Jun. 1876, *Speeches of Surendranath Banerji*, Madras, not dated, p. 1.
128. Speech at annual dinner of Traders' Association, 30 Jan. 1880, R.C. Palit, ed., *Speeches and Minutes of Kristo Das Pal*, p. 316.
129. *Sadharani*, 23 Dec. 1877, *Report on Native Press, Bengal*, 5 Jan. 1878, p. 3

we do. We are not so foolish as to imagine that the English, French, Russian, or the German will ever deliver us from the burden of our sorrows:...

National consciousness was implicit in such awareness, and it seemed logical that Indians 'must not abandon their religion and must not forget their past history, if they again wish to rise in the world'.[130]

Hindu reform movements also fell under the spell of the past; it often was the driving force behind them. Debendranath Tagore, for instance, hoped that through Brahmoism 'all India' 'would be united in a common brotherhood, her former valour and power would be revived and finally she would regain her freedom'.[131] He expected to remove dissensions by conceiving of the Brahmos as belonging to 'the great Hindu community' whose duty it was 'by example and precept to hold up as a beacon the highest truths of the Hindu Shastras'. Only in their light had the Brahmos to 'purify our heritage of customs, usages, rites and ceremonies', and to avoid 'proceeding too fast in matters of social change, lest we be separated from the greater body whom we would guide and uplift'.[132] This cautious reformism found institutional expression in the Adi Brahmo Samaj. The conformism of its members became evident in their opposition to the Special Marriage Bill.[133]

Even Keshab Chandra Sen (1838-84)—instrumental in the introduction of the Special Marriage Bill, once suspected to be a Christian at heart and as such the best bet of the advocates of Christianity in India, and the leader of the revolt against the circumspection of the older Brahmos—ultimately sparked off by his revivalism the second split in the Brahmo Samaj. For, besides his megalomania, it was the influence on Sen of Ramakrishna Paramahamsa, deified by many as the embodiment of the beauty of popular Hinduism, that brought about this split.

Being spiritually inclined, Tagore and Sen admired instinctively what they believed was the pristine purity of Hinduism. But Hindu society kept bound to itself even those who seemed to have burned their boats while denouncing it. The career of Ram Gopal Ghosh, whose 'apotheosis' was claimed to symbolise the progress made by Hindu society,[134] illustrates the hold of tradition. An admirer of the

130. *Arunodaya*, in G.W. Kurkaray's report, 24 Jun. 1880, Home Department, Public Proceedings, B, Jul. 1880, No. 181.

131. *The Auto-Biography of Maharshi Devendranath Tagore*, Calcutta, 1909, p. 40.

132. *Ibid.*, p. 152.

133. Tagore's *National Paper* refuted Sen's claim to represent to government the wishes of all Brahmos. *Native Opinion*, 18 Oct. 1868. At a meeting held on 18 Oct. 1868 the Adi Brahmo Samaj resolved that the proposed law was unnecessary as the greater number of Brahmos accepted Hindu customs and institutions. *Ibid.*, 22 Nov. 1868.

134. M.N. Ghosh, ed., *Selections from the Writings of Girish Chunder Ghose*, Calcutta, 1912, p. 36.

meteoric Derozio (1809-31), young Ram Gopal delighted in outraging Hindu orthodoxy and professing to be an atheist. He became such a notorious non-conformist that marriage with him caused his wife's family the forfeiture of a pension from the millionaire Day family. Subsequently, however, he saw the infusion into Hindu society of a good deal of tolerance. Caste came to mean 'a simple refraining from the open embracement of Christianity', and Hindus became 'a community of vast latitudinarian principles and habits'. Beef was openly eaten, without losing social influence, by 'some of the foremost' Bengali Hindus.[135] These were, however, deviations from externals which failed to touch the essence of Hindu social and religious system; and in the bargain Hindu society reclaimed most of its rebels, but not without exacting a price from them.

That Ghosh's apotheosis was not without compromise with orthodoxy is clear from his role in the burning *ghat* controversy. Viewing as an outrage on 'public health and decency' the burning of corpses at the Nimtalla and Cassey Mitter's *ghats* in the heart of Calcutta, Beadon (1816-80), the lieutenant-governor of Bengal (1862-67), addressed the chairman of the justices about the immediate 'necessity of putting a stop to the practice of burning the dead within the limits of the town, or on the banks of the River ... and also to prevent the skinning of animals at Nimtolla Ghat or elsewhere'.[136] Earlier, through talks with notable Hindus, he had been 'led to believe that though the measure would be distasteful to the Hindu Public on the ground of inconvenience and perhaps of sentiment, yet if another suitable place of cremation were provided the proposal would be acquiesced in'.[137]

Ghosh was not consulted; for, as Beadon explained to Lawrence, he should as soon have 'thought of consulting... any European justice as Ram Gopal Ghosh, who has long abjured Hindooism, drinks freely and otherwise affects European manner and himself avowed in his speech at the meeting that he did not care whether his own body was burned or buried or what became of it'.[138]

But the sanguine lieutenant-governor overlooked the anxiety of the Europeanised Hindu Justice of the Peace to make his peace with the society that had ostracised him. Supported by the Hindu Press and by fellow caste men like Prasanna Kumar Tagore, Ramanath Tagore and Ishwar Chandra Vidyasagar, all of whom affected to be or were social reformers, Ram Gopal successfully employed his formidable eloquence to oppose the measure.

Here was a compromise between the rebel and the Establish-

135. *Ibid.*
136. Beadon's Minute of 1 Jun. 1864, Home Department, Public Proceedings, A, 14 Jun. 1864, Nos. 27-8.
137. Beadon to Lawrence, 3 Jun. 1864, *Lawrence Collection*, reel 7.
138. *Ibid.*

ment. Neither had retained in the 1860s the rigidity of the 1830s and
1840s. Both had shown resilience to make possible the *rapprochement*. But whereas the rebel and thrown 'himself at the feet of dolo-
potees for the sake of caste',[139] the Establishment had just winked at
insignificant, though spectacular, 'offences'.

Even the apostates whose disillusionment with Hinduism had
taken them to the fold of Christianity were fascinated by their cultural heritage. These restless, gifted souls discovered a spiritual void
within themselves. But centuries of a continuing religious tradition
had made scepticism that followed loss of faith a terrifying state of
mind.[140] Isolation from near and dear ones aggravated the torture of
a spiritual vacuum. Something more positive than scepticism seemed
necessary to escape the terror of negation. But what they would accept depended on their immediate circumstances. While Debendranath
Tagore fell upon a *sloka* from the *Upanishads*, and Tarachand Chak-
ravarty (1804-55) met Rammohan Roy (1772-1833), the young persecuted Hindus who accepted Christ as their Saviour happened to be
under the constant and solicitous care of Christian missionaries. No
sordid considerations motivated these early converts; visions of Lu-
ther and Knox had inspired them. 'Blessed are we', they believed,
'that we are to reform the Hindoo nation.'[141]

Acceptance of Christianity was the rejection of an unsatisfying
religion, not the renunciation of their own culture. Rev. K.M. Banerji,
one of the first converts, used his profound knowledge of Sanskrit to
reconstruct the Indian past. As Rammohan Roy went back to the *Upanishads*, and Dayananda (1827-83) to the *Vedas*, Banerji argued, in his
The Aryan Witness, that the *Bible* had been anticipated in the *Vedas;*
the sacrifice of Jesus had its forbear in Prajapati.[142] He appealed to his
countrymen to give up caste and idolatry, and advanced 'the Testi-
mony of Aryan Scriptures in corroboration of Biblical History and
the Rudiments of Christian Doctrine'.[143] This was an indigenous
Christian call to return to the *Vedas*. Continuing his Brahman-Pandit
family tradition, Banerji edited and wrote works on ancient Indian
religion and philosophy.[144] Instead of being cut adrift from his community, he became one of its venerable leaders. When the middle
classes revolted against the British Indian Association, he became
successively the president of the Indian League and the Indian Association. Other Indian Christians also, like K.C. Banerji, Rev. L.B. Day

---

139. *Hindoo Patriot*, 27 Jan. 1868. Dolopotee means a caste leader.
140. Mahesh Chandra Ghosh, the first convert of Alexander Duff, wrote: 'Scep-
     ticism has made me too miserable to wish my dear brother the same.'
     G. Smith, *The Life of Alexander Duff*, London, 1879, vol. I, p. 158.
141. K.M. Banerji quoted *ibid.*, vol. I, p. 156.
142. S.K. De, *Bengali Literature in the 19th Century*, Calcutta, 1962, pp. 588-89.
143. G. Smith, *op. cit.*, vol. I, p. 207.
144. S.K. De, *op. cit.*, pp. 587-88.

(1824-94) and G.M. Tagore, the disinherited son of Prasanna Kumar, were actively associated wtih political movements for obtaining increasing rights for Indians.

Their treatment as racially inferior by the European Christians in India strengthened the patriotism of the educated Indian Christians. This gave birth to the idea of a National Church of India in order to ensure equality between Indian and western Christians and to minimise dictation from abroad. A significant move in the direction was the meeting held at the house of G.M. Tagore to form an association 'for the promotion of Christian truth and goodliness and for the protection of the rights of Indian Christians'.[145] Thus emerged the Bengal Christian Association, of which K.M. Banerji became the first president. Two years later, in 1870, was started the *Bengal Christian Herald* to act as the exponent of Indian Christians. The Association 'sought to consolidate and extend the movement' for the National Church.[146] Though it cracked before the 'forceful personality' of Rev. Alexander Duff (1806-78), the Scottish missionary in Bengal, strong men like Lal Behary Day kept up the fight for equality and independence.[147]

In western India, though young Bombay derived inspiration from Young Bengal,[148] the orthodox phalanx faced a much feebler challenge. Early in the 1860s, the Maharaja libel case highlighted the superstitious character of sections of the Bombay Hindus. A debate to resolve a protracted controversy about widow marriage was arranged between the reform party led by Narmadashankar (1833-86), the stormy petrel of Gujarati literature, Javerilal Umiashankar Yajnik and Karsondas Mulji (1832-71) and the orthodox party led by Jadunath Brijratanji Maharaja. This ended in a deadlock following the Maharaja's insistence on accepting the authority of the *Shastras,* and Narmadashankar's refusal to do so if these were inconsonant with reason.[149]

The deadlock was broken by a strife. Karsondas, writing in the *Satya Prakash,* accused the Maharajas of having 'wilfully altered to their own advantage the fundamental rules and practices of their religion' and 'systematically perverted their actual position (which in the eyes of their bigoted followers is that of deified humanity) to the most gross and infamous debauchery'. Thereupon Brijaratanji, who was named in the article, was stung into bringing an action for libel. In his deposition Karsondas, elaborating the charges, said:[150]

145. *Friend of India, in Native Opinion,* 2 Aug. 1868.
146. *Indian Christians,* Madras, not dated, p. 23.
147. L.B. Day, *Recollections of Alexander Duff,* London, 1879, pp. 240-42.
148. *Bombay Times,* 7 Dec. 1860.
149. *Times of India,* 28 Feb. 1862.
150. *Ibid.,* 5 Feb. 1862.

> It is a matter of general reputation in the sect that all the Maharajas have
> carnal intercourse with the wives and daughters of their more zealous
> devotees. Girls are sent to the Maharajas before being touched by their
> husbands...During the 'Ras' festival, wives and husbands collect promis-
> cuously in a room, and have carnal intercourse promiscuously among them.
> The 'Ras' festival is held three or four times in a month. The Maharaja
> has actual sexual intercourse with many women.

Medical practitioners of unimpeachable character like Dr Bhau Daji
and Dr Dalpatram, who had earlier attended on Brijaratanji Maharaja, deposed that he had been suffering from syphilitic ulcer on the
glans penis; the former also disclosed that he had attended on three
Maharajas for venereal diseases.[151]

Unruffled by such revelations, some prominent Hindus supported
the Maharaja. Seth Varjivandas Madhowdas, J.P., was the Maharaja's
chief supporter.[152]   On his own evidence he was castigated as 'the
thoughtless driver of a Maharaja's coach', and his dismissal as J.P.
was demanded.[153] But the crowning piece of the show was the deposition of his brother, Gopaldas Madhowdas, who said: 'If the Shastras
enjoined the offering of women, I would believe in the doctrine.'[154]
Equally revealing of the state of contemporary society was the action
of Narayan Dinanathji, that early bloom of English education in
Bombay, who abused his official position as an interpreter in a vain
bid to protect the high priest; he only managed to earn censure from
Sir Joseph Arnould (1814-86) in the judgment.[155]

As for smaller men, the crowds of Bhatias who thronged the
supreme court during the trial 'saw in Jadoonathjee Brizruttonjee
nothing morally offensive'. Rather, they seemed to regard him 'as a
precious individual raised above common mortality'.[156]

Though the case was described at the time as 'one of the first
fruits of education and the free press',[157] its actual effects were later
discovered to have been negligible.[158] Even those who had appeared
for the defendant in the case were orthodox Hindus. Mangaldas Nathubhai, for example, was a confirmed conservative who simply aimed
at avoiding reactionary excesses for which Gopaldas Madhowdas
worked as a missionary. Thus, when in 1873 an excommunicated
Kapol Bania died, leaving behind him a seven-year old daughter,
Gopaldas insisted on *prayaschitta* by the child; but Mangaldas advocated her entry without the silly fuss.[159] That more than a decade

151. *Times of India,* 29 Apr. 1862.
152. *Ibid.,* 28 Feb. 1862.
153. *Bamdad,* quoted *ibid,* 4 Mar. 1862.
154. *Ibid.,* 6 Mar. 1862.
155. *Bambad,* quoted *ibid.,* 29 Apr. 1862.
156. *Ibid.,* 3 Mar. 1862.
157. *Ibid.*
158. *Native Opinion,* 3 Sep. 1871.
159. *Ibid.,* 30 Nov. 1873.

after the Maharaja case such trifles were magnified into public controversies engaging the foremost caste men indicated the measure of the achievements of education and free Press.

While banias thus behaved, brahmans were scarcely more progressive. In 1861 the return from England of Mahipatram Rupram (1829-91), one of the earliest Gujarati social reformers, caused considerable excitement because the treatment accorded him would set the pattern for the future.[160] The verdict, not surprisingly, declared him guilty, with the inevitable sentence, banishment from the community. Six years later Mahipatram Rupram was readmitted to caste on paying a fine of Rs. 1,500 and holding a community feast. He was also subjected to the indignities of having his moustaches shaved off, and of undergoing a penance that entailed the partaking of the *panchgavya*, the five products of the cow.[161]

The reform party was outraged by this apostasy.[162] The controversy found its echoes in Calcutta also where the *Indian Mirror* dismissed Mahipatram Rupram's defence as stereotyped.[163]

Yet, Bombay was not static. As late as the 1850s, young reformers, wanting courage to 'openly say a word against idolatry', had to hold clandestine confabulations.[164] That within a decade reforms had begun to be discussed in public indicated a significant advance that denoted the infusion of both courage and tolerance in the Hindu society of western India. But the reformers there were particularly effete. In 1869, to offer an illustration, seven leading Hindus, who had arranged the marriage of a brahman widow were dragged to a court of law on a false criminal charge and later on excommunicated. To decide the issue of the legitimacy or otherwise of widow remarriage, a great council of *Shastris* was convened by the Shankaracharya in March 1870 at Poona. This lasted nine days. At the end three arbiters belonging to the reform party voted for remarriage; but two were either cowed down by threats of ostracism or lured by pecuniary promises.[165] But the denouement was the penance performed by

---

160. *Times of India*, 1 Jan. 1862.
161. *Native Opinion*, 22 Sep., 20 Oct. 1867. The five products included cow dung and urine.
162. *Rast Goftar* and *Indu Prakash*, representing the reform party, assailed Mahipatram Rupram, *Native Opinion*, 6, 20 Oct., 3 Nov. 1867.
163. This referred to Mahipatram Rupram's letter of defence, *ibid.*, 3, 17 Nov. 1867.
164. In fact, 'some of them were almost terror-stricken when the proceedings of one of these meetings were accidentally disclosed and began to be publicly talked of and they preferred putting a stop to that meeting rather than it should attract any public notice'. *Ibid.*, 8 Nov. 1868.
165. *Indu Prakash*, in *Hindoo Patriot*, 15 May 1867. For details see C.Y. Chintamani, ed., *Indian Social Reform*, Madras, 1901, pp. 298-306; G.R. Havaldar, *Ravsaheb Vishwanath Narayan Mandlik Yanche Charita* (in Marathi), Bombay, 1927, vol. I, pp. 302-13.

Gopalrao Hari Deshmukh, president of the Widow Remarriage Association, for his part in the marriage of the brahman widow.[166] The reform movement could be little more than a laughing stock if its president was to undergo penance for doing what was implicit in his position. It has been suggested that Deshmukh was forced to do this because the mother-in-law of his daughter had threatened to turn her out of the house if he refused to recant.[167] In any case, this serves to reveal the effective sanctions possessed by orthodoxy to check transgression. In Deshmukh's case its success was complete. When asked to give evidence before the Finance Committee in England, he declined to cross the seas. He had been persecuted, he said, for having sheltered his English-returned son. So obstinate was Hindu orthodoxy in Bombay that Deshmukh was persecuted in spite of having taken his son immediately to Banaras for the requisite purification.[168] And the deterrent was so successful that not even Ranade and Mandlik could fulfil their desire to visit England.

Even Parsis, apparently the most westernised community in India, stuck to their religion and culture.[169] Experiencing early the threat from English education and Christian proselytisation, they learnt the necessity of presenting a solid front to thwart cultural inroads. The conversion, in 1839, of two young Parsis, Dhanjibhai Naoroji (1822-1900) and Hormasji Pestanji, had offended and excited the entire community as it had never been in India.[170] From this moment Parsis began to set their house in order by means of reforms, though reaction also retained a few pockets. When the Special Marriage Bill was introduced, the Bombay Parsis petitioned against it,[171] expressing their refusal to let their social and religious institutions be encroached upon.

It is this synchronisation of progressivism and anachronism, not in different persons or groups of persons but in the same person, that offers a key to the understanding of the 19th century Indian mind. What made this possible, besides the instinct to survive and the human proclivity to avoid radical change, was the fact that most of the reformers belonged to the upper castes and the middle classes. They might, in response to the ideas imbibed from the western contact, talk of reform. But in the absence of a material propulsion, limited and often only intellectual advocacy of reform, rather than total emotional commitment to the cause, sufficed to keep their conscience clear. And maybe somewhere at the back of their mind they felt not unhappy that their privileged position in society continued. This sup-

166. *Native Opinion*, 5 Jun. 1870.
167. C.Y. Chintamani, ed., *op. cit.*, p. 306.
168. *Native Opinion*, 11 Jan. 1874.
169. M.M. Murzban, *The Parsis in India*, vol. II, pp. 313 ff.
170. Karaka, *op. cit.*, vol. II, pp. 291-92.
171. *Native Opinion*, 7 Feb. 1869.

position gains strength from the fact that while the supposedly egali-
tarian Parsi and Muslim communities in India failed to throw up a
single radical reformer, the one person entitled to such a description
was Phule who, a *mali* by caste, stood low in the *varna* hierarchy.

Moreover, the slow pace of industrialisation and of the growth
of professions kept within the incipient stage group contacts
that would cut across caste or denominational lines. People from
different castes and religious communities but belonging to one class
or profession did meet, more so when required to safeguard some
common interest. But by far the larger part of their life moved within the age-old caste grooves, making them vulnerable to the *pancha-
yat* of their community. Excommunication then did not mean just
a social slight that could be compensated for by a self-elating awareness of dedication to a noble cause. It meant, for self and the biological
family, isolation from near and dear ones, an isolation that became a
living nightmare because of the near impossibility of forging relationships outside one's caste or sect. For life even in the 19th century
Indian cities was in many respects an extension of the communal
rural life. The logic of gregariousness proved invincible.

Implicit faith in the superiority of their own culture, which was
a common constituent in the mental makeup of Indians of all shades
of opinion, produced and sustained the fundamental conservatism of
the Indian mind. It acted as a bulwark against the alien cultural
thrust. But this cultural component carried within it inconvenient
implications for the fusion of various Indian communities under the
pressure of non-spiritual forces. The natural susceptibility of a subject people to romanticise their past particularly threatened to viti-
ate relations between Hindus and Muslims in view of the different
pasts they chose to derive inspiration from. Every time Hindus
evoked their ancient glory, they could not but lament its eclipse following the Muslim conquest. Muslims, on the contrary, could scarcely
feel attached to an Indian past prior to their arrival and revelled in
the memories of their ascendancy. Here was a potential danger to the
development of common national consciousness, though during 1858-
85 it did little to widen the gulf between the two comunities.

Still, it was not an atmosphere of trust that prevailed between
educated Hindus and Muslims, though they might at times work together in response to a political necessity. The *Hindoo Patriot*, for instance, blamed Muslims for being 'deficient in public spirit and patriotism', and for their 'sole ambition' to serve 'not the principle but
the man of authority'. Abstaining from movements opposing the
authorities, Muslims joined every movement 'in which praise and not
censure was the object'. In order to propitiate the men in power, complained the *Patriot* superciliously, they could even adopt an independent course, notwithstanding the superior wisdom and better
counsel of their Hindu brethren'. It advised Muslim leaders to en-

courage English education. This would improve the condition of their co-religionists and bring them closer to Hindus. But it did not like what it alleged was the official policy of conciliating 'the Mahomedans by inviting them to offices of honour and emolument, notwithstanding their admitted inferior qualification' and 'want of appreciation of and unfitness for the favours conferred and promised'.[172] So, when the Mahomedan Literary Society was founded, educated Bengali Hindus welcomed it as likely to 'exercise the healthiest action on Mahomedan thoughts and feelings all over the country'. They also favoured the utilisation of the Mohsin Trust for the education of Muslims.[173]

While backing the efforts made by Muslims for their own advancement, Hindus opposed preferential treatment by the government in which they saw a threat to their own prospects. Muslims, equally naturally, resented this opposition as an attempt to bar their advancement. They also denied having been accorded preferential treatment, and turning the Hindu charge upside down, alleged that the government was unduly favouring Hindus. However, being dependent on government service,[174] and even otherwise convinced of the expediency of keeping the government in good humour, they normally eschewed politics that would demand collaboration with other communities at the risk of displeasing the rulers.

In such a state of relations it seemed natural for a shrewd observer like Kristo Das Pal to favour fixing 'by law the number of representatives of each section of the community, so that there might be no misunderstanding or confusion'.[175] Pal, it may be added, was referring to the adoption of the elective principle for municipal government in Calcutta.

IV

A factor that constantly agitated Indians and acted as a cohesive force among them sprang from the existence of Europeans in India. Relations between the two communities were perhaps never cordial. A sense of superiority and *hauteur* among resident Europeans developed proportionately with the growth of their political power. By the first decade of the 19th century, every Briton in India seemed 'to pride himself on being outrageously a John Bull'.[176] Anxious to secure

172. *Hindoo Patriot*, 26 May 1862.
173. *Bengalee*, 24 Jun. 1863.
174. Temple, *Story of My Life*, vol. I, p. 276; Blunt, *op. cit.*, pp. 27-30, 86-113, 289-92.
175. Pal's speech of 13 Nov. 1875, Palit, ed., *Speeches and Minutes of K.D. Pal*, p. 67.
176. D. Kincaid, *British Social Life in India, 1608-1937*, London, 1938, p. 113

'the quiet preservation' of their power, the British would not 'suffer a man of their nationality to appear before the natives except on a footing of superiority and grandeur'.[177] Since this also satisfied the natural vanity of the ruling community, the feeling of superiority often overstepped administrative exigencies and produced a variety of excesses in practice.

Since all Indians could not persuade themselves to submit quietly to the resultant humiliation, friction ensued between them and Europeans. Recalling that man 'doth not live by bread alone', the *Hindoo Patriot* ruled out the possibility of proper relations between the two communities 'so long as to meet an Englishman is to be insulted and dishonoured, as is undoubtedly the case now;—so long as all that is noble and brave and aspiring in human nature is crushed and trodden down in us by English pride;—so long as it shall be the Anglo-Indian creed that the fattest is for their board, and the fairest for their bed.'[178]

The legacy of blood, hatred and suspicion bequeathed by 1857 aggravated the situation beyond control; and it became a trite observation that Europeans, while coming out to India, are generally in the habit of leaving their consciences at the Isthmus or at the Cape'.[179] The problem of racialism was created by an inextricable complex of psychological, political and economic factors. As Stanley, the secretary of state for India, put it, 'a conquering race almost inevitably displays a certain sense of superiority—a certain arrogance, if that be not too harsh a word to use—a certain disregard of the feelings of others'.[180] Grant Duff, who dismissed as 'idle cant' the idea of racial equality between the rulers and the ruled, offered a simple explanation for European aggressively. '...our attitude must be usually an attitude of command; and an attitude of command, if prompt obedience is not rendered, is very apt to become an attitude of harshness and menace'.[181] Writing in a similar strain, James Stephen (1829-94), former law member and the arch priest of imperialism, even warned that because 'the European (cant apart) really is the superior of the native and is in this country only by virtue of that superiority', any 'attempt to alter the real relations between the two will produce the most bitter resentment in the Europeans'.[182]

177. V. Jacquemont, *Letters from India, 1829-1832*, London, 1936, p. 23.
178. N.C.Sen-Gupta, *Selections from the Writings of Hurrish Chunder Mookerji*, Calcutta, 1910, p. 38.
179. *Rast Goftar*, 17 Oct. 1858.
180. Speech at Fishmonger's Hall, 29 Sep. 1858, in *Hindoo Patriot*, 18 Nov. 1858.
181. Grant Duff, *op. cit.*, p. 264.
182. Stephen to Lytton, 30 Nov. 1876, *Stephen Papers*, Roll I, Box I. Blunt witnessed the transformation of racial relations in Egypt. Before the occupation 'the best possible relations existed between Englishmen and native Egyptians'. Suddenly, after 1882, this gave way to a relationship of 'rulers and ruled, the rulers being aliens and affecting the airs of race superiority

The notion of ethnic superiority, which tended to be an article of European faith in India, invested the assumption of superiority with a pseudo-scientific aura. 'Not only the "twice-born" civilian considers himself a demi-god', fretted the *Rast Goftar*, 'but the thorough donkey...will swell himself into importance, simply because he had the accident of being born of a European parentage.'[183] Even those Europeans who were, as individuals, disposed favourably towards Indians, tended to subscribe to the group paranoia. The *Hindoo Patriot* scarcely exaggerated when it wrote.[184]

> The European Press is pledged to abuse, systematically abuse, our race. The pulpit echoes the press, and even our warmest friends who in their personal speech and behaviour are the soul of honour and the glass of courtesy are not unfrequently the authors of the most violent diatribes against the nation.

If Europeans naturally assumed superiority, equally naturally did Indians, especially the educated ones, demand equality. Stanley could appreciate that Indians were 'apt to be all the more tenacious of their intellectual independence and national customs because of the political subjection'.[185] Accentuating the sensation of inferiority and the need for psychological compensation, English education rendered Indians 'less submissive in tone and language than formerly, more erect in mental and moral stature in the presence of Europeans, even jealous of the superior position held by European in the country'.[186] He who had 'appreciated the genius of Shakespeare and Bacon' and 'read and discussed so much about the equality of men' could not 'bear the insolence of the civil servant or of the lowborn English merchant'. He would neither put off his shoes nor kiss the earth when *salaaming* the *Huzur Bahadur*. He preferred to converse in English which contained 'no words so sweet as *Khodawand, Junabali etc.*' This angered the European who had been spoiled by 'oriental adulation and could be content with nothing less'.[187]

English education thus created what an Anglo-Indian paper apprehended was 'the most inevitable and unmanageable' threat to British rule. It elevated Indians to the level of Europeans in respect

over the natives'; *op. cit.*, p. 234.

183. *Rast Goftar*, 15 Aug. 1858.
184. *Hindoo Patriot*, 5 Jun. 1861.
185. Speech of 29 Sep. 1858, *Hindoo Patriot*, 18 Nov. 1858.
186. Temple, *Men and Events*, p. 431.
187. *Calcutta Monthly Review*, May 1858. Lawrence made the same point when he wrote that race feeling was 'more or less strong everywhere but perhaps stronger in Calcutta than in most places'. He explained: 'The educated Bengallees are sensitive and irritable and dislike the bearing of the English towards them, many of whom are inferior to them in wealth & position & also in intellect & knowledge.' Lawrence to Cranborne, 19 Dec. 1866, *Lawrence Collection*, reel 2.

of attainments and ambitions. But instead, and at times in spite, of recognition which they were entitled and bound to look for, they received social slights. The situation implied that unless Europeans were prepared to recognise the principle that equal virtues and accomplishments demand equal respect, they were 'but sharpening weapons' for their own destruction.[188]

The sharpening, however, continued unabated inasmuch as the racial prejudice was inherent in the imperial position, and posed a refractory problem for the authorities in India and England. Wood, the secretary of state, could 'hardly see how the country is to be administered unless a good and kindly feeling towards the natives is entertained by our official servants'.[189] Lawrence, who did his best 'to cultivate kindly feelings towards the Natives' as a measure to deal 'with the great danger to which our rule in India is exposed', despaired of success and commented: 'What it will all end in God only can tell.'[190] Salisbury even forecast that the only enemies 'who will ever seriously threaten England's power in India, are her own sons';[191] and Lytton agreed 'that the greatest danger we have to deal with in India is from the whites'. Assessing the magnitude of the problem, he added that if to 'this prevalent brutality towards natives of the lower order' was added 'the crytallised official formality towards natives of the highest class', the marvel would be why British rule was not more unpopular than it was.[192]

Salisbury laid his hand on the economic aspect of the problem when he admitted that it was 'very difficult—almost impossible—to do anything which shall conciliate and benefit the natives without exciting a considerable amount of Anglo-Indian spleen'.[193] Resident Europeans actually tended to regard higher offices, business and exploitation of the country's natural resources as their preserve. They even thought it derogatory—thought basically in response to an instinctive aversion to material deprivation—to be required to pay taxes in the land of conquest.[194]

But concern at the top level could not bring the two communities together. G.H.R. Hart, private secretary to Fergusson (1832-1907), the Bombay governor from 1880 to 1885, struck a realistic note by recognising that even if promotion of social intercourse between Indians and Europeans had commended itself to all, there existed 'practical difficulties in the way of inaugurating a reform in this respect'.[195] The difficulties being inherent in the ruler-ruled relation-

188. *Bombay Times*, 2 Nov. 1860.
189. Wood to Frere, 2 Sep. 1860, in Martineau, *op. cit.*, vol. I, p. 330.
190. Lawrence to Mcleod, 5 Apr. 1866, *Lawrence Collection*, reel 11.
191. Salisbury to Lytton, 30 Aug. 1876, *Salisbury Papers*, reel 822.
192. Lytton to Salisbury, 28 Sep. 1876, *ibid.*, reel 814.
193. Salisbury to Lytton, 27 Oct. 1876, *ibid.*, reel 822.
194. See Chapter 3.
195. Hart to Tyabji, 26 Jan. 1885, *Tyabji Papers*.

ship, Blunt was not being cynical in prophesying better relations only after India's emancipation.[196]

However, so long as they ruled, the British had to attend to the problem. Wood was thus compelled by the virtual impunity of European violence against Indians to suggest that as against Europeans, the government of India should be 'the protector of the natives and their representatives'.[197] This was a near impossible role. Most of the officials were 'averse to act decidedly' because the 'whole influence of the non-official English community, of nearly all the Press' was arrayed against the man who attempted to protect an Indian vis-a-vis a European.[198] Moreover, it was 'difficult enough to get an English Jury, more particularly in Calcutta, to convict an Englishman of a crime perpetrated against a native: but still more difficult to get a Court Martial to do so'.[199]

Henry Maine, the law member, plainly pronounced the evil beyond eradication. The only law under which a European British subject could then be tried in the mofussil was Act XII of 1865, which required a jury of 12 persons of whom 7 (if the prisoner so demanded, which he was sure to do) must be European or American. As 'sympathy with justice is always greater on the Bench than in the Jury-box', non-official votes could be relied upon to effectively screen the defendant. In fact Maine saw no reason for the government of India 'to be ashamed' of its inability to strip Europeans of this privilege. Even if 'most unreasonable', their distrust of the 'ordinary Criminal Courts of the country' had been respected by governments 'far better able than we are to neglect the discontent of the European community'. And the 'timidity of each successive Government' had further diminished the amenability of the problem to a solution.[200]

In spite of its inability to modify the existing law, the government intervened from time to time to prevent gross miscarriage of justice. But rather than create a moral effect, sporadic interference served to explode anti-Indian feeling 'into a paroxysm of illogical fury' as Europeans heartily detested and sharply reacted to the theory that Indians were their 'equal in the eyes of the law'.[201] On the other hand, alarmed by 'the settled doctrine of the European malcontents that the European should not be punished for doing injury to a Native',[202] Indians expected the government to effectively protect their person, property and rights.

Placed between the diametrically opposed claims of superiority

196. Blunt, op. cit., p. 235.
197. Wood to Frere, 17 Aug. 1861, Martineau, op. cit., vol. I, p. 344.
198. Lawrence to Wood, 4 May 1865, Lawrence Collection, reel 2.
199. Lawrence to Northcote, 21 Sep. 1867, ibid., reel 3.
200. Note by Maine, 10 May 1866, ibid., reel 4.
201. Trevelyan, Competition Wallah, p. 272.
202. Hindoo Patriot, 30 Jun. 1862.

and equality, as advanced by Europeans and Indians respectively, the government could hope to satisfy neither. Mayo's predicament exemplifies this. Wishing that 'this horrid habit of striking natives would go out of fashion',[203] he was called upon to deal with the action of Cowen and Forsyth against the Kukas. Mayo believed that the blowing of '49 of these wretched people from guns' without trial and the hanging of '14 or 15 more' after trial had exceeded 'in violence almost anything that was done in the Mutiny'. He explained his stand to the secretary of state:[204]

> I cannot tell you how much I lament this occurrence. It must weaken authority and bring disgrace on our Govt. I am quite ashamed of the way many of my countrymen talk of the deed. They call Cowen a fine vigorous fellow, and trust that he will be supported—but I cannot help that. The act was one of great and unnecessary cruelty, and I must condemn it... I am quite prepared to face the outcry that will be made—for I know I am right.

Yet Mayo could not satisfy Indians. Resenting the fact that instead of being prosecuted on a criminal charge, Cowen had been dismissed with pension, they attributed 'this undue leniency on the part of the great authorities to race-partiality'.[205] After dismissing an official in the teeth of organised European opposition, Mayo could earn from Indians only a charge of race-partiality. For, overly sensitive to their subjection and seeking recompense in absolute equality, most Indians were psychologically capable of appreciating neither the viceroy's impartiality and courage, nor the exigencies that ruled out the institution of criminal proceedings against an administrator.

Lytton had a similar experience when Indian reactions seemed to frustrate the very ends that had induced his minute on the Fuller case. For weeks together Anglo-Indian Press, as expected, attacked the government and teemed 'with the most virulent and brutal abuse of the whole native population'. But Indian Press did not prove helpful to the government either. Though 'unanimously applauding the conduct of the Govt.', complained Lytton, it indicted, 'in language scarcely less objectionable', 'the whole administration of justice in British India'.[206]

Executive interference really offered no solution; it only highlighted the impunity of European crime. Indians could at best be grateful to those who tried to shield them. But their real hope lay in a fundamental reform of the legal system, and they could not but criticise the authorities for not undertaking it. Ripon alone attempt-

---

203. Mayo to Argyll, 1 Feb. 1871, *Argyll Papers*, reel 314.
204. Mayo to Argyll, 24 Jan. 1872, *ibid.*
205. *Indu Prakash*, 3 Jun. 1872, *Report on Native Press, Bombay*, 8 Jun. 1872, p. 3.
206. Lytton to Salisbury, 27 Aug. 1876, *Salisbury Papers*, reel 814.

ed the overhaul. He failed. But he left India as the most loved viceroy.

Indians suspected even the highest courts of law. The *Indu Prakash* dramatised the despair resulting from the perennial 'mock-
ery'[207] of justice by magnifying it into the apprehension that Indians
had 'in store for them the same fate which befell the red aborigines
of America under the rule of the European settlers'.[208]

The stock subterfuge of diseased spleen and madness removed
the last vestige of faith, giving rise to the allegation that medical
practitioners had become the *de facto* judges. Whenever an Indian
was killed 'knowingly or unknowingly by a European', the doctor
was at hand 'to state either that the accused committed the act in a
moment of temporary insanity, or that the spleen of the deceased
was diseased or enlarged'.[209] Bitter, damaging satires were written
to ridicule the law and to lampoon the judges, doctors and lawyers.[210]
The *Oudh Punch* published an imaginary Act, an article of which
laid down that 'medical evidence should show that the deceased suffered from an enlargement of the spleen, or some other severe disease'.[211] Also forthcoming were plain warnings that 'a continuance
of this state of things will ultimately prove a scourge and bring about
the destruction of British rule in this country'.[212]

The form of European violence that agitated Indians the most
was the raping with virtual impunity of Indian women by low, dis-
orderly Europeans. Initially such acts produced warnings like the
one that it was this outrage which had rendered the government of
the last Peshwa an object of odium and hatred; and that for the greater portion of the Indian populace every European being a part of
the government, outrages by individual Europeans were attributed
to the government.[213] Discontent mounted as the evil continued, and,
towards the end of the period under review, the acquittal of Webb[214]

207. *Indu Prakash*, 17 Jul. 1871, *Report on Native Press, Bombay*, 22 Jul. 1871,
     p. 5.
208. *Indu Prakash*, 27 Mar. 1871, *ibid.*, 1 Apr. 1871, p. 3.
209. *Gujarat Mitra*, 6 May 1877, *ibid.*, 12 May 1877, p. 4.
210. *Sulabh Samachar*, 29 Dec. 1877, *Report on Native Press, Bengal*, 12 Jan.
     1878, pp. 9-10.
211. *Oudh Punch*, 10 Jul. 1877, Home Department, Judicial Proceedings, B, Jun
     1878, No. 81.
212. *Som Prakash*, 11 Feb. 1878, *Report on Native Press, Bengal*, 16 Feb. 1878,
     p. 9.
213. *Bombay Samachar*, 23 Jun. 1868, *Report on Native Press, Bombay*, 27 Jun.
     1868, p. 9. Compare: 'In this country no Englishman is a private indivi-
     dual'. *Iris*, in *Bombay Times*, 8 Aug. 1860.
214. Planter Webb had kept a woman in a cabin for the whole of night. On
     coming out the following day she had shown blood marks and complained
     of pain in abdomen. Yet the magistrate had refused to believe that Webb
     had had connection with her. Webb was let off with a fine of Rs. 100 which
     he had been ready to pay for a compromise.

caused 'universal indignation and dismay'.[215] For the first time, perhaps, the decision of the high court was openly challenged and the
people were exhorted 'to bestir themselves in the matter'.[216] Even
Malabari, the moderate of moderates, was obliged to give the warning: 'Should ever a day of reckoning come (which God forbid!) such
violence unpunished may be terribly avenged.' He thought it necessary to ask the Bengali coolies, 'where was their manhood when they
allowed the girl to be dragged to the cabin'?[217] If Malabari could
hint at extra-legal methods to obtain redress, it was not surprising
that the *Sahas* wrote what had not been seen earlier in the Indian
Press:[218]

> If the High Court has proved itself unworthy...and affords us not that
> protection which entitles it to its existence, are we to continue to be mute
> and inactive? What is more valuable to us than the honour of our females?
> And when this is attacked, what is left to us? The Government of India,
> it is said, has called for the papers of the case: is any reliance to be placed
> upon its proceedings? Have we not been already too shabbily treated by it?
> Our hope now centres in combined action and in stimulating that public
> opinion without which all efforts must prove futile. Let every Indian, in
> distinct and unmistakable language, demand vengeance and we are quite
> confident the handful Englishmen will yield...Sukurmony was an Indian,
> and as Indians, they should avenge her wrongs.

Expressions like vengeance, combined action and Indians *versus*
Europeans, heard together for the first time, manifested a new spirit
that emerged from cumulative discontent against continued denial
of justice. Racialism was fast forging a link to bind Indians together.

The only effective solution of the problem of European violence
was totally unacceptable to Europeans. This was the removal of the
legal exemption enjoyed by them from trial by an Indian judicial
officer in the moffusil, as also of their privilege to claim a jury with
a majority of Europeans. To Indians it was not merely the only way
of obtaining justice but also a matter of national self-respect. Because the existing law simply meant that a 'person, no matter he be
an adept at thieving, a reckless spendthrift, a drunkard, a confirmed
gambler, a robber, or even a murderer, if he happens to have been
born in Europe or to be a descendant of one born there, that mere
accident confers upon him privileges which are denied to natives
however highborn or however elevated in official position'.[219]

But Indian insistence on this reform stood no chance against
organised European obstinacy. Europeans had weathered attacks on

215. *Voice of India*, 31 Aug. 1884, p.516.
216. *Bengalee*, 9 Aug. 1884.
217. *Indian Spectator*, 17 Aug. 1884.
218. *Sahas* (Weekly published from Allahabad in English), 18 Aug. 1884, in
     Voice of India, 31 Aug. 1884, pp. 537-38.
219. *Native Opinion*, 7 May 1871.

this privilege in 1836, 1849 and 1857. The matter came to a head again in 1859 with Trevelyon (1807-86), as governor of Madras (1859-60), suggesting 'a larger proportion of purely Native jurors being usually empanelled'. As he refused to change his views in spite of protests and demonstration by the Europeans and Eurasians of Madras, Trevelyan was attacked from the heights of the Calcutta supreme court by Justice Wells. In July 1859, addressing a Grand Jury that included some prominent Indians, Wells said that the proposal amounted to 'nothing more or less than equivalent to leaving the property and lives of Europeans comparatively unprotected'.[220] To justify his contention, Wells delivered from time to time scathing invective against Indian character. He said, *inter alia*, that he had discovered among Indian witnesses 'a mass of false evidence which it was astonishing and revolting to behold'; and also that 'forging in India is as common as iron forging in England! A workshop can be found within a few miles of another.'[221]

Tempers were frayed and counter-charges hurled against Englishmen as a reaction against the 'foulmouthed rhapsodies' of the 'Judicial Don Quixote'.[222] Launching a wordy offensive, the *Hindoo Patriot* asserted that grater crime prevailed in London than in Calcutta, and advised the 'terrorist Puisne of the Supreme Court' to weed the mother country of atrocious crimes before tackling forgery and perjury in Bengal. He was also reminded that in Calcutta itself heinous crimes lay upon the head of the European, and 'all the petty theft upon that of the native.'[223] The *Patriot* thought it necessary that the country should 'make its feeling on the subject known in all its fulness to the British public in order that future Judges may take warning'.[224] The public meeting held to petition the secretary of state against Wells was attended by 5,000 persons,[225] a remarkable figure for 1861.

Nothing, however, resulted. The lives and property of Europeans continued to be as well protected as before; and Indians continued to resent the existence of the law. They took advantage, in 1872, of the amendment of the Indian criminal procedure code to press for reform. The three leading political associations of the time called for the abolition of discrimination between Europeans and Indians. The Bombay Association reminded the authorities how a 'large number of Europeans scattered over the country, and residing in the interior,

220. *Bengal Hurkaru*, 14 Jul. 1859.
221. Memorial of the British Indian Association to secretary of state for India, 26 Aug. 1861. Home Department, Public Proceedings, B. 24 Sep. 1861, Nos. 137-38.
222. *Hindoo Patriot*, 5 Sep. 1861.
223. *Ibid.*
224. *Ibid.*, 22 Aug. 1861.
225. *Ibid.*, 5 Sep. 1861.

violate the law with impunity whilst only a limited number of offenders, who are sent to the High Court at a heavy charge to the State and serious inconvenience to the people, are brought to trial before a purely European British jury'. Justice miscarried even in the cases that did reach the court. Of the 43 cases that were sent up to Bombay during the preceding two years, only three related to murder and two to forgery. The accused in two of the murder and one of the forgery cases were convicted. Of the remaining 38 cases of 'misdemeanours and petty offences', only 16 ended in conviction, and the punishment was ridiculously mild. In many cases people had to come from far off places like Nimbahera in Rajasthan, Jabalpur, Jacobabad and Karachi. The witnesses, who numbered from five to 32 in individual cases, were detained for a fortnight to three months. The jury, being European, sometimes gave 'verdicts of acquital contrary to the evidence and against the summing up of the presiding judge'. The Bombay Association regretted that 'this opportunity for remedying a great wrong is about to be thrown away; and that the perpetuation of race distinctions is to be again recognized by the highest legislature in India'. It entreated the governor-general in council on behalf of its countrymen 'to amend the proposed criminal procedure Bill so as to abolish the exclusive privilege and inconvenient jurisdiction enjoyed by European British subjects, which militates against an inflexible adherence to broad principles of justice and perfect equality of all classes of Her Majesty's subjects of whatever race, color or creed'.[228] The Poona Sarvajanik Sabha petitioned both the viceroy and the secretary of state for India.[227] The British Indian Association argued that 'a distinction between Natives and Europeans filling the same office' was 'contrary to the terms of Her Majesty's Proclamation'.[228]   The *Native Opinion* stressed the absurdity of not allowing an Indian official in the mofussil to try 'even a European loafer' or a 'common pickpocket' although in the presidency town or the high court he could do that.[229] This anomaly, later on precipitated towards an issue by B.L. Gupta, was to occasion the ill-fated Ilbert Bill.

Voices were raised within the governor-general's council, too, against making distinction between European and Indian J.P.s, and the clause was carried by a majority of only two.[230] But Stephen, the law member, who wrote off racial equality as idle cant, defended it as a compromise which the European community had accepted and beyond which it was not possible for the government to go.[231] Making

226. Petition of the Bombay Association, 1 Feb. 1872, in *Native Opinion*, 18 Feb. 1872.
227. First Annual Report of the Poona Sarvajanik Sabha, *ibid.*, 11 May 1873.
228. Petition of the British Indian Association to the governor-general, 3 Aug. 1872, *Argyll Papers*, reel 317.
229. *Native Opinion*, 11 Feb. 1872.
230. *Argyll Papers*, reel 317.
231. *Memo on the Code of Criminal Procedure*, p. 5.

light of the Indian objection regarding the violation of the royal proclamation, he counter-argued:[232]

> All that the Queen's Proclamation says (if I remember rightly) is that no one is to be excluded from office on account of his religion or race. It does not say that every one admitted to office is to have the same duties.

For a decade the law remained unmodified, aggravating tension and despair among Indians, till Ripon determined to remove the anomaly. The convulsions that paralysed his effort left a profound impression on the Indian mind which marked a distinct phase in the development of national consciousness.[233]

Prohibition of carrying arms, unavoidable in the circumstances of 1857, appeared to Indians, when continued thereafter, as another perverse aspect of the race problem. While Europeans resisted equality with Indians in this respect on grounds of prestige, Indians demanded it mainly because of the same consideration. Prasanna Kumar Tagore expressed Indian feeling on the subject when to the observation of a member of the legislative council that the obnoxious clauses of the Arms Bill would not apply to respectable Indians like him, he replied: 'I ask no advantage that is to be denied to my countrymen. I rise or fall with them.'[234]

Equality with Europeans apart, on no subject were many Indians 'more sensitive than the right of carrying arms' since it was to them 'a prescriptive privilege of caste or birth, the ancestor's sword being a cherished heirloom'.[235] Moreover, to deprive people of means of self-protection was sheer oppression; even 'under the tyrannical Government of the Mahomedans, the country was not so disarmed'. There was also the moral issue whether the government could 'inflict on native life and property injury our wretched police cannot or will not remedy'.[236]

The working of the Arms Act of 1860 made it clear that it had given Indians a deceptive legal equality. In practice it meant uninhibited supply of arms to Europeans and acute shortage for Indians who were exposed to increasing depredations of wild animals. The number of human victims in 1870 alone was 12,500.[237] But Lytton's

232. *Ibid.* Earlier, Barnes Peacock, chief justice of the Calcutta supreme court, had argued that the statutory provision of 1833 removing discrimination on grounds of colour or creed 'did not qulify every Native to hold every office'. It simply removed disqualifications on the basis of religion, colour or race. *Proceedings of the Legislative Council of India*, vol. VIII, col. 373.
233. See chapter 4.
234. Mitter, ed., *op. cit.*, pp. 24-5.
235. *Bombay Times*, 24 Jul. 1860.
236. *Ibid.*
237. *Jame Jamsed*, 29 Nov. 1871, *Report on Native Press, Bombay*, 2 Dec. 1871, p. 4.

government found the 1860 Act ineffective. It passed a more stringent measure because 'cheap arms were in fact bought or sold to an
extent quite incompatible with the maintenance of peace and good
government'.[238] Unconvinced, Indians contended that 'no facts or
arguments had been adduced to establish the necessity for such rigo-
rous legislation'.[239] Rather, it would aggravate the existing scarcity
of arms and render the people more defenceless. Indians rejected
the official contention that the annual import of 20,000 arms constituted a danger. In terms of population it came to the ridiculous
figure of one weapon for 12,500 persons. To put it differently, supposing 300 to be the average population of a village, there would be
one weapon for 40 villages, or one weapon for a village after every
40 years.[240]

The Act of 1878 touched Indians where they were most sensitive. By drawing a legal line between them and Europeans it underscored their station as members of the vanquished race.[241] With hurt
pride and maintaining their claim to equality as loyal subjects of
Her Majesty, they dramatised the existing state of things in which
while 'British criminal tribes can in all immunity arm themselves
with every sort of weapon and even shoot down the peace-preserv-
ers, natives of this country, however high their character or position, are not entitled to carry a single weapon of defence for fear of
the law'.[242] They also argued that if people became disloyal, they
would not think much of the want of arms; even stones in the streets
would serve them.[243]

Opposition to this measure was particularly vehement, coalesce
as it did with irritation against the general tenor of Lytton's viceroyalty. Feelings were sufficiently exacerbated for Ripon to attempt to heal them. He admitted that the Act of 1860 had 'nowhere
been fully and clearly stated to be insufficient to meet the wants of
the country under the peaceful conditions of 1878'. Lytton's Arms
Act, applied in a 'very anomalous and unequal' manner, had proved
'undoubtedly vexatious and burdensome to the people in cases in
which the possession of arms is necessary for the protection of themselves and their property'. Initially inclined towards administrative
action, Ripon was convinced by the tenor of the answers he received
from local governments that moderation would not be possible 'so
long as they are possessed of the powers which the present law confers on them'. He, therefore, prescribed the introduction of 'a sys-

238. *Abstract of the Proceedings of the Council of the Governor-General of India*, vol. XVI, p. 523.
239. *Ibid., vol.* XVII, p. 139.
240. *Arunodaya*, 27 Jan. 1878, *Report on Native Press, Bombay*, 2 Feb. 1878, p 5.
241. *Bharat Mihir*, 25 Jul. 1878, *Report on Native Press, Bengal*, 3 Aug. 1878, p. 5.
242. *Native Opinion*, 21 Oct. 1883.
243. *Kiran*, 3 Feb. 1878, *Report on Native Press, Bombay*, 9 Feb. 1878, p. 5.

tem of general permission with special prohibitions', instead of the existing 'system of general prohibitions with special permission'. His idea was to 'deal with the subject boldly and place the law relating to the possession and use of arms upon a sound permanent footing calculated to secure the public safety and to afford at the same time the utmost amount of individual freedom consistent with that safety, and also to remove the individious and irritating distinctions which are one main cause of the unpopularity of the existing system'. A despatch was sent to the secretary of state for India on 2 May 1882 and a draft Bill was prepared.[244] Nothing came of it.

Consequently, though they thanked Ripon for reducing the oppression caused by the Arms Act,[245] Indians refused to forget that they had been let down on such a sensitive issue.[246]

Besides enjoying prescriptive rights in regard to criminal cases and possession of arms, Europeans also arrogated to themselves privileges that exposed Indians to further humiliation. Unlike European violence which was mainly directed against lower classes of Indians, the arrogance and exclusivism behind these privileges primarily affected the higher classes. It should be, in fact, an achievement to ferret out one contemporary Indian of some note who was never insulted by a European. And one such experience of inferiority was sufficient to rankle for a life-time and produce, in many, a will to fight against such inequity.

The railways offered ample scope for the display of European pride. Ejection of an Indian from a first class compartment—sometimes from second class also—was no abnormal occurrence. The privilege to deny Indians the comfort they had a right to purchase was enjoyed, in spite of the law, on the strength of belonging to the ruling race. G. O. Trevelyan explained this by asking: 'How is it that there are no tradesmen's sons at Eton or Harrow?'[247] Lawrence apprehended that this could 'one day be productive of much political mischief'.[248] Only the docility of people had prevented a conflagration, and Lawrence had 'no hesitation in saying that a Railway so managed running through Peshawar would certainly be damaged, and the Englishmen connected with it murdered'. But he felt helplessl as the men managing the railways in India tended 'to look to their Boards in England rather than to the local Govt.'[249]
chological revolution.

But the docile Indian was fast ceasing to be docile, particularly the Indian who travelled in first class. For example, Shripad Babaji

244. Home Department, Public Proceedings, A, May 1882, Nos. 174-95, K.W.
245. *Native Opinion*, 30 Apr. 1882.
246. Banerjea, *op. cit.*, p. 58.
247. Trevelyan, *Competition Wallah*, p. 25.
248. Lawrence to Cranborne, 31 Aug. 1866, *Lawrence Collection*, reel 2.
249. *Lawrence to Cranborne*, 31 Aug. 1866, *ibid.*

Thakur, the first Indian from Bombay to become a covenanted civilian, refused to budge when asked by a European army officer to vacate his compartment.[250] This was symptomatic of an incipient psychological revolution.

Indians were also expected to put up with European exclusivism in regard to clubs, hotels, public roads and even barbers' shops. Required to visit Poona in connection with the Bombay legislative council, Tyabji discovered that no decent hotel there would lodge him. Inviting Tyabji to stay with him, M.A. Rogay (1848-?) a member of one of the leading aristocratic families of Bombay and a member of the Bombay Association who had resigned in 1878 from the Bombay legislative council, wrote that in 'Napier' and 'Poona' 'our Countrymen are not admitted because *they are* Natives'.[251] How this came about is clear from a letter to Tyabji from C. C. Shapurjee, the Parsi proprietor of the Fountain Hotel, who wrote:[252]

> I am sorry Europeans object our taking any other Lodgers,...your money is just as good as their but as I have more patronage from them have to pay attention towards their wish.

Blunt found a worse state of affairs in Bengal and northern India where 'no native gentleman, whatever his rank, age, or character may be, can visit a place of public resort frequented by Englishmen, especially if he be in native dress, without a certain risk of insult and rough treatment'.[253]

The favouritism shown in matters of appointment and promotion to Europeans at the cost of deserving Indians added to racial discontent. The career of the first Indian to qualify for the covenanted civil service, a Bengali posted in Western India, was vigilantly followed. His abilities were commended and his supersession was attributed to the only drawback he possessed—that he was an Indian.[254] Similarly, there was considerable agitation when Peterson (1847-99) was called from England to supersede Bhandarkar as professor of Sanskrit in the Elphinstone College. The scholarship of Peterson in particular and European Indologists in general was ridiculed. Peterson was said to have been 'as good a Sanskrit teacher as most of the European professors of Sanskrit and of the Oriental languages are—he has but a slight acquaintance with Sanskrit'. With obvious glee—a balm to soothe ruffled sensibility—it was reported that after assuming charge of his office, Peterson had asked Bhandarkar to teach all the other Sanskrit classes and leave for the professor the boys who studied the *Pancha Tantra*. On enquiry why only the lowest class

250. *Report on Native Press, Bombay*, 3 Jan. 1874, p. 10.
251. Rogay to Tyabji, 25 Aug. 1882, *Tyabji Papers*.
252. Shapurjee to Tyabji, 14 Oct. 1884, *ibid.*
253. Blunt, *op. cit.*, p. 263.
254. *Native Opinion*, 19 Mar. 1871.

met him, the Englishman was surprised to learn that the other classes had already read the *Pancha Tantra*, and a good deal more.[255] When Bhudev Mukerji, to cite another example, was not appointed director of public instruction, the reason was found in the race bias of the Bengal government.[256]

As racialism seemed to be based on the supposed inferiority of Indians, they became inordinately touchy about attacks on Indian character. Anxious to uphold it, they even suspected motives where none existed. But when Europeans denounced Indian character wholesale, Indians not only offered self-defence but often attacked their critics for possessing similar defects. On their own they might recognise, even condemn, defects in the Indian character; they would brook no criticism from foreigners. When G. O. Trevelyan and Northcote alleged want of morality among Indians, the *Arunodaya* invoked history to observe 'that those who now plume themselves so much upon their morality were once the most corrupt of nations'.[257] The *Indu Prakash* made a frontal attack saying that Indians had 'seen enough in this country to convince us how far the English are swayed in their dealings by the love of truth, regard for promises, kindness to the weak, &c.'[258] The *Som Prakash* even claimed superiority for Indians, holding that between European and Indian judicial officers 'the tendency towards a higher standard of morality' predominanted among the latter.[259]

Prone to repel any attack on their cultural heritage, Indians were particularly sensitive about religion. Their religion, whether Hinduism, Islam or Zoroastrianism, was to them 'the purest and the holiest'; and they viewed any interference with their religion or any 'injudicious or obtrusive efforts' at their conversion as 'an encroachment on their rights and liberties.'[260]

After the thirties and forties of the 19th century, when Christian proselytisation had appeared as a serious threat to Indian religions, reorganised orthodoxy and reform movements had begun making Indians more confident of themselves and less apprehensive of Christian missionaries. But although the tangible results of Christian propaganda no longer held many terrors for Indians, its crude logic and disparaging language piqued them. In their 'ignorance of proportions' and 'mischievous idea of the equality of heathenism', observed Harish Chandra Mukerji, the Christian missionaries ap-

255. *Dnyan Prakash*, 24 Feb. 1873, *Report on Native Press. Bombay*, 1 Mar. 1873, pp. 3-4.
256. Home Department, Public Proceedings, B, 8 Jun. 1885, Nos. 269-72, p.8.
257. *Arunodaya*, 7 Jun. 1868, *Report on Native Press, Bombay*, 13 Jun. 1868, pp. 5-6.
258. *Indu Prakash*, 15 Jun. 1868, *ibid.*, 20 Jun. 1868, p. 3.
259. *Report on Native Press, Bengal*, 18 Jun. 1868.
260. *Native Opinion*, 9 Apr. 1868.

plied the same policy to New Zealanders and Patagonians, with obvious success, and to the Hindus and Muslims, with obvious irritation and worse effects. They forgot that there were 'Hindoos and Mohamedans, vast in their erudition, profound in metaphysical speculations, and who might give lessons in logic to all the pious gentlemen in Exeter Hall'. They further alienated Indians by presuming that they had only to teach and nothing to learn. Learn from heathen Indians! They might as well learn from a weed! This was perhaps logical to the extent that it was 'of the essence of Evangelicalism to condemn the world out of their circle to perdition'. But they failed to use logic or reason in their mission; they relied on abuse and ridicule. In an attempt to discredit Vedantism, Dr Alexander Duff, for example, adverted to the representation of the Brahma as a hateless, loveless, feelingless and passionless Being, and concluded that such a deity was his shoe or stocking. Warning Duff that he could be paid back in his own coin as Christianity presented no 'fewer themes for the comic genius than Hindooism, or perhaps any other religion', Mukerji ended with the riposte:[261]

> When the missionary expresses commisseration for our degraded moral and religious being, all we do is to laugh at the presumption of a man, poor in knowledge and poorer in thought, the great-grand-father of whose great-grand-father was, we know, a painted savage.

The Christian missionary, however, could not long avoid a repayment and got it, maybe with compound interest, in the *Satyartha Prakash.*

Anger against Christian preachers at times manifested itself in assaults on them.[262] The protection sought by them and given by the government further detracted from their dignity and added to the Indian irritation. In no way could it become Europeans to have their missionaries protected by the police and to complain, as Tudor Trevor did in the police court of Bombay, against Hindus for public denunciation of Christianity;[263] or to have Melville, a Panjab civilian, removed from service because of his conversion to Islam.[264]

261. Sen-Gupta, ed., op. cit., pp. 330-31.
262. Report on Native Press, Bombay. 20 Feb. 1869, p. 8, 14 Aug. 1869, p. 10.
263. Bombay Samachar, 21 Jun. 1877, ibid., 23 Jun. 1877, p. 6.
264. Dnyan Prakash, 4 May, 1874,ibid, 9 May, 1874, p. 3, R.G. Melville wrote in his defence: 'I never really adopted the Mahomedan faith. The only explanation of my having for a short time professed the faith appears to be that a 3-years' residence at Sirsa had so far acted on my brain that I was ready to do anything for the sake of a little excitement, without reflecting on the consequences. Those who have seen Sirsa will have no difficulty in crediting this.
   'Of course I soon repented of my folly, and have long since ceased to profess a faith in which I never believed; but I was hurried out of the service without a chance of retracing my steps.
   'I should be glad to have it generally known that I am a Christian and not a Mahomedan.' Bengalee, 2 Oct. 1875.

Some of this hostility was directed against the government, the ecclesiastical expenditure being the chief count in the indictment against it. Indians did not appreciate the diversion to a particular sect of even a fraction of the public money contributed by the followers of different religions. They resented that in their country admidst 'a vast teeming population of Hindus, Mahomedans, Parsees, Jews, Sikhs, Buddhists, and a score of other sects there existed the Established Church of England for the benefit of a few thousands, and at the cost of the people at large'. In certain districts these persons numbered from three to 20; yet they 'enjoyed the support of government, and the millions had to shift for themselves'. The government also bore half, at times the whole of, 'the heavy annual cost for the repairs of churches, and the building of new churches'. Though churches were 'raised with heathen money', never was 'a single pie spent for a mandir, or a mosque, a fire temple or a Baptist chapel'.[265]

A distressing feature of this 'standing source of heart-burning to the people' was that it remained untouched even when the state of Indian exchequer made clipping 'the order of the day' and necessitated fresh financial burdens or closure of colleges. It also negated the professed official policy of religious neutrality which implied not merely accordance of the freedom to follow any religion but also refusal to favour any creed. The expenditure began to appear all the more iniquitous after Catholic Ireland had been divested of the expenses of the Anglican Church. Demand gained ground for similar action in India.[266]

This was the most charitable view that Indians could take of the official religious policy. But there also existed people who argued that protection and propagation were often synonymous terms.[267] Whatever its degree, dissatisfaction did exist, pointing to the inability of Indians to control their finances.

With its myriad manifestations, racialism became for Indians a permanent reminder of subjection, and in a great measure welded 'into one bond of union' 'the multitude of tribes, castes and religions of India'.[268] It also offered an area of emotional identification between the politically developing upper and middle classes in spite of the existence of mutual tension caused by different interests and aspirations. Though this emotional affinity could crack under the pressure of vital material interests, racialism considerably aided the transformation into a collectively shared sentiment of a national consciousness which, as the next chapter will show, began as the rationalisation of material group interests.

265. R.L. Mitra, 'The Dis-establishment of the Church in India', 24 Jan. 1877, Mitter, ed., *op. cit.*, pp. 75-77. This speech was favourably noticed in Bombay; *Dnyan Prakash*, 26 Feb. 1877, *Report on Native Press, Bombay* 3 Mar. 1877, p. 3.
266. *Report on Native Press, Bombay*, 29 Jan. 1870, p 4.
267. *Arunodaya*, 10 May 1868, *ibid.* 16 May 1868, p. 5.
268. *Native Opinion*, 13 Aug. 1871.

3   The Economic Aspect

B RITISH rule in India presented two aspects, the political and economic. The main interests of the British being economic, the
political structure was meant to ensure economic advantages. If concessions to Indians became unavoidable, these were to be made pre-
ferably in the political and not in the economic sphere. The anxiety
to safeguard British economic interests, which was of the essence of
imperialism, entailed a conflict with Indian interests. However,
neither British nor Indian interests were fixed and monolithic. They
involved, depending upon the issues at stake, a variety of groups and
alignments, and reflected varying degrees of social cohesion.

Indians first became seriously aware of this discordance of interests because of the taxation measures of the government. After
1857, apart from the huge deficit bequeathed by the war, civil expenditure tended irresistibly to increase.[1] Public works, education,
law and justice, defence, and numerous other branches of the administration called for larger expenditure than before;[2] so did the de-
creasing value of money, the consequent rise in prices, and the difficulties of exchange.[3] The military expenditure, which did admit of
reduction, could not be touched because of the concern of the War
Office for British taxpayers' interests; remonstrances from the highest Indian authorities notwithstanding.[4]

The inability to control expenditure meant increased taxation,
and, as a sequel, 'more or less discontent in every class both of Euro-

---

1. *Proceedings of the Legislative Council of India*, vol. VI, pt. I, cols. 84 ff.
2. Frere to Lawrence, 7 Jan. 1864, *Lawrence Collection*, reel 9.
3. Cranborne to Lawrence, 3 Nov. 1866, *ibid.*, reel 1; Denison to Lawrence,
   18 May 1864, *ibid.*, reel 10.
4. *Speech of the Earl of Northbrook in the House of Lords on the 5th August
   1878 on Presenting a Petition from the Inhabitants of Calcutta*, pp. 6-7,
   ibid., reel 14.

peans and of natives'.[5] But what added to the difficulties of the government was the fact that the sections which could best afford this extra burden—resident Europeans and well-to-do Indians—were also capable of organised articulation. Acting in response to the natural human aversion to taxation, they reacted to the imminence of additional taxation by devising ways to avoid it.

Even before 1858, in fact, Indians had criticised taxation as unnecessarily oppressive and its collection as vexatious.[6] Land revenue and salt tax were especially attacked.[7] But the incidence of taxes on affluent and middle class men had been light, and they had no direct taxes to pay. The situation, however, changed for them after 1857 with the possibility of the introduction of direct taxes.

Indians questioned the justification for increased taxation. The financial difficulty, they argued, could be surmounted by pruning 'the public expenditure' as it was maintained 'on a very high and even extravagant scale in more than one department'.[8] The salaries of covenanted civilians, constituting 'an awful drain upon the finances of the country',[9] could be substantially reduced 'without impairing the efficiency of the service'.[10] Further economy could be effected by larger employment of Indians. In any case, the people were 'already overtaxed' and unable to 'bear a single pie in addition to it'. Of the alternatives suggested by 'some maudlin politicians', succession duty would be 'impolitic' and income tax 'a positive oppression';[11] the tax on tobacco would also fall heavily on the people.[12]

If, however, fresh taxation was really unavoidable, the *Hindoo Patriot* suggested that non-official Europeans, being rich and virtually exempt from taxation, should be taxed.[13] The *Patriot* betrayed its concern for the rich zemindars by maintaining that instead of introducing new taxes, the salt tax could be raised 'without calling forth more than a meaningless murmur from the community'.[14]

Europeans also resisted taxation so far as they could. Though they acquiesced eventually, their initial reaction was sharp. They did not 'emigrate to be taxed';[15] and under no circumstances would

5. Frere to Wood, 10 Apr. 1861, Martineau, *op. cit.*, vol. I, p. 337.
6. Petition from the inhabitants of Bombay to Parliament on the eve of the renewal of the Charter in 1853. Tracts, India Reform No. 1. *The Government of India Since 1834*, London, Undated, p. 26.
7. Ibid., pp. 24-5; *Report of the Proceedings of a Public Meeting held on Friday, the 29th July 1853*, Calcutta, 1853.
8. *Rast Goftar*, 22 May 1859.
9. *Hindoo Patriot*, 3 Mar. 1859.
10. *Rast Goftar*, 22 May 1859.
11. *Hindoo Patriot*, 3 Mar. 1859.
12. *Rast Goftar*, 22 May 1859.
13. *Hindoo Patriot*, 24 Mar. 1859.
14. *Ibid.*, 17 Mar. 1859.
15. *Friend of India*, 26 Aug. 1858.

they allow themselves to be saddled with taxes which the 'mutiny' had occasioned. The liability for its expenses ought to fall primarily on the mutineers and then, if necessary, on the people of India. Before anyone was 'called upon for a farthing', the 'last brass pan and the dhotee' of the mutineer 'ought to be sold'. About half the required sum could be raised 'if justice were done sternly and systematically'. The remaining 'damages must be obtained' from Indians 'like the cost of war'. The Bengali baboos might claim immunity for having remained 'more loyal than Englishmen'. But it was their concern 'that their throats should not be squeezed by the sepoys, and they must help to pay the expenses of preventing it'. India had to pay for her apathy as much as for her defence. This could be easily done because the rich classes paid 'nothing to the support of the State, nothing for their exemption from imposts such as fell upon the wretched citizens of Bareilly from their rebel governors'.[16]

The first measure to meet the financial crisis was welcomed by Indians when, on 14 March 1859, the import duties were raised. But Europeans complained, *inter alia*,[17] that the additional burden fell on them alone—a complaint which the government had anticipated and requested them not to make in view of its financial embarrassment and their light tax obligations.[18] Indians, on the other hand, claimed that they were 'the largest consumers of most of the articles on which enhanced duty has been levied'. In the European cry of exclusive burden they detected a strategy 'to purchase exemption from the taxation which the Government propose hereafter to impose on Europeans in common with Natives'. The government, they hoped, would 'not be deceived by this ruse'.[19]

The other official proposal was to license trades and professions. This was condemned by resident Europeans and middle class Indians. A public meeting in Calcutta, attended by Europeans and Indian businessmen, demanded that the proposed tax should be converted into an income tax; that yearly budgets should be published; and that a committee should be sent from England to enquire into the causes of the prevailing economic discontent. Allusions were made to the American War of Independence in order to drive home the moral that 'when the British Lion or the offspring of the British Lion, is roused to a sense of injustice, he will prove too many for the full-fledged Civilian Eagles of the Governor-General's Council'. The zemindars were warned that 'no political expediency will ultimately screen them from an Income Tax'. Exception was also taken to the

16. *Ibid.,* 7 Jan. 1858.
17. See section II of this chapter.
18. *Bombay Gazette,* 6 May 1859; *Proceedings of the Legislative Council of India,* Calcutta, 1859, vol. V, col. 114.
19. *Rast Goftar,* 8 May 1859; even *Friend of India,* 26 Mar. 1859, admitted that the duties fell more heavily on Indians.

exemption of fundholders 'many of whom are wallowing in wealth'.[20] The Bombay Chamber of Commerce also organised a widely attended public meeting to oppose the progress of the Bill.[21]

Glad at having escaped taxation, but worried by the agitation against the license tax, the Bengal zemindars lent warm support to the government.[22] The British Indian Association recommended the proposed tax for being 'so well adapted to the state of the country and the traditions and feelings of the people, and likely to prove remunerative'. In a puerile bid to disarm European criticism and strengthen official resolution, the Association added that the license tax would be 'in accord with the opinions and feelings of the British public'.[23]

But there were dissentient voices within the British Indian Association as well. The Calcutta protest meeting was requisitioned, apart from Europeans, by 22 Indians, all businessmen. Four of them withdrew their names on the day of the meeting, and the action was attributed to their fear of the *Hindoo Patriot* and the *Indian Field*. Yet, among those who favoured the agitation against the license tax were at least four members of the British Indian Association, *viz.,* Durga Charan Law, Digambar Mitra, Peary Chand Mitra and Madan Mohan Auddy.[24] This shows that though economic motivation was politicising people, they were being brought together by essentially personal interests. However, as they were being politically charged, and moved uncertainly from one point to another, the individuals also coalesced into groups which of necessity permitted considerable choice of action to their members.

The *Rast Goftar*, representing the middle classes, criticised the license tax as 'the most cruel and oppressive that can be conceived'. It chastised the Bombay Association for its inactivity while 'consternation and alarm' had spread 'throughout the length and breadth of the country'. The *Rast Goftar* preferred a well-regulated succession duty, tax on marriage and caste feasts or an equitable income tax.[25] This explains why the affluent Indian businessmen in Bombay chose to keep quiet rather than invite greater trouble in the form of an income tax. It is doubtful whether but for the exemption enjoyed by the Bengal zemindars, even European businessmen and their Indian counterparts in Bengal would have pressed for the more 'equitable'

20. *Bengal Hurkaru*, 14 Sep. 1859; for adverse comments on the meeting see *Indian Field*, 17 Sep. 1859.
21. *Bombay Times*, 24 Sep. 1860.
22. *Hindoo Patriot*, 17 Sep. 1859.
23. *Report of a Monthly General Meeting of the British Indian Association*, 21 Sep. 1859, p. 2.
24. *Bengal Hurkaru*, 9, 14, 28 Sep. 1859.
25. *Rast Goftar*, 2 Oct 1859.

income tax.[26]

The Indian financial scene was altered by Wilson, the finance member, who thought that the defective financial system needed overhauling.[27] The three years following the 'mutiny' had produced a deficit of £30,547,488.[28] The deficit for the current year was estimated at £6,500,000.[29] Given a total deficit of £37,047,488 on an annual income of £37,706,209, the prospects promised ill even if the standard of 1857 could be regained.[30] Earlier statistics also offered no comfort. During the 46 years between 1814-60, there had been only 'thirteen years of surplus at an average of £5,540,000 a year'. The normal state of the Indian finance had thus been 'deficiency of income and addition to debt'.[31] Moreover, the annual income of about five millions from opium was a source of uncertainty and alarm.[32]

In order to justify his mode of dealing with the financial crisis, Wilson argued that India was 'the lightest taxed country in the world, in proportion to the good Government which it enjoys'. The per capita taxation was 1s. 4d. without land revenue and 5s. with it as against £2-3 in England. Since this taxation had particularly affected the poor, Wilson wanted that further additions to it 'should fall mainly upon upper classes'.[33]

Of the three taxes proposed by Wilson, the tobacco and the license taxes were shelved; the income tax was levied for five years. The minimum taxable income was fixed at Rs. 200 a year. Incomes upto Rs. 500 were to be assessed at 2%, and beyond that at 3% for the public treasury and at 1% for local purposes.[34]

The immediate reaction of Europeans was to welcome the income tax.[35] Having realised the impossibility of escaping taxation, they had been anxious to get a portion of the inevitable burden imposed on the zemindars, who had now been roped in. Moreover, the income tax had made possible the reduction of import duties on the principal articles of European consumption, and the repeal of export

26. Exemption of the zemindars and fundholders was especially resented at the Calcutta meeting of 12 Sep., see *Indian Field*, 17 Sep. 1859.
27. *Proceedings of the Legislative Council of India*, vol. VI, pt. I, col. 103.
28. *Ibid.*, cols. 89-91.
29. *Ibid.*, col. 94.
30. *Ibid.*, col. 99.
31. *Ibid.*, col. 100.
32. *Ibid.*, cols. 100-01.
33. *Ibid.*, cols. 111-12.
34. *Ibid.*, col. 129.
35. *Englishman*, 22 Feb. 1860. Richard Temple, an eye-witness, records that Europeans, realising the gravity of the situation, acquiesced in the tax, and Indians yielded to the current of approbation which had set in. *Men and Events*, p. 192. This is an incorrect representation.

duty on indigo, the trade in which was monopolised by Europeans.

Among Indians, the zemindars were the first to attack the income tax as 'a desperate expedient of an impoverished tyranny'. Instead of making reductions in the expenditure, the government had fallen on a device calculated to 'breed a large amount of real discontent'. Viewed 'as a government of foreigners' making itself and its countrymen 'rich at the expense of a conquered race', the zemindars suggested, it had added substance to the charge by its measures relating to the import and export duties.[36]

While the income tax was still on the anvil, the British Indian Association had prayed for exemption of the zemindars on the ground that the tax militated against the Permanent Settlement.[37] The Association sent a petition to the legislative council denying that the need for increased taxation had been established. Even if its urgency could be shown, 'the new modes are unnecessary, inexpedient, and dangerous.' The income tax was sure to prove 'a perennial source of perjury peculation, fraud, and extortion'. Legislation would be impotent to remove this drawback for it was 'the result of ages of despotism, of the vast and various differences between the manners and habits, the mind, the social organization, of Europe and of Asia, between the material of Government in the two hemispheres'. As an alternative, the Association suggested addition to the salt tax as follows:

Bengal and the North West Provinces 8 annas per maund,
Madras and Bombay 12 annas per maund,
and Panjab 1 rupee per maund.

This would yield a crore and a quarter, and, added to the gains from the license tax, obviate recourse to the income tax.[38]

The middle classes were initially inclined to accept the tax though they complained that the minimum taxable income was too low. Only incomes above Rs. 600 per annum should have been taxed; but on the surplus. There was no reason for reducing the import and repealing the export duties. Also objectionable was the fact that Wilson was 'very vague and obscure' about reduction of expenditure, in which lay 'all hopes of effective measures'.[39] Nor was

36. *Hindoo Patriot,* 25 Feb. 1860.
37. 'Petition of certain inhabitants of Permanently-settled Estates in Bengal and Behar to the Legislative Council', not dated, *Publications of the British Indian Association,* vol. II.
38. 'Petition of the British Indian Association to the Legislative Council of India', 26 May 1860, *ibid.*
39. *Rast Goftar,* 11 Mar. 1860. Wilson argued that the import duties had been reduced owing to diminution of consumption and revenue; he defended the repeal of export duties on the basis of competition in the world market, adding that these had been raised where India monopolised the supply. *Proceedings of the Legislative Council of India,* vol. VI, pt. I, cols. 366-67. The *Rast Goftar* argued that the fall-off in the consumption of luxuries, even if real, was not 'much to be deplored and averted'. It thought that the alleged competition of Mexico indigo was 'at best but doubtful'.

it possible to accept that India was the least taxed country in the world. An Indian contributed one-fourth of what an Englishman paid 'for a superior and national Government and better security'. The proportion could be equitable only if the wealth of India were one-fourth of that of Great Britain and Ireland. In the absence of other data, the foreign commerce of the two countries could be compared. Indian foreign trade amounted to 60 million pounds sterling for a population of 120 millions, and that of England to 300 millions for a population of 30 millions. In view of this poverty, India was 'neither lightly taxed nor paying little for the Government it has fallen under.'[40]

This attitude of reluctant acceptance of the income tax was transformed by the publication of Trevelyan's minute against it. Having earlier believed the finance member regarding the impossibility of reducing the civil expenditure and the necessity of the income tax, the *Rast Goftar* admitted to have been 'led away by the magniloquent but delusive oratory of Mr. Wilson'. But Trevelyan had disproved the necessity of fresh taxation and laid bare its perils. The *Rast Goftar* even persuaded itself that only Trevelyan's remonstrance had '*gubh-rowed*' Wilson into limiting the duration of the tax to five years. It hoped that the people of Bombay would 'follow in the wake of Madras and Calcutta and give all support to Sir Charles Trevelyan, the statesman and philanthropist, whom it will be a calamity for India to lose.'[41] Even the timid leaders of the moribund Bombay Association felt constrained to protest against the tax.[42]

Trevelyan began to be echoed. Feeling that they were 'about to be grossly wronged and cruelly plundered', Indians contended 'that the threatened bankruptcy of the Indian Government can be averted by existing means, and that the proposed remedy is worse than the disease'. In 1856-57, the cost of the Indian army was £ 11,491,905. In 1860 it was nearly 17 millions and Wilson thought that it could be reduced to £ 14,662,232. This was excessive. Indians had been disarmed, the frontiers well defined and offering a natural barrier, and the Indian States more loyal than ever before. Moreover, the military expenditure for 1856-57 had included the cost of stores and the expense of the Persian war. For the following three or four years, however, no stores would be required. Wilson, 'backed by the Viceroy', might assure Indians that utmost retrenchment had been effected; but they were 'neither prepared nor justified to accept the assurances'.[43]

---

40. *Rast Goftar*, 15 Apr. 1860.
41. *Ibid.*, 13 May 1860.
42. *Ibid.*, 1, Jul. 1860. The *Rast Goftar* criticised the *Englishman* as the 'reputed organ of our Financial Director of Indigo Planters' for its attack on the Bombay petitioners, especially Dr Bhau Daji.
43. *Rast Goftar*, 10 Jun. 1860; also see petition of the British Indian Association to the legislative council of India, 26 May 1860.

The Indian exchequer was also being drained as a result of 'the maintenance of a huge European Army in India, and the appropriation of the Indian money to the service of Regiments not even stationed here'.[44] Further, Wilson had given no account of the gains from 'the confiscation of public securities belonging to the rebels' and from the forfeiture of pensions and stipends. The public works charges, more than three million and a half in 1856-57, were 'mainly suspended in the last year' and the works could be resumed without further taxation. Economy, moreover, could be effected by means of 'a thorough reformation' in this 'notoriously corrupt' department.[45] Even otherwise, it was 'wrong in principle', oppressive in practice and 'unsupported by any precedent in the history of British legislation' to impose an income tax for promoting public works. The zemindars of Bengal repeated their general argument about the 'ill-adaptedness' of the income tax to 'the circumstances of the people of this country' and the special plea that it tended 'to infringe upon the perpetual settlement'.[46]

Isolated demonstrations, too, were provoked by the income tax. In Bombay the piece-goods merchants and petty dealers in cloth in the market near the Jama Masjid closed their shops on 1 August 1860, although the cocoanut fair, symbolising the opening of the season, fell on that day. They decided to transact no business on a day that presaged ill-luck for the whole year. More than 100 shops remained closed.[47] In Poona, on 14 November, people assembled 'in a tumultuous manner in large numbers, intimidating the officers of Government, and tearing up and trampling under foot the Income Tax Forms in the public streets.' Though quiet followed and returns were made, it is notable that telegraphic communication by means of a secret cypher was suspected between the organisers of the agitation in Poona and Bombay.[48]

The excitement against the income tax impressed Laing (1812-97), Wilson's successor as finance member, 'with a sense of the political disadvantages attending fiscal measures of this nature among the people of India.[49] He saw no objection to the enhancement of the salt tax,[50] and pronounced the income tax to have miscarried.[51] This encouraged the British Indian Association to send a deputation to Canning. In view of the retrenchments proposed by Laing, 'the harassment, misery and discontent' produced by the income tax, and

44. Proceedings of the 9th Annual General Meeting of the British Indian Association, 29 Jan. 1861, *Indian Field*, 9 Feb. 1861.
45. *Rast Goftar*, 10 Jun. 1860.
46. *Indian Field*, 9 Feb. 1861.
47. *Bombay Times*, 2 Nov. 1860.
48. *Poona Observer*, 21 Nov. 1860, quoted *ibid.*, 24 Nov. 1860.
49. Temple, *Men and Events*, p. 213.
50. *Proceedings of the Legislative Council of India*, vol. VII, col. 354.

its condemnation as a failure, the deputation prayed that the people be relieved of this 'oppressive impost'. But the viceroy gave a deft turn to the argument and saw in the partial failure of the tax and prevalance of 'abuses and unnecessary vexations' a case not for repeal but for amendment 'to correct these failures'. He also refused to abolish the income tax by enhancing the duty on salt because that 'would be to relieve the rich at the expense of the poor'.[52]

Meanwhile Europeans, too, were growing anxious to get rid of the income tax. Taking advantage of the opportunity to welcome Elgin, the new viceroy, the Bengal Chamber of Commerce and the British Indian Association separately urged its abolition at the first opportunity.[53] This was on 1 April 1862. Exactly a fortnight later, relief was extended to nearly two-thirds of the assessees, who numbered between 500,000 and 600,000, by remitting the 2% rate of the tax.[54]

This partial remission and the subsequent appointment of Trevelyan, who had opposed the income tax at the time of its introduction, to succeed Laing were looked upon as 'gladsome tidings'.[55] Although Trevelyan only reduced the tax from four to three per cent.,[56] the concession was gratefully received.[57]

Anticipating the expiry of the income tax after the completion of five years, the British Indian Association petitioned the viceroy for its repeal; and to ensure that the tax was not renewed, reiterated the suggestion that, if necessary, the salt tax could provide 'the least objectionable mode of raising increased income'. The Association favoured equalisation of the salt duty.[58] In this, however, it went against the interests of Bombay and Madras where the duty on salt was lower.

Though committed to drop the income tax in 1865, the government was forced by the 'very gloomy' financial outlook to reckon the possibility of giving it a fresh lease of life. Moreover, it had at hand

51. *Ibid.*, col. 357.
52. Address of the British Indian Association to Canning, 5 Jun. 1861, *Report of the Monthly General Meeting of the British Indian Association, 26 Jul. 1861*, pp. 7-9. The British Indian Association stuck to its guns, observing: 'It is a mistake to suppose that the poorer classes would not feel relief by the substitution recommended, inasmuch as the poor and middle classes are suffering the more from the operations of the Income Tax Assessment than the rich who have the means and are generally well able to cope with oppresion and annoyance.' *Ibid.*
53. *Times of India*, 11 Apr. 1862.
54. Financial Statement, 16 Apr. 1862, *Proceedings of the Legislative Council of India*, vol. I, pp. 114-37.
55. *Bengalee*, 6 Jan. 1863.
56. *Proceedings of the Legislative Council of India*, vol. II, p. 80.
57. *Bengalee*, 6 May 1863.
58. Petition of the British Indian Association to the viceroy and governor-general in council, 30 Mar. 1865, *Report of a Monthly General Meeting of the British Indian Association held on 19 July 1865*, pp. 16-7.

a lavish plan to erect new military barracks, and there was a general 'furore for expenditure'. Constantly 'in the minority in Council' on the subject of economy, Lawrence wondered 'how any considerable addition is to be made to the ways and means of the State, without much discontent and infinite obloquy'.[59] He complained that while irresponsible in supporting 'increased expenditure of various kinds', non-official Europeans resisted 'their share of the burthen' 'to meet the extra cost'.[60]

Lawrence was convinced that reduction of the military expenditure offered the only escape from further taxation, and that this could be accomplished only in England. Whatever little clippings the government of India made 'after much trouble' vanished 'in the general increase in the whole department'.[61] Though willing to 'see the military expenditure diminished as far as practicable', Cranborne, the secretary of state, made his willingness meaningless by shifting back to the government of India 'the responsibility of deciding when and how that can be done'. He felt that in the public works department, where alone reduction was possible, the government of India had persistently ignored productive works and pledged itself 'to a huge expenditure on barracks'. Eschewing all considerations of economy, it had allocated £ 150,000 for irrigation as against £ 2,500,000 for barracks. Besides being unproductive, expenditure on barracks was of temporary utility and might be 'found to have been thrown away a few years hence'. Cranborne regretted that 'matters have gone too far to suffer me to attempt any reversal of this policy'.[62] Eventually, the barracks produced a deficit of £ 2,500,000 and added £6,500,000 to the public debt of India during Lawrence's viceroyalty.[63]

Ceaseless shuffling of responsibility between Calcutta and London having made moonshine of economy, need for fresh taxation remained an inconvenient reality. But the supreme executive council would not permit the renewal of the income tax. Unwillingly, Lawrence had to submit.[64] Surprised at the repeal, Wood complained to Lawrence that it 'had been a great deal too bad of the Civilians, landholders and merchants forcing your hand on the Income Tax, and trying to shift the load on to the natives in salt.'[65]

As if to justify the complaint, the zemindars kept up the strain of increased salt duty.[66] But Lawrence, who knew that the rich preferred

59. Lawrence to Wood, 4 Feb., 1 Jul. 1865, *Lawrence Collection*, reel 2.
60. Lawrence to Northcote, 28 Mar. 1867, *ibid.*, reel 3.
61. Lawrence to Wood, 1 Aug. 1865, *ibid.*, reel 2.
62. Cranborne to Lawrence, 3 Nov. 1866, *ibid.*, reel 1.
63. Temple, *Men and Events*, pp. 335-36.
64. Lawrence felt outraged by Trevelyan who had agreed to retain the income tax. Lawrence to Wood, 4 Feb. and 17 Apr. 1865, *Lawrence Collection*, reel 2.
65. Wood to Lawrence, 16 May 1865, *ibid.*, reel 1.
66. *Hindoo Patriot*, 1 Jan. 1866.

'indirect taxation particularly when it did not fall on them', was determined not to raise the salt tax after it had doubled in his own time in upper and central India. He had seen the cost of this necessary condiment go up 'at least 12 times in Punjab, and perhaps 8 times in the North West Provinces'. And the incubus, stressed the viceroy, gripped those who barely earned six to eight shillings a month and had to sustain their families.[67]

None the less, the shortfall caused by the withdrawal of the income tax had to be made good. So the simple-minded viceroy suggested export duties on sugar, silk, tea, coffee and jute; his justification being that in spite of a flourishing business, European planters contributed little to an administration that was put to a considerable cost for roads, police and postal arrangements on their account'.[68] Predictably the entire European mercantile community was 'open-mouthed against the export duties';[69] and these were prudently disallowed by the secretary of state.

The search and need for money continued. Work on the barracks was on, and for two years there had been a debt of a million per annum. In spite of Lawrence's preference for an income tax, a license tax was levied for 1867-69. The minimum taxable income in 1867 was Rs. 200 a year on which Rs. 4 was charged; the maximum amount payable by an individual was Rs. 500.[70] The maximum amount payable by a joint-stock company was Rs. 2,000 a year.[71] In 1868 the minimum taxable income was raised to Rs. 500, exempting four-fifths of the original assessees who now numbered 1,16,000 as against 5,56,230 in 1867. The maximum amounts payable by individuals and companies were raised to Rs. 1,600 and Rs. 6,400 respectively.[72]

Both Europeans and Indians opposed the tax and denied its necessity. Massey, the finance member, was criticised for levying a tax in spite of an affluent exchequer. It was pointed out by way of contrast that in 1862-63, his 'most prosperous financial year', Laing had shown a surplus of £ 1,827,345 with receipts worth £ 45,143,752. But with an estimated income of £ 46,783,110, a million and a half more than that of 1862-63, Massey expected a deficit of more than half a million. The British Indian Association 'forwarded a memorial objecting to the principle as well as the details of the Bill, but it arrived a little too late'. This led to condemnation as 'outrageous' of the 'hot haste' of the passage of the License Bill.[73] The Association further petitioned

---

67. Lawrence to Cranborne, 6 Sep. 1866, *Lawrence Collection*, reel 2.
68. *Ibid.*
69. Lawrence to Wood, 14 Apr. 1865, *ibid.*
70. *Abstract of the Proceedings of the Council of the Governor-General of India 1867*, Calcutta, 1868, vol. VI, pp. 186-91.
71. P. Banerjea, *A History of Indian Taxation*, Calcutta, 1930, pp. 53-4.
72. *Ibid.*, p. 58; *Abstract of the Proceedings of the Council of the Governor-General of India, 1868*, Calcutta, 1869, vol. VII, p. 172.
73. *Hindoo Patriot*, 11 Mar. 1867; for the memorial which reached 'exactly an

Northcote, the secretary of state, on the 'propriety of providing some agency for the purpose of bringing public opinion to bear upon the consideration of measures of taxation and the general administration of the finances of the Queen's Indian empire.' As things were, the public in India had 'no voice in the management of the finances or even sufficient opportunities of discussing financial measures until when too late'. The Association suggested, 'in the absence of representative system', the creation of a consultative council 'sufficiently numerous, and composed of competent Native and European gentlemen, drawn from all parts of the empire'.[74]

The Traders' Association objected to the exemption granted to 'the rich zemindar, the householder and the fundholder'.[75] At a public meeting in the Calcutta Town Hall on 27 March 1867, organised by Europeans but attended by Indians also, the absurdity of a situation was highlighted in which the Maharaja of Burdwan would not pay a penny and every employee of his earning Rs. 200 a year would be taxed. This was a real indignation meeting, which is what its organisers had meant it to be. The finance member was publicly reviled: 'the lowest boy in Dr. Duff's Academy or any other school, would not be guilty of such errors in figures, and fallacies in reasoning as Mr. Massey had been, or if he was, he would deserve to be flogged.' The tax was variously condemned as 'one which shackles trade and commerce, frightens the poor and exempts the rich'; 'as giving the minimum of revenue with a maximum of unfairness'; as 'a disguised Income Tax characterised by iniquitous inequality'; and as 'legalised extortion'. No wonder that a speaker was led away to wish that the government 'be at once thrown overboard'.[76] But the speakers at the meeting had no alternative to offer except the increase of the salt tax which, as Massey bitterly remarked, already amounted to six millions and was 'paid almost exclusively by the naked wretches, who cannot get up petition and public meetings to protect themselves'.[77]

Indians also criticised the license tax as unnecessary and inequitable, but without employing violent language. The *Indian Mirror* asserted: 'Nothing but the consciousness of possessing absolute and irresistible might in enforcing it, and of utter irresponsibility in the exercise of such power, would have inspired the obstinacy with which any attempt at amendment has been withstood.'[78] The *Native Opinion* lamented that, unlike Calcutta, Bombay was politically dead

hour after the adjournment of Council', see *Report of a General Meeting of the British Indian Association held on 18 September 1867*, pp. 1, 12-3.
74. Memorial of the British Indian Association to Northcote, 20 Jan. 1868.
75. Petition of Traders' Association to governor-general, 19 Mar. 1867, *Hindoo Patriot*, 25 Mar. 1867.
76. *Ibid.*, 1 Apr. 1867.
77. Massey to Lawrence, 30 Mar. 1867, *Lawrence Collection*, reel 5.
78. *Indian Mirror* in *Native Opinion*, 31 Mar. 1867.

and no public protest was being organised there.[79]

Particular annoyance was caused by the new barracks. By squandering eleven crores of rupees on these, it was argued, Massey had unnecessarily increased taxation.[80] The occasion was ideal for a credible juxtaposition of economic discontent and racialism. It was 'really sickening', wrote the *Hindoo Patriot,* that as against the heavy outlay on barracks for sanitary reasons, 'not a pice' was 'spent upon the improvement of the epidemic-stricken villages'. Soldiers were valuable no doubt, 'but does it never occur to our rulers that those who contribute revenue have a claim to it for the elevation of their lives'?[81] Convinced as Indians were beginning to be of the *mala fide* intentions of their rulers, even absurd charges were made and believed. In spite of the European outburst against it, the license tax was compared to the *jaziya.*[82] The real object of the rulers was alleged to have been to plunder Indians in order to enrich Europeans.[83]

Perplexed by the 'frightful state' of the Indian finances, Mayo, who had succeeded Lawrence, dizzily complained: 'Year after year of Deficit has taken place and absolutely nothing has been done to stop it.' What was more shocking, these deficits had occurred 'in seasons of profound peace' free from 'any particular Natural Misfortune'. Faced with a net shortage of £ 3,900,000 for 1868-69 and 1869-70, Mayo proposed to save two millions through economy and raise one million by taxation.[84]

Meanwhile, Temple had succeeded Massey as finance member, and provoked, by his antecedents,[85] speculations about the revival of the income tax.[86] His first budget, presented in March 1869, included an income tax of one per cent. on incomes of Rs. 500 or above a year.[87] The low rate kept non-official Europeans silent, and a section of the Indian Press favoured it.[88] But the zemindars of Bengal—despite Temple's appeal to them[89]—apprehended in it the thin end of the wedge;

79. *Ibid.*
80. *Bhaskar,* 28 Mar. 1868, *Report on Native Press, Bengal,* 4 Apr. 1868, p. 10.
81. *Hindoo Patriot,* 11 Mar. 1867.
82. *Amrita Bazar Patrika, Report on Native Press, Bengal,* 26 Apr.—9 May 1868, p. 6.
83. *Arunodaya,* 31 Oct. 1869, *Report on Native Press, Bombay,* 6 Nov. 1869, p. 6.
84. Mayo to Argyll, 2, 9 Sep. 1869, *Argyll Papers,* reel 312.
85. Temple has recorded a graphic account of how his old master, Lawrence, while retiring as governor-general, urged upon him the necessity of reimposing the income tax, *Men and Events,* p 337. Temple had also served under Wilson.
86. *Amrita Bazar Patrika,* 25 Feb. 1869, *Report on Native Press, Bengal,* 13 Mar. 1869, p. 3.
87. *Abstract of the Proceedings of the Council of the Governor-General of India, 1869,* Calcutta, 1870, vol. VIII, pp. 124-28.
88. *Bengalee,* 20 Mar. 1869.
89. *Abstract of the Proceedings of the Council of the Governor-General of India, 1869,* p. 128.

and the fear was soon confirmed, in November, by the doubling of the rate.[90] They warned Europeans against their myopic and sadistic 'ecstasy' that the zemindars, 'an eye-sore to them', had fallen within the orbit of taxation. Weak opposition being an incentive to official extravagance, the tax was bound to increase. The zemindars also used this opportunity to remind the government of their favourite panacea, enhancement of the salt tax.[91]

In spite of the low rate, resentment was caused by Temple's admission that the income tax had become necessary because of the expenditure on barracks and the demands of England on India.[92] This made the tax an indication 'much more of the impotency of our financiers than of the poverty or barrenness of the ordinary sources of the state's revenue'. Temple was called to account for his silence on the military expenditure, 'the heaviest drain on the country's resources', depriving it of 12½ crores of rupees or one-fourth of its total revenues. The Abyssinian expedition, originally expected not to exceed five million pounds sterling, was likely to cost eight and a half millions, and even this figure could not be treated as final. This was 'Indian financial management all over'; though such a mistake or oversight could bring about a change of government in England.[93] It was Temple's 'theory of ordinary expenditure' which had saddled the revenue with a million and a half of pounds sterling for barracks in a year. With a loan for these, he could have shown, without the income tax, a better surplus than he had contrived to obtain with it. In England a deficit had been met with liberalisation of taxes. But the Indian financiers thought that everything was in order. 'Our soldiers are hardly a man too many—our railways are constructed on the most economical scale—our Public Works expenditure would delight the heart of a man like Joseph Hume, and the only thing therefore for our Financiers is to have recourse to fresh taxation whenever the accounts are a puzzle to them.' The moral was obvious. But 'for the absence of anything like public opinion', income tax could not have

90. *Abstract of the Proceedings of the Council of the Governor-General of India, 1869*, pp. 321-59.

91. *Hindoo Patriot*, 8 Mar. 1869. Referring to the 'iniquitous proposal' about the salt duty, the *Bengalee* of 20 Mar. 1869 indignantly remarked: 'If our vaunted knowledge of politics comes to this, we better give up politics altogether.'

92. *Som Prakash*, 29 Mar. 1869, *Report on Native Press, Bengal*, 3 Apr. 1869, p. 1. See *Abstract of the Proceedings of the Council of the Governor-General of India, 1869*, pp. 108-14.

93. *Native Opinion*, 4 Apr. 1869. Earlier, finding Temple almost on his knees to show that every effort has been tried in the direction of retrenchment and of indirect taxation and that the tax on incomes is imposed as a clear and pure matter of necessity', *Native Opinion* of 21 Mar 1869 had 'no help but to believe the Finance Member'. It had favoured Rs. 1,000 as the minimum taxable limit and also doubted whether the rate would not be raised.

been needlessly imposed.[94]

Realising the interrelatedness of expenditure and taxation, and of the need to check the arbitrary character of the administration, Indians naturally thought of 'the reorganisation of the whole system of government' while agitating against the income tax.[95]

In 1870 there was a combined opposition from Indians and Europeans when the income tax rate was raised to 3¼ per cent.; an opposition that was first expressed bluntly within the council chamber.[96] The government was censured for having created a crisis by 'gross mismanagement', and for inflicting 'a heavy war tax in time of peace'. The army, the 'Home' charges and the public works had 'entirely eaten up the resources' of the country. The 'patent' fact was that Indians were 'made to pay'.[97] The agitation this time was 'not so much against the Income-tax in particular, as against the financial management of the country in general'.[98] Of the four resolutions passed at the Calcutta protest meeting of Indians and Europeans on 18 April, only one directly criticised the income tax as 'impolitic, unjust and uncalled for by the present state of the finances of the country'. Another resolution objected to a quarter of the revenues raised from the Indian tax-payers being expended in England; it demanded 'an effective control in India over such expenditure'. The third resolution favoured discontinuance of the practice of charging the cost of permanent public works to ordinary revenues. The fourth resolution deprecated the 'precipitation with which Budgets and measures founded thereon are passed'.[99] Realisation of the wisdom of possessing an effective voice in the legislature was gaining ground.[100] A protest meeting was organised by the Bombay Association on 2 May.[101] Petitions were sent to the secretary of state from Bombay and Calcutta.

The combined pressure of Indians and Europeans kept on gaining strength. But Temple, though prepared to raise the minimum assessable income from Rs. 750 to Rs. 1,000,[102] stuck to the income tax. His argument was: 'If we had not taxed the Europeans and the better classes of natives, we must have taxed the mass of the people: which was worse still.'[103] Turning the tables on the zemindars, who had talk-

94. *Ibid.*, 9 May 1869.
95. *Som Prakash*, 26 Apr. 1869, *Report on Native Press, Bengal*, 1 May 1869, p. 2.
96. *Abstract of the Proceedings of the Council of the Governor-General of India, 1870*, vol. IX, Calcutta, 1871, pp. 211-15. 270-316.
97. *Hindoo Patriot*, 11 Apr. 1870. Even *Bengalee*, 23 Apr. 1870, attacked the income tax this time after having supported it in 1869.
98. *Native Opinion*, 24 Apr. 1870.
99. *Bengalee*, 23 Apr. 1870.
100. *Bombay Samachar*, in *Native Opinion*, 17 Apr. 1870.
101. *Ibid.*, 8 May 1870.
102. Temple to Argyll, 16 Feb. 1872, *Argyll Papers*, reel 319.
103. Temple to Argyll, 5 Jan. 1872, *ibid.* Temple argued that 'all persons who

ed, in 1869, of weak opposition inducing official thriftlessness, the finance member asserted that if the 'rich and clamorous classes' escaped taxation, 'the pressure exerted by the Income tax to ensure economy of expenditure will be removed.'[104]

Temple claimed that the income tax was really popular. Referring to the *Amrita Bazar Patrika,* he said that only one in 800 was affected by the tax, and though this one person might abuse the government, the rest would bless it.[105] He overlooked an essential difference between the one who paid the income tax and the 799 who did not: the former was politically articulate while the latter were not. The question was not one of according justice to the poor, but of the inexpediency of antagonising non-official Europeans and the politically awakening upper and middle class Indians. Northbrook, Mayo's successor, realised this. He recognised 'the evil effects produced by the Income tax' not only among resident Europeans but also among Indians in general.[106] Eventually, decision to remit it was taken on 20 March 1873; Temple, Ellis and Napier dissenting.[107]

The government did not forget for more than a decade the lesson learnt from the income tax agitation. Requiring two million pounds sterling, Lytton, for instance, could do no more than toy with the idea of an imperial taxation that would 'indirectly meet the purpose of an income tax without directly exciting from the European and official community the opposition' to which the income tax had been sacrificed.[108] He was not afraid of Indian landlords; but non-official Europeans scared him.[109]

Even earlier, alarmed by the discontent produced by the income tax, Laing had proposed the allocation of some of the taxation to provincial governments.[110] Constitutional changes in the provinces had, however, precluded the implementation of the idea,[111] which was next taken up by Massey. But Lawrence, unable to differentiate between 'local taxation as compared with general taxes', found in it 'a great political fallacy'.[112] The fallacy was removed by Cranborne who argued that discontent from taxation could shake the government of India only in case the discontent was concentrated against it. If 'split

could be called poor or needy in the ordinary sense, would be fully excluded from the operation of the Tax: and all just cause of complaint would be removed.'

104. Temple to Argyll, 8 Mar. 1872, *Argyll Papers,* reel 319.
105. Temple to Argyll, 26 Sep. 1872, *ibid.*
106. Northbrook to Argyll, 26 Sep. 1872, *ibid.,* reel 317.
107. Northbrook to Argyll, 21 Mar. 1873, *ibid.*
108. Lytton to Salisbury, 22 Jul. 1876, *Salisbury Papers,* reel 814.
109. Lytton to Salisbury, 1 Nov. 1877, *ibid.,* reel 816.
110. *Proceedings of the Legislative Council of India,* vol. VII, cols. 359 ff.
111. *Abstract of the Proceedings of the Council of the Governor-General of India,* vol. I, p. 118.
112. Lawrence to Cranborne, 5 Oct. 1866, *Lawrence Collection,* reel 2.

up into a number of local grievances, and directed at different times against subordinate local officers', this discontent could not be 'a serious political danger'. Local taxation did not produce 'in any shape half the hatred which the same amount of the tax would have produced if levied simultaneously, & by a central authority'.[113] This was the political motive behind financial decentralisation, though it had fiscal advantages too.

An experiment in decentralised taxation was made in 1868 with the levy of a cess for roads on land in Bengal. The British Indian Association was up in arms against what the zemindars characteristically considered a violation of the Permanent Settlement. A public meeting was organised by the Association on 2 September.[114] Even Girish Chandra Ghosh, who told the zemindars to their faces that he would not 'hesitate to spurn' the Permanent Settlement with his feet for 'standing in the way of national progress', opposed the cess. He feared that the cess would be extorted from the ryot by the zemindar who would justify himself on the plea that 'as the Government had broken faith with him, he was not bound to extend mercy towards his tenants'.[115] But the *Som Prakash* alleged that the zemindars used the Permanent Settlement as an excuse for evading obligations that devolved on them. They squandered the ryot's hard-earned money on week-end debaucheries.[116] Educated Indians in Bombay also found the agitation of the zemindars unreasonable and unjust.[117]

The opposition, hitherto confined largely to the zemindars, spread to other sections of Indians with the formal inauguration of financial decentralisation on 14 December 1870. They immediately saw through the imperialistic stratagem and feared that since local taxes would be confined to different regions, Indians as a whole would not unite to protest against these taxes, thereby minimising the chances of obtaining relief.[118] Motivated by the fear of growing discontent against increasing taxation, the scheme made possible the transference of 'the disagreeable work of imposing new taxes to the local governments and administrations'.[119]

---

113. Cranborne to Lawrence, 3 Nov. 1866. *ibid.*, reel 1.
114. Supplements to *Hindoo Patriot*, 7, 14 Sep. 1868.
115. *Hindoo Patriot*, 14 Sep. 1868. *Friend of India*, 10 Sep. 1868, while denouncing the promoters of this meeting, shared this fear.
116. *Som Prakash*, 16 Mar. 1868, *Report on Native Press, Bengal*, 21 Mar. 1868, p. 1. Rev. James Long (1814-87), the popular Christian missionary of *Nil Darpan* fame, attributed this agitation to the zemindars' fear that 'serfdom and knowledge cannot work together'. Long to Lawrence, 15 Sep. 1868, *Lawrence Collection*, reel 6.
117. *Dnyan Prakash*, 1 Aug. 1870, *Report on Native Press, Bombay*, 6 Aug. 1870, p. 3.
118. *Jame Jamsed*, 17 Mar. 1871, *ibid.*, 18 Mar. 1871, p. 6.
119. *Hindu Reformer*, 15 Feb. 1871, *ibid.*, 18 Feb. 1871, p. 3.

Indians criticised financial decentralisation because its 'first fruits' were local taxes which 'neutralised' the reduction of the income tax.[120] In Bombay three taxes were proposed. When the Bombay Association asked for time to make a representation, only 48 hours were granted.[121] In a hastily prepared communication, the Association submitted that the proposed feast tax, municipal police cost tax and family tax on non-agricultural classes would fall on Indians and scarcely affect Europeans. For this petition the Association was chastised by the governor in the local legislative council, and its secretary, Naoroji Fardunji, who was sitting in the council, was also implicated.[122] Instead of being cowed down, the Indian Press retorted that busy hunting and unable to answer the petition, the authorities had indulged, like vulgar people, in personal attacks on the Association and its secretary.[123] It was argued that economy being the aim of the new scheme, the deficit of Rs. 1,42,730 could have been made up by reductions. On the contrary, the deficiency had been enlarged by an increase of Rs. 4,09,101 in the expenditure on provincial services and by the formation of a reserve fund of Rs. 4,50,000.[124] The scheme was obviously causing extravagance on the part of the local government without any benefit to Indians.[125]

The authorities, admitted the Bombay governor, could no longer 'afford to neglect' the discontent produced by increased taxation 'throughout the length and breadth of the country'.[126] One of his councillors made it plain that Bombay could not 'contribute anything more in the shape of taxation'. Discontent was confined to no particular class. Even the trading and agricultural classes, so far 'well affected towards the Government in this Presidency, are making use of language punishable in a Court of Justice.' There loomed in 'the continued augmentation of the burden of the people a source of political danger'. People made no distinction between local and imperial taxes; for them every tax was 'taken by the sirkar'.[127] In Bengal also feeling against local taxation was 'very strong', and the governor-general was obliged to direct the lieutenant-governor 'to act with the greatest caution'.[128]

120. *Native Opinion*, 19 Mar. 1871.
121. *Ibid.*, 23 Apr. 1871.
122. *Ibid.*, 30 Apr. 1871.
123. *Indu Prakash*, 24 Apr. 1871, *Report on Native Press, Bombay*, 29 Apr. 1871, p. 7.
124. *Indu Prakash*, 1 May 1871, *ibid.*, 6 May 1871, p. 5.
125. *Native Opinion*, 29 Dec. 1872.
126. Fitzgerald to Argyll, 18 Jun. 1871, *Argyll Papers*, reel 320.
127. Minute by Mansfield, 1 Sep. 1870, *ibid.*
128. Northbrook to Argyll, 26 Sep. 1872, *ibid.*, reel 317. For widespread 'consternation' in Bengal as a result of local taxation, see Rev. J. Bhattacharjye, *Observations on the District Road Cess and the Municipality Acts, ibid*, encl.

Like provincial taxation, municipal reform also came to be suspected as a device to relieve the imperial exchequer of certain ugly obligations. Local cesses were introduced to build roads, bridges and rest houses and to provide for education in rural areas; the municipal reform was intended to charge the people with police, educational and other expenditure.[129] Particularly, the power given to the local governments of imposing municipal government even on reluctant people was 'an engine' to molest and oppress them.[130]

For once since 1858, however, Indians were grateful to a viceroy for his 'manful stand' against 'unnecessary taxation'. They praised Northbrook's fidelity to his avowed object of reducing taxation in so far as he had remitted the income tax, advised the Bombay government to remove the non-agricultural and municipal rates, and vetoed the Bengal Municipal Act.[131] That he had achieved this without starving necessary public works, retarding progress and pressing upon the springs of industry was a proof of 'the mismanagement of the finances' in previous years.[132]

The reprieve was short. Indian finances deteriorated during Lytton's stormy viceroyalty. Menaced by the Tory determination to have the import duties on the Manchester goods removed, the finances were thrown into confusion by famine and depreciation of silver. Taxation was imminent. The measures eventually taken to impart some cheerfulness to the financial prospect brought to the boiling point the simmering economic discontent.

The new viceroy intimated his 'Chief' rather nervously that the financial prospects were 'terrible'. Fresh taxation seemed certain as the rupee threatened to stay at 1s.6.9d. till March 1877. The estimated deficit of two millions could even soar up to five if silver continued to fall. Lytton spied a silver lining in the crisis if the deficit stood at two millions. He hoped to use it 'to reconcile the great taxpayers to some new impost in which the State may find—what at present it sorely needs—a permanent source of revenue sufficiently elastic to bear stretching in case of any great emergency.' He wished not to touch the poor.[133]

The silver lining was a mirage. The viceroy ended up with famine cess and license tax, both of which fell mainly on the poor and the middle classes. Incapable of risking European resistance to income tax, which he would have liked to introduce, Lytton offered the callous justification that the new taxes would be 'received with a general feeling of relief, by all who can make their voices heard in India'.

129. *Native Opinion*, 14 Sep. 1873.
130. *Indu Prakash*, 15 Sep. 1873, *Report on Native Press, Bombay*, 20 Sep. 1873, p. 9.
131. *Bengalee*, 2 May 1874.
132. *Ibid.*, 27 Apr. 1874.
133. Lytton to Salisbury, 9, 22 Jul. 1876, *Salisbury Papers*, reel 814.

He gave his timidity the masquerade of strategy by rationalising that he had 'purposely stimulated' a false dread of the imminence of income tax in order that its eventual non-introduction might come as a relief to these vocal sections.[154]

The famine cess and license tax were allotted to the provincial governments as fixed sources of revenue for famine insurance and public works. In March 1877 a cess on land was levied in Bengal and a license tax was introduced in the North Western Provinces.[135] As more revenue was needed, Strachey, the finance member, proposed in December, an unusual time for taxation, a land tax in the North Western Provinces and a tax on commercial classes in Bengal. He proposed to introduce these taxes in the Panjab and Oudh also. For Bombay and Madras, exempt from land cess, license tax and increased salt duty were chosen to bring in more money.[136]

The minimum assessable income for the license tax was Rs. 100 in Bombay and Bengal, and Rs. 200 in Madras. In 1878-79 it was raised to Rs. 250 in Bengal. In 1880 the minimum assessable income was raised to Rs. 500 for the whole of British India.[137] During the first two years, the license tax was indeed a harsh measure. The agricultural cess was one per cent. on the rental, and the additional salt duty was 11 annas a maund.[138]

Up against the new taxation, Indians assailed its 'wisdom, propriety and humanity'.[139] The infliction of additional burden on the people of Madras and Bombay, still groaning under the ravages of famine, made it difficult to believe that they were 'the same people, the tale of whose distress evoked the sympathy of almost all the nations of the world'.[140]

Jotindra Mohan Tagore (1831-1908) conveyed to the legislative council 'the strong impression' of Indians that without attempting retrenchments, for which 'considerable room' existed, 'no additional tax ought justly to be imposed on the people'.[141] Belonging to the more affluent branch of the Tagore family, Jotindra Mohan, however, betrayed his personal and class selfishness when he ended his criticism with a whimper. He agreed that the license tax was 'the best that could be suggested—next perhaps to an income tax with a high

134. Lytton to Salisbury, 1 Nov. 1877, *Salisbury Papers*, reel 816.
    India, vol. XVI, pp. 123ff.
135. *Abstract of the Proceedings of the Council of the Governor-General of*
136. *Ibid.*, pp. 568 ff.
137. P. Banerjea, *op. cit.*, pp. 64-70.
138. *Bengalee*, 5 Jan. 1878.
139. *Indu Prakash*, 14 Jan. 1878, *Report on Native Press, Bombay*, 19 Jan. 1878, p. 3.
140. *Amrita Bazar Patrika*, 3 Jan. 1878, *Report on Native Press, Bengal*, 12 Jan. 1878, p. 6. This referred to the late famine in the two presidencies.
141. *Abstract of the Proceedings of the Council of the Governor-General of India*, vol. XVII, p. 9.

minimum of incidence'. He proposed that the license tax and the land cess be levied for two or three years during which period the grievances of the people could be represented to the British government and public. The professed preference of Tagore for income tax was no more than a simulated concern for the people, induced by the confidence that the tax proposals were final. On the two previous occasions when the income tax had been introduced, the British Indian Association had attacked it vehemently, and, to anticipate events, was to do so again in 1886. Relieved that its members had been spared the dreaded income tax, the British Indian Association, in fact, took a lukewarm stand at the public meeting convened by it in conjunction with the Indian Association. This obliged the disgruntled petty traders to organise a separate protest meeting. The British Indian Association was consequently dubbed the landholders' association which had 'left the poor to take care of themselves'.[142]

Strachey tried in vain to convince Indians that the civil expenditure was irreducible and the military expenditure could be curtailed in England alone.[143] They doubted whether the government of India was really so helpless.[144] Military charges could be scaled down by at least a million sterling, and 'another million, if not more', could be saved 'by abolishing the Cooper's Hill College, amalgamating the different branches of the Public Works Department, employing natives more largely in the services of the State, and making a territorial redistribution of local governments.'[145] Reduction to the extent of the deficit that had occasioned fresh taxation being possible, it was 'imperatively necessary that the growing demand upon the Indian Exchequer for ordinary wants of the State and for insurance against famine should be provided by judicious retrenchments and economical administration, without permanently adding to the burdens of the people by further heavy taxation.'[146]

The new taxation was objectionable not only because no reduction had been attempted, but also because it had left 'the richest mercantile classes almost free and the official and professional classes altogether free'.[147] The maximum amount of Rs. 200 a year, payable as license tax, represented 'too low a figure' for a rich merchant or firm.[148] The tax fell 'but lightly on rich merchants and heavily on the petty dealers'.[149] The 'moral cowardice' of the authorities, who had

142. *Sadharani*, 23 Jun. 1878, *Report on Native Press, Bengal*, 29 Jun. 1878, p. 3.
143. *Abstract of the Proceedings of the Council of the Governor-General of India*, vol. XVII, pp. 79-80.
144. *Bengalee*, 29 Dec. 1877.
145. *Ibid.*, 5 Jan. 1878.
146. Resolution passed at a public meeting convened by the British Indian and Indian Associations on 2 Mar. 1878, *ibid.*, 9 Mar. 1878.
147. *Native Opinion*, 10 Feb. 1878.
148. *Bengalee*, 5 Jan. 1878.
149. *Native Opinion*, 20 Jan. 1878.

been deterred from introducing the income tax by 'the apprehended opposit:on of the powerful members of the Civil and Military Services and of the rich mercantile classes',[150] was actually responsible for this 'invidious class taxation'.[151]

The strongest and the best organised opposition to these taxes came from Bombay. There the protest meeting of 19 February 1878 was a 'signal success',[152] being 'nothing more nor less than the first public demand for representative government in India'.[153] The governor having refused the use of the Town Hall for this meeting, it was held in the tent of Wilson's circus on the Esplanade. Four thousand Indians and Europeans expressed their dissatisfaction by attending it in spite of the governor's disapproval. Even the wary Bombay Association sent a letter of sympathy. The sheriff, Dr Atmaram Pandurang, initiated the proceedings with a speech severely condemning the governor as 'the lackey on the heels of Lord Lytton'.[154]

The Indian Press in Bengal, unhappy over the imbecile and selfish conduct of the political associations there, derived inspiration from the Bombay leaders. The *Som Prakash* was led to predict that if any good ever accrued to India, it would be through the exertions of the people of Bombay, and not of the indolent inhabitants of Calcutta who merely aped Europeans. Recalling an old historical allusion, it discerned a promise for the future in the antagonism of the Bombay government towards the agitation:[155]

> The more arbitrary its conduct, the greater will be the earnestness and courage with which the people will strive to obtain their lawful rights and privileges. In the hostile attitude of the Government of Bombay towards the promoters of the recent meeting, we see but a repetition of the struggle which long continued to rage in ancient Rome between the Patricians and the Plebians, and which at last ended in the submission of the former.

Here was struck a new note of hope and determination that tended to bring closer people belonging to different parts of the country. This was further evidenced by countrywide sympathy for the two Surat editors and a lawyer who were being tried for having instigated riots against the new taxes.[156]

The enhanced salt tax even provoked slander. Driven by thoughtless avarice, it was alleged, the government had embarked on under-

150. *Bengalee,* 5 Jan. 1878.
151. *Quarterly Journal of the Poona Sarvajanik Sabha,* vol. II, no. 1. p. 30.
152. *Hindoo Patriot,* 4 Mar. 1878.
153. *Times of India,* in *Native Opinion,* 24 Feb. 1878.
154. *Kashinath Trimbak Telang, 1850-1893,* Bombay, 1951, p. 25.
155. *Som Prakash,* 25 Feb. 1878, *Report on Native Press, Bengal,* 2 Mar. 1878, p. 8.
156. *Native Opinion,* 7, 14 Apr., 29 Sep. 1878; *Bengalee,* 13 Jul. 1878.

mining the health of the people by rendering salt too costly to be easily procurable. This ominously resembled the extirpation of the American aborigines by Europeans; 'the only difference being that the European settlers put the American Indians at once to death, while the Englishmen in India are killing the Natives by a slower process'.[157] Such wild charges, though an aberration, expressed the indignant frustration of at least some Indians.

Taxation inspired discontent that acted as a magnetic field to which a variety of people with a common grievance felt attracted. It provided a plane and a compulsion for them to get together. The getting together was an occasion for a none too clear, often unconscious, awareness of being in a group that was distinct from the immemorial fixtures on the *varna* graph. The group was not yet a sovereign unit. It represented, in terms of its shifting membership, the extent and power of the magnetic field which varied in accordance with the taxation measures of the government. The impulsion, however, was personal. The group did not attract the individuals so much as they veered towards it.

Besides aiding in the emergence of an incipient class consciousness that cut across traditional social divisions, taxation also gave an extra dimension to political awakening by indicating the inseparability of economic and political issues. Seen in the total Indian perspective, the discontent, though economic, admitted of a remedy that had very much to do with political power. Taxation, not treatises on political economy, ensured that the truth of the dictum that 'taxation without representation is tyranny' should be 'more and more realised in the fiscal and financial arrangements of the country'.[158] Popular control of finances was necessary because the official policy was worked on two different lines: in relation to income 'a truly European system, evincing much skill and thought', was adopted; but the pattern of expenditure was irresponsibly thriftless. This dichotomy in the financial management could be removed by empowering the legislative councils to control 'both the income and expenditure of the Imperial and Provincial Governments'.[159] But this was not enough. The legislative councils, in order to be really responsible, had to be answerable to the people. And agitation was afoot for obtaining popular representation.

II

Taxation necessitated by increasing expenditure produced, as

157. *Suryodaya*, 28 Jan. 1878, *Report on Native Press, Bombay*, 2 Feb. 1878, p. 3.
158. *Native Opinion*, 20 Jan. 1878.
159. *Som Prakash*, 7 Jan. 1878, *Report on Native Press, Bengal*, 12 Jan. 1878, p. 8.

we have seen, recurrent clashes of interest between the government and sections of the people including resident Europeans. We shall now deal with an aspect of taxation which brought out in sharp relief the conflict between Indian and British interests. It related to the import duties on British manufactures. Indians began to be conscious of it in the early 19th century. If Britain expected India to be a market for British goods, murmured the *Bengal Herald* in the wilderness, 'reciprocity of trade' demanded that 'she must remove the restrictive, almost prohibitory duties on Asiatic produce'.[160] But the combined pressure of power-looms and protective tariff operated inexorably to reduce India from an exporter to an importer of cloth.

The tariff would have continued to favour the cotton magnates of Manchester, but for the depletion of Indian finances after 1857. The government of India was obliged to raise to 20 per cent. the import duty on 'all articles of luxury, and not of prime necessity'. On the generality of articles the duty was fixed at ten per cent., and on cotton yarn at five per cent.[161] The move was welcomed by Indians as the partial redress of a wrong done long back by the adoption of free trade.[162] But European businessmen in India assailed it as a setback to British imports in India, and as an artificial stimulus to Indian production. Within three days of the announcement of the enhanced duties the Bengal Chamber of Commerce met and prepared seven resolutions to be adopted at a public meeting which was fixed by the sheriff for 26 March 1859. Besides criticising the new duties and calling for their reduction at the earliest opportunity, the resolutions demanded that, 'as in other British possessions', 50 per cent. members of the legislative council should be independent of the government; viewed 'with alarm the enormous increase' in expenditure and pressed for retrenchment 'in every department of the Government at home and abroad, with as little delay as possible'; suggested loans, not taxation, with imperial guarantees in the English money market; favoured the construction 'as much as possible' of reproductive public works; and asked for a parliamentary committee 'to investigate into and report upon the finances, as well as upon all other important questions-in relation to India on which information may be necessary with a view to future legislation'.[163] It is significant that while Indians in general welcomed the enhanced tariffs, two leading members of the British Indian Association, Ram Gopal Ghosh and Durga Charan Law, both businessmen by profession, supported the

160. *Bengal Herald,* 13 Jun. 1829.
161. *Proceedings of the Legislative Council of India,* vol. V, cols. 113-14.
162. *Hindoo Patriot,* 17 Mar. 1859.
163. *Bengal Hurkaru,* 18, 21, 24, 26, 28, 30 March 1859; *Friend of India,* 31 Mar. 1859. The Bombay Chamber of Commerce also organised a meeting of the mercantile community which was attended by 'Europeans and Natives interested in the object'. *Bombay Gazette,* 16 Mar. 1859.

agitation. Ghosh even moved the fourth resolution that related to loans with imperial guarantees. Personal material interests, as we saw earlier also, constituted the primary moving factor.

Even Wilson, who introduced, a year later in 1860, a uniform rate of ten per cent.,[164] failed to allay European fears. His budget was seen as an impetus to the Bombay cotton textile industry. The history of the budding industry was recounted to make the point. The first venture, London's Broach Mill, had failed on account of faulty construction and distance from skilled labour. But the Bombay mills of Cowasji Nanabhoy and Manockji Nasserwanji Petit 'realised handsome returns in spite of indifferent machinery, expensive management, and high cost of fuel'. This success naturally engaged the attention of the Bombay capitalists. At this juncture came Wilson's measure. By doubling the import duty on yarns, it 'directed a rush of capital in this direction' and caused 'the formation of seven or eight new companies within less than as many months'.[165] This rapid advance placed Bombay 'in a fair way to distance Manchester, in the production of coarse grey yarn and fabrics'. As against 82,566 spindles and 240 looms then working, the new tariff brought forth 200,740 new spindles and 3,560 looms over and above the 27,536 spindles and 225 looms added in the old establishments. The expected outturn from these was 15,592,100 lbs. of yarn No. 20 and 13,443,050 lbs. of yarn No. 30. This almost trebled the total import of all numbers of grey in 1859 which was 9,767,578 lbs., and far exceeded the requirements of the Indian market. Thus Bombay rivalled Manchester not only in the production of low yarn, but also posed a threat with respect to coarse cloth. Having produced yarn in such a large quantity, the manufacturers were sure to convert it into fabrics suited to the Indian market. Already, because of their superior finish, the Indian dealer had begun to prefer the Longcloths and Maddapolams of the Oriental Spinning and Weaving Company 'to the produce of the Lancashire looms'.[166]

Manchester moved quickly to avert this danger to a portion of its Indian supply. In a petition to the secretary of state, the Manchester Chamber of Commerce referred to the opposition of the Bengal, Bombay and Madras Chambers of Commerce to the tariff and submitted that this would seriously injure its Indian trade. It denied Wood's contention that the Indian cotton mills were being chiefly financed by British capital. Rather, if British money ever found its way to the Indian industry, that would be because of the heavy duties. Gilding its demand with altruism, the Manchester Chamber appealed to the interests of the Indian exchequer and consumers. The enhancement would defeat its own purpose by diminishing the returns; and the

164. *Proceedings of the Legislative Council of India*, vol. VI, cols. 115-23.
165. *Bombay Times*, 1 Aug. 1860.
166. *Ibid.*, 2 Aug. 1860.

consumers would resent having to pay more. Abandonment of the high scale of duties was, concluded the Chamber, 'absolutely necessary for the interests of India, as well as those of England'.[167]

Wood's reference to the investment of British capital in the Indian industry was significant. It implied a readiness to act if the industry was entirely indigenously financed. Free trade was an intellectual camouflage to promote British economic interests, and Indians were not slow to realise this.[168]

For Indians, cn the other hand, the emerging cotton textile industry was 'a source of prosperity to the country' which had aroused the anger and jealousy of 'the Brobodignacs[169] of Manchester'. Only three mills were in working order, they maintained, as if hoping to allay the fears of Manchester, and nearly half a dozen existed merely on paper. Local European merchants, however, seemed to have 'perceived the future competition of the Indian looms and written letters "home" to their principals'. Hence the spectacle of 'a free trader like the Hon'ble Member for Manchester' stooping to ask for 'an excise duty on manufactures in India, which are only in their infancy'. Yet, it was added to ward off pessimism, Indian mills were destined 'to stand their ground'. Cheap labour and saving in the freight, despite the increased cost of coal, were 'calculated at 15 per cent. in favour of the Indian produce'. Long after 'England had dealt very unfairly towards Indians in regulating the tariff and destroyed a flourishing Indian industry, Indians rejoiced that 'a Nemesis has come' in the form of the Bombay textile industry.[170] But they also knew that the British manufacturers would not 'tamely allow themselves to be gradually displaced in the Indian markets'.[171]

Indian protests notwithstanding, Laing thought that the Bombay Liliputians did have an unfair advantage over the Brobdingnagians of Manchester, especially in regard to yarn. So in spite of his realisation that the annual yield of £400,000 could not be sacrificed 'without imprudence', he reduced the duty on twist and yarn to five per cent. in 1861-62.[172] The following year a similar reduction was made for

167. *Home News*, 27 Aug. 1860, in *Hindoo Patriot*, 3 Oct. 1860; cf. *Times*, 4 Jul. 1860, in *Bombay Times*, 16 Aug. 1860.
168. *Hindoo Patriot*, 17 Mar. 1859; *Rast Goftar* 16 Sep. 1860.
169. Obviously for Brobdingnagians in Swift's *Gulliver's Travels*.
170. *Rast Goftar*, 16 Sep. 1860.
171. *Ibid.*, 11 Nov. 1860. This was natural as the activities of the British manufacturers and the writings in the English Press were freely reported in India. For example, the *Bombay Times* of 25 Oct. 1860 quoted from the *Overland News* of 10 Sep. 1860: 'Can Mr. Wilson suppose that Lancashire, the cradle of free trade, which has built up, by her own brain and muscles, the mightiest commercial fabric in the world, will sit down in tame submission to witness the ruin of all that her genius and enterprise has achieved, without a murmur?'
172. *Proceedings of the Legislative Council of India*, vol. VII, cols. 351-52.

piece-goods and the duty on yarn further curtailed to 3½ per cent.[173] In this Laing ignored the Indian advice that his duty was towards 'poor and prostrate India, powerless and dumb', not towards the 'shrieking Manchester with its thousand and one engines of political pressure.'[174] Tariff reduction, therefore, brought upon him the charge of having cared for his 'inconveniently importunate' Manchester friends, though 'he was called upon to legislate for India and not for Manchester.'[175]

Still unsatisfied, Manchester pressed for the remission of the remaining five per cent. duty on the ground of its being protective. The authorities in India repudiated the charge. If the Bombay mills, asked Frere, could live 'with only five per cent. duty on English goods what chance will the English goods have against a factory in the Nerbudda districts, in sight of both coal and cotton fields and with food and labour so much cheaper than in Bombay?'[176] However, Frere accepted Dinkar Rao's proposal for an equivalent excise duty on Indian cloth.[177] So did Wood.[178] But Trevelyan thought differently. The 5 per cent. *ad valorem* duty, he pointed out, actually amounted to 2½ per cent., charged as it was on a valuation fixed when the prices were nearly half of the existing ones.[179] Lawrence, too, resisted the Manchester pressure for a reduction, or rather for the abolition of the import duties on cotton goods'.[180]

Signs of renewed activity by Manchester appeared in 1872. Mayo saw a premonitory letter in which 'one of the very best and most influential of the Manchester men' had written: 'I begin to fear we are producing Cotton Goods faster than our Eastern Consumers can buy, and pay for them and that we may before long have again to complain of bad Trade and stir up the India Office for further changes.' The viceroy took it to mean that 'the Blacks' were to pay 'when by over speculation these Gentlemen begin to trade at a loss'.[181]

This overspeculation coincided, unluckily for the Manchester men, with the rapid growth of the Bombay industry. While they aimed at increasing their exports to India, these stood at the 1859 level. In the latter year, cotton piece-goods worth Rs. 11,04,10,000 and yarn valuing Rs. 2,30,60,000 had been imported.[182] These figures

173. *Abstract of the Proceedings of the Council of the Governor-General of India*, vol. I, pp. 128-33.
174. *Hindoo Patriot*, 24 Mar. 1862.
175. *Ibid.*, 21 Apr. 1862.
176. Frere to Elgin, 1 Jul. 1862, Martineau, *op. cit.*, vol. I, p. 399.
177. *Ibid.*, pp. 400-01.
178. S. Gopal, *British Policy in India 1858-1905*, Cambridge, 1965, p. 54.
179. *Abstract of the Proceedings of the Council of the Governor-General of India*, vol. II, pp. 81-3.
180. Lawrence to de Grey, 5 Mar. 1866, *Lawrence Collection*, reel 2.
181. Mayo to Argyll, 20 Jan. 1872, *Argyll Papers*, reel 314.
182. *Proceedings of the Legislative Council of India*, vol. VI, pt. I, col. 120.

for 1872-73 were Rs. 11,99,17,000 and Rs. 2,14,09,000 respectively.[183] In 1874 the Bombay industry made a spurt as 16 new mills came into existence with an aggregate investment of Rs. 1,50,37,500. That this included British capital as well as a part of the fabulous fortunes of the Sassoons[184] must have convinced the worst sceptic that the Bombay industry would prosper in spite of Manchester. But what alarmed Manchester even more was the risk, evident from the reported plan of Bombay to import long stapled Egyptian cotton, to its monopoly of fine fabrics in the Indian market.

The project to manufacture fine fabrics in India was really ominous for Manchester. In view of its ebbing goodwill, even repeal of the import duties was unlikely to help it regain the Indian market in coarse cloth. Its Long cloths, T cloths, Domestics and lower counts of yarns had 'of late been in a large measure driven out of the market by the local manufacturers'. Adulteration having 'become a science' in England, the consumer was sure not to be taken in a second time.[185] Nor could Manchester offer competitive rates after the duty had been taken off. Comparing the cost in England and the price in India, the loss suffered by Manchester was 'very much more than 3½ per cent. or 5 per cent.' Moreover, the Bombay manufacturer was, with new machinery, making 'as much as two annas a pound or from 25 to 30 per cent.' He was even shipping, after paying a 3 per cent. export duty, 'large quantities of goods to Arabia, Persia, Africa and China in competition with the England manufacturer' who had no export duty to pay.[186] The prospect for Manchester in these circumstances seemed bleak once Bombay had taken to manufacturing superior cloth.

Bombay was at this stage manufacturing yarns upto 24s and 'grey, that is, rough, unbleached, and undyed cotton cloths made from such yarns'.[187] In this Manchester could not re-establish itself. In fact, leaving aside grey cloth sent by reckless shippers whenever the money market was easy, 90 per cent. of the English yarns and piece-goods imported into India consisted of 'qualities not attempted by the native spinning mills'. Only 10 per cent., 'perhaps, strictly speaking, little more than five per cent.' of these imports was covered by the 'protective' duty.[187] There was much comfort in the thought that no

183. *Abstract of the Proceedings of the Council of the Governor-General of India*, vol. XVI, p. 213.
184. *The Times of India Calendar and Diary for 1875*, pp. 379-86.
185. Letter from M/s. W. Nicol & Co. to Bombay Chamber of Commerce, 27 Nov. 1873, *Times of India*, 29 Nov. 1873. Even Hugh Mason, president of the Manchester Chamber of Commerce, admitted dishonesty on the part of the manufacturers there; see *Bombay Gazette*, 29 Nov. 1873.
186. Speech by J. K. Bythell of M/s. Gaddum & Co. at a special general meeting of the Bombay Chamber of Commerce, 27 Nov. 1873, *Times of India*, 29 Nov. 1873.
187. *Ibid.*, 5 Dec. 1873.
188. *Ibid.*

less than 90 per cent. of Manchester's Indian supply would remain un-challenged. The Surat cotton was expensive to work 'beyond a certain fineness in yarn'. Though, during the American civil war, even 40s had been made from Surat, the process was not financially feasible because of the hard twisting that the staple had to sustain. But this was in England. As things were in India, Surat could not be worked upto 30s with profit, while by making 20s the manufacturer made 'a very handsome return'.[189]

But the Bombay manufacturer aspired higher than his rivals had imagined. He 'proposed to strike out new paths in industrial enterprise by importing and adapting cotton and machinery to the making of finer yarns and cloths'. He conceived of a 'variety of efforts and experiments' in order to combine 'cotton with silk, hemp, jute and other indigenous fibres' and to attempt 'dyeing and calico-printing the colouring stuffs for which abound extensively in this country'.[190] The anxiety of Manchester to nip in the bud what could be disastrous to it was natural.

Equally natural was the vigilance of Indians in watching every movement of 'the Princes of Cottonopolis', while apparently ridiculing their concern for 'their rotten piece-goods'.[191] When the British fina-nced Anglo-Indian Spinning and Manufacturing Company became 'an accomplished fact', Bombay manufacturers were advised to 'look sharp'.[192] Also when a deputation of the Manchester Chamber of Com-merce urged upon Salisbury the repeal of the import duties, relief was found in his statement that this could not be done for the time being. Yet, beneath the uncertain safety 'for the present' lurked the fear of a breeze 'from the opposite direction'.[193] Finally, when it be-came known that a revision of tariffs was under consideration, Indians declared, half desperately and half hopefully, that the revised duties would determine 'whether India is governed for Manchester or for the millions of the soil'.[194]

The revision, when it came, shocked Indians like nothing under the Crown had done. Since in its latest clamour Manchester had stres-sed the consequences of the imminent import of long stapled cotton in India, the Indian government, instead of abolishing the import du-ties which it had refused to regard as protective, levied an equivalent 5 per cent. import duty on raw cotton not produced in Continental Asia or Ceylon.[195] The countervailing duty on the import of long stapl-

189. *Ibid.*, 29 Nov. 1873.
190. Petition of the Bombay Branch of the East India Association to the gover-nor-general in council, 20 Aug. 1875, in *Native Opinion*, 5 Sep. 1875.
191. *Bengalee*, 2 Jan. 1875
192. *Native Opinion*, 13 Sep. 1874.
193. *Ibid.*, 8 Nov. 1874.
194. *Ibid.*, 31 Jan. 1875.
195. See L. Gujral, 'Sir Louis Mallet's Mission to Lord Northbrook on the Ques-tion of the Cotton Duties', *Journal of Indian History*, Dec. 1961, pp. 474 ff.

ed cotton hammered into the Indian mind a painful consciousness of political subjection. Here was an utterly deliberate sacrifice of 'the interests of the voiceless millions of India' to 'the Moloch of Cottono-polis'.[196] 'No free people would have thus drawn the knife across their own throats'.[197] Recalling the American War of Independence, Indians derived satisfaction from the thought that though they might not 'throw into the sea ship-loads of piece-goods and kindle a war of inde-pendence, this new bantling of the Legislature must at least create an equal amount of dissatisfaction and furious indignation throughout the land'.[198] The secretary of state had 'bowed his head to King Cotton' and secured for Manchester 'a perpetual lease of manufactur-ing finer sorts of cotton'. No longer could they believe that their interests were 'in safe keeping'.[199] Talk of justice to India was fiddle-sticks.[200] The make-believe of the identity of Indian and British in-terests lay exposed; as did the nostrum of free trade—that dirty de-vice to retain 'a gigantic monopoly' and constringe Indian commercial ambitions.[201] The duty itself did violence to free trade.[202]

The suspense was over. Manchester had won against India.

More ominous than the duty was the official justification for it. T.C. Hope, an official member of the supreme legislative council, had declared that 'it was in accordance with sound policy to prevent the cotton manufacturers of India "from assuming undue proportions" ', and that 'the only measure at present required appeared to be the im-position of a duty upon raw cotton.'[203] This implied that the Indian cotton industry would be artificially dwarfed. Should it, unruffled by the duty, 'assume more important dimensions than at present', the next curb would be an excise duty. Which meant than no effort would be spared to help Manchester, 'the *real* rulers of India', put 'our money into her pocket and have the gratification of seeing our infant cotton industry destroyed'.[204]

The Bombay manufacturers got alarmed. They formed the Bombay Mill-Owners' Association and petitioned the governor-general against the duty.[205] Indians could do little else. In an incensed piece

196. *Bengalee*, 14 Aug. 1875.
197. *Native Opinion*, 15 Aug. 1875, quoted this from the *Englishman* and added: 'And if the people at this moment feel that they are not a free people and that the Government to which they owe their allegiance is despotic and alien, the Government must thank themselves'. See *Englishman*, 6 Aug. 1875. However, another Anglo-Indian paper, the *Indian Daily News*, found the duty 'completely equitable'; 7 Aug. 1875.
198. *Hindoo Patriot*, 9 Aug. 1875.
199. *Native Opinion*, 15 Aug. 1875.
200. *Hindoo Patriot*, 9 Aug. 1875.
201. *Mookerjee's Magazine*, New Series, vol. V, Jan.-Jun. 1876, pp. 47, 64.
202. *Supplement to Bengalee*, 25 May 1875.
203. *Hindoo Patriot*, 16 Aug. 1875.
204. *Bengalee*, 14, 21 Aug. 1875.
205. *Native Opinion*, 24 Oct., 21 Nov. 1875.

of sarcasm the *Hindoo Patriot* exemplified the compulsive chasm between the passion of their feelings and the ineffectiveness of their
means[206]:

> England boasts that she has a mission in the East. and the new Tariff affords
> a glorious exemplification of it. It stands forth as an emblem of the justice,
> conscientiousness and righteousness, which characterize her dealings with
> this poor dependency...Whatever she ordains is of course always for our
> best.The people of India are mere childern; they do not understand their
> interests....We do not hesitate to say that this measure will remain a
> standing monument of righteous legislation...We hope our countrymen
> throughout the Indian continent will combine, and send forth to Parlia-
> ment a humble and respectful address, expressive of their gratitude for
> this inestimable boon....

Their distrust of official motives having been confirmed, Indians
quickly surmised from Louis Mallet's mission[207] that Salisbury was
intent on forcing Northbrook to repeal the import duties.[208] The pre-
sumption became a conviction following Salisbury's disclosure to a
Manchester deputation that he had directed the government of India
to fix a time limit for removing the duties on piece-goods and yarns.
This coincided with Northbrook's resignation which created an impression that Manchester would brook no procrastination. The departing viceroy was hailed as a friend of India 'who was conscientious
enough not to minister to the mercantile greed of England' at the
cost of India. But more troublesome than feeling for an individual
was the realisation that Manchester was strong enough to override.
even a viceroy. Further, since Northbrook's exit was ascribed to interference from England, it was reasonable to expect the new viceroy
to obey the secretary of state faithfully.[209] Of course, if he wished 'to
remain long in his appointment',[210] there being no reason to suppose
that he would not. Salisbury's assurance, repeated by Lytton, that the
duties would be taken off without recourse to fresh taxation was irrelevant. The issue really was that were reduction of taxation feasible,
the oppressively taxed Indian, not the opulent Manchester manufacturer, deserved relief. Also, irrespective of what free trade might re-

---

206. *Hindoo Patriot*, 9 Aug. 1873.
207. Mallet, the under secretary of state, had been sent to India by Salisbury in
     order to thrash out a scheme for the progressive repeal of the duties on
     British cotton goods. But he found Northbrook 'very sore, very sensitive,
     and under the impression that due consideration has not been given to
     his difficulties'. He also found 'a universal conviction, that the remission
     of Cotton duties is a simple concession to Manchester'. Everywhere,
     excepting Strachey, he met 'either with warm opposition, or absolute indi-
     fference'. Mallet to Salisbury, 6 Jan. 1876, *Salisbury Papers*, reel 819.
208. *Hindoo Patriot*, 6 Dec. 1875.
209. *Native Opinion*, 27 Feb. 1876.
210. *Shubh Suchak*, 24 Mar. 1876, *Report on Native Press, Bombay*, 1 Apr. 1876,
     p. 5.

102 Dependence and Disillusionment

quire, the nascent Bombay industry needed the retention of the duties.[211]

Behind the curtain of verbal stipulations, the stage was being set for abolishing the duties. Temple had observed that 'the manner in which the Manchester people were to take the case up' would determine the 'urgency, or otherwise of the case'.[212] And the Manchester people were pressing relentlessly, unmoved even by famine which, they alleged, had been conjured up by the authorities 'on purpose to disappoint them'. Nor did the secretary of state or the viceroy carry a less callous heart. Referring to the proposed abolition, Salisbury warned his protege, in March 1877, that the Tories would be in trouble 'unless we can make a step in that direction next year'.[213] Lytton, oblivious of Temple's warning 'not to combine' tariff relief with a new tax,[214] proposed the famine cess to facilitate the liquidation of the import duties.[215] When Hobhouse (1819-1904), then a member of the supreme council, inconveniently insisted on the precondition of a surplus for the removal of the duties, Lytton twisted it to mean 'a reasonable prospect of a surplus'.[216]

Indians got an inkling of the impending repeal when Strachey (1823-1907), the finance member, recklessly testified before the legislative council on 15 March 1877'.[217]

I have not ceased to be an Englishman because I have passed the greater part of my life in India....The interests of Manchester, at which foolish people sneer, are the interests not only of the great and intelligent population engaged directly in the trade in cotton, but of millions of Englishmen...I believe that our countrymen at home have a real and very serious grievance...if I had not confidently expected to take a part in this great reform [abolition of the duties]. I doubt whether anything would have induced me to accept my present office;...

Sharp reactions within the council[218] brought home to Strachey the mischief his statement could create. To avoid this he mendaciously explained that he had expressed, not the official policy, but his personal ambition; and that the removal of duties yielding two and a half crores was 'totally unjustifiable, and indeed preposterous' be-

211. *Bombay Samachar*, 1 Mar. 1876, *Report on Native Press, Bombay*, 4 Mar. 1876, p. 8.
212. Temple to Salisbury, 4 Feb. 1876, *Salisbury Papers*, reel 819.
213. Salisbury to Lytton, 22 Mar. 1877, *ibid.*, reel 822.
214. Temple to Salisbury, 4 Feb. 1876, *ibid.*, reel 819.
215. Lytton to Salisbury, 1 Nov. 1877, *ibid.*, reel 816
216. Lytton to Salisbury, 19 Jan. 1877, *ibid.*, reel 815. Lytton contended that if the finance member, with the concurrence of the viceroy, thought 'that a certain reduction of the duties may safely be made, and ought in his opinion to be made, at once, the Government is bound to act on that opinion'.
217. *Abstract of the Proceedings of the Council of the Governor-General of India*, vol. XVI, pp. 163-64.
218. *Ibid.*, pp. 254, 325.

cause that would necessitate fresh taxation.[219] Less rash than his finance member, Lytton attempted to soothe the public mind and yet prepare it for the repeal. Though the cotton duties ought to go in the interest of India, he equivocated, the government had at hand no measure 'even remotely connected with' them.[220]

Seeing through the equivocation, Indians suspected that provincial taxation was 'not unlikely to prepare the way for that complete extinction' of the import duties which the viceroy and the finance member so 'avowedly desired'. The suspicion was deepened by 'the absence of any intimation in the Budget that, the famine charges being now classed as ordinary expenditure, the revenue yielded by these new taxes will be devoted in the first instance to the redemption of the famine loans, or a like amount of other loans, when possible'.[221] The suspicion could as well have been an *expose* of Lytton's tactics. Barely a few months back, he had confided to Salisbury that the principle of local responsibility for famines—leading to provincial taxation—would enable the government to 'safely pledge ourselves to an immediate reduction of the Cotton duties without interruption in the progress towards their ultimate abolition'. He had warned that if the principle was disallowed, the duties might not be touched 'at all'.[222]

Self-interest inspired the Indian opposition to the repeal of the import duties, though other arguments were also thrown in. Indians were never taken in by the solicitude Manchester paraded for the Indian poor; nothing could be more 'nauseating and detestable' than the cant uttered by jealousy 'in the guise of philanthropy'.[223] Most Indians were forthright and pragmatic. Telang, for example, laconically stated his belief that 'protection to native manufacturers' was not only unobjectionable, but 'even desirable. in the circumstances of our country'.[224] Within the legislative council, Narendra Krishna Deb pleaded for 'the fostering care of the British Government' without which the nascent Indian industry would come to grief. He honestly argued that 'all principles should not necessarily be acted upon simply because they were good and sound, without a due regard to their adaptability to the times and the circumstances of the people'.[225]

There were, however, Indians with a doctrinaire bent of mind who debated the matter without referring to the interests of India. S. S. Bengali, for instance, denied that the duties were protective.

219. *Ibid.*, p. 247.
220. *Ibid.*, pp. 338, 340.
221. Letter from S. S. Bengali to Lytton, in *Native Opinion*, 6 May 1877.
222. Lytton to Salisbury, 19 Jan. 1877, *Salisbury Papers*, reel 815.
223. *Bengalee*, 20 Mar. 1875.
224. See K.T. Telang, *Free Trade and Protection from an Indian Point of View*, Bombay, 1877.
225. *Abstract of the Proceedings of the Council of the Governor-General of India*, vol. XVI, p. 255.

There was no competition, he argued, between Manchester and Bombay. The competition was internal, between handlooms and cotton mills. The duties represented, moreover, the only taxation that fell on the rich and the poor in proportion to their means, and also on the people of the Indian States—the lone levy they paid for the benefits they reaped at the expense of British India.[226]

As the repeal hung fire and Indians demurred at it, the deadline fixed by Salisbury in March 1877 was drawing near. But the finances would not permit total remission. So Lytton decided, in September 1877, to take off the duties on coarse cloth.[227] In December, an unusual time as noticed above, provincial taxation was extended to make good the prospective loss to the exchequer. The repeal was announced in the *Gazette of India* on 19 March 1878.

Indians read into this chronology proof of bad faith on the part of the government. They accused it of imposing taxes ostensibly for famine insurance but actually to benefit Manchester.[228]

Rumours of remission of duty on finer fabrics renewed the objection that this would be unjustified by the supposed surplus which represented not a legitimate balance but the famine insurance fund. Indians had contributed to the fund in spite of considerable hardships on the understanding that it would be diverted to no other account. It was strange that having a short while earlier spoken of a strained treasury to impose 'tyrannical and barbarous taxes', the government was now justifying the repeal and the expenses of the Afghan war on the strength of overflowing finances.[229]

The excitement was widespread when, in the teeth of popular opposition and the dissent of four executive councillors, Lytton extended tariff exemption to cotton goods not containing yarns finer than 30s. Thinking it 'necessary to raise the national voice in emphatic protest',[230] the Indian Association decided to summon a public meeting on 27 March 1879. That the meeting was convened, and attended by 3,000 persons in spite of Lytton's rebuke to the British Indian Association revealed some measure of defiance in the otherwise subdued constitutional agitation.

On 8 March 1879 a deputation of the British Indian Association had waited on the viceroy. Contemplating 'with feelings of regret and alarm the pressure sought to be exerted from England for the repeal of the Indian import duty on cotton goods', the deputation had submitted:

226. *Native Opinion*, 6, 27 May, 22 Jul. 1877.
227. Lytton to Salisbury, 15 Sep. 1877, *Salisbury Papers*, reel 816.
228. *Bombay Samachar*, 21 Mar. 1878, *Report on Native Press, Bombay*, 28 Mar. 1878, p. 6.
229. *Rast Goftar*, 5 Jan. 1879.
230. *Third Annual Report of the Indian Association, 1878-79*, Calcutta, 1880, p. 2.

Regarding as we do the import duty as a potential fiscal engine, we venture to solicit your Excellency whether in the present state of Indian finances this duty can be repealed without detriment to the vital interests of this country.

The duty, they had added, possessed 'a double advantage'. It was 'almost nominal in its incidence' and yet 'highly productive'. Referring bluntly to the position of the zemindars and the 'long standing debt of loyalty and gratitude they owed to the British Indian Government', the viceroy had accused the deputation of mis-representation and selfishness.[231]

It was feared that the viceregal admonition would not let anyone 'as much as squeak'.[232] Yet the Indian Press jeered at and condemned the viceroy.[233] It was determined not to allow 'to go unheeded' 'such misbehaviour on the part of authorities—the biggest in the land though they be.'[234] The Calcutta meeting of 27 March, held as it was in a sullen atmosphere, became 'the occasion of a great demonstration of national feeling, for from all parts of India letters and telegrams had been received'.[235] Even the circumspect leaders of the Bombay Association, who had been disconcerted by Lytton's snub to put off a projected public meeting in March,[236] eventually held a protest meeting on 2 May.[237]

For the first time, perhaps, Indians made personal attacks on the viceroy and the secretary of state. They capitalised on the dissenting minutes of Stokes, Rivers Thompson, Arbuthnot and Clarke[238] to attack Lytton as 'peculiarly a man of the present Ministry' whose 'adoration of the higher authority is unbounded', and Cranbrook as 'a great offender' who had sanctioned an 'unrighteous and inexpedient measure'. Cranbrook was also criticised for disregarding the majority of the India council.[239] Turning to political advantage the literary prowess of the poet-viceroy, Telang quoted from him a couplet on the paradox of human nature:

'Heights measures he in depth, seeks peace in strife
And calls all this the poetry of life'

and concluded that the viceroy had 'undoubtedly sought peace in strife both in our North-West...and also in this affair of domestic

231. *Publications of the British Indian Association* vol. III.
232. *Native Opinion*, 6 Apr. 1879.
233. For comments in the Indian and Anglo-Indian Press on Lytton's reply see *Publications of the British Indian Association*, vol. III.
234. *Native Opinion*, 13 Jul. 1879.
235. *Third Annual Report of the Indian Association*, p. 2.
236. *Native Opinion*, 30 Mar. 1879.
237. *Ibid.*, 8 Jun. 1879.
238. *Ibid.*, 15, 22 Jun. 1879.
239. *Ibid.*, 13 Jul. 1879.

106   Dependence and Disillusionment

administration.'[240]

Far from accepting the surplus as genuine, Indians saw 'serious financial embarrassments' in the form of a deficit of five million sterling which they showed by including in the ordinary expenditure the outlay of three millions and a half on reproductive public works. Scarcely bringing in any return, only by a misnomer could these works be called reproductive and charged to extraordinary expenditure. Besides this, the estimated official shortfall for 1878-79 was a million and a half; the gross revenue of £ 64,400,000 being offset by a gross expenditure of £ 65,900,000. The total deficit of five millions was faced by the economy at a time when its capacity to recoup had been particularly damaged by the exchange difficulty. From half a million in 1874-75, the loss by exchange had leapt up to three and a half millions in 1878-79. The other incubus on the Indian economy was the Afghan war. Having cost £ 670,000 in 1877-78, it was estimated to swallow up a good two millions during 1879-80. Nor was the Indian revenue remarkable for its elasticity. Four-fifths of it was derived from land, salt and opium, all of which presented a cheerless outlook. The Bengal settlement could not be disturbed; and the cultivators in Bombay and Madras were already rack-rented. The duty on salt could not be raised further, and the Chinese government was thinking of cultivating opium in China.[241]

Yet, 'in such a season of financial embarrassment, when every available source of income has to be husbanded', the government 'in the plenitude of its wisdom and in its conscientious regard for the welfare of the teeming millions whom Providence has placed in its care, has abolished the import duty' worth two million pounds sterling per annum.[242]

This underscored, as the import duty on superior cotton had earlier done, the meaning of subjection and evoked thoughts of a national government. Surendranath Banerji was not alone when he asked:[243]

> was there ever a more wanton sacrifice, a more utter disregard of the interests of the people of this country? If we had a native Government, would such a Government, I put this question to my countrymen, venture upon a thing of this kind in reckless defiance of public opinion and in total forgetfulness of the interests of the people?

Indians also decided to carry the agitation on in England. The East India Association and Lal Mohan Ghosh were entrusted with

240. Speech at the Bombay meeting, 2 May 1879, *Selected Speeches and Writings of K. T. Telang*, Bombay, 1916, pp. 190-91.
241. Speech by S. N. Banerji at the Town Hall meeting on 27 Mar. 1879, R. C. Palit, ed., *Speeches by Babu Surendra Nath Banerjea*, vol. I, pp. 193-202.
242. *Ibid.,* pp. 198-99, 201-02.
243. *Ibid.,* p. 202.

the task.[244] But the way the Liberals vied with the Tories to woo Manchester boded ill for the agitation. The advent of the Liberals to power brought little change in the tariff policy. That Hartington had acknowledged his 'obligation' towards his Lancashire friends and appreciated 'the moderation' of their demand showed that the Liberals also were bowing 'in submission to the demand of Manchester'.[245] This became clear when the exemption enjoyed by fabrics containing yarns upto 30s and 'affording protection to Manchester' was extended to *dhoties* and dhotibordered piecegoods with borders not more than 4½ inches wide and containing yarns of higher numbers.[246] The following year was completed, four years after it had been initiated, the process of progressive remission of the import duties.

Like the Ilbert Bill fiasco[247] and the retention of the Arms Act, the final abolition of the import duties during Ripon's viceroyalty did much to erode Indian faith in the Liberals. That the repeal was completed to ensure 'the Lancashire vote'[248] while the license tax continued, seemed 'most unjustifiable and derogatory to the good intentions of the present Government'.[249] Hartington's next step, it was suggested in sheer chagrin, would be a law reducing railway fares if his 'servant had occasion for travelling in India'.[250]

The last instalment of repeal completed the exposure of the duplicity underlying free trade. For while free trade was forced upon India, 'import duties on foreign goods, on Indian silver goods, for instance, were levied in England, the land of free trade, under the political ascendency of Gladstone, Bright and Fawcett'. This was 'free trade indeed!' British customs were contrived purely to serve national interests. Free trade was brought into play in regard to articles, like corn and iron, which were badly needed but not produced internally; for the rest, Britain quietly made 30 millions a year through import duties.[251] This was the Indian rejoinder to the British assertion that India had been 'an enormous gainer by the Free Trade policy of England'.[252]

The tariff question crystallised more than any other official measure, the irreconcilability between Indian and British interests. What was a conflict between a government anxious to increase and

244. Jeejeebhoy to Mehta, 20 May 1879, *Mehta Papers*, reel 1.
245. *Native Opinion*, 16 Jan. 1881.
246. *Ibid.*, 13 Feb. 1881.
247. See chapter 4.
248. *Sahachar*, 14 Jun. 1882, *Supplementary Volume of Reports on Native Press, Bengal*, 1869-95, p. 209.
249. *Native Opinion*, 12 Mar. 1882.
250. *Sahachar*, 14 Jun. 1882, quoted above.
251. *Sadharani* and *Sahachar*, quoted in Home Department, Public Proceedings, B, Aug. 1883, Nos. 95-6.
252. Salisbury to Lytton, 20 Apr. 1877, *Salisbury Papers*, reel 822.

a people endeavouring to avoid taxation was elevated to a struggle aimed at upholding national *vis-a-vis* imperial interests. National consciousness was beginning to flavour the rising discontent against the taxation policy of the government.

Group interests, which taxation did much to bring to the surface, fused more or less at least on one point. A collective interest which could be, and was actually, called Indian was recognised. Politically conscious Indians sincerely believed that whatever their other differences, they formed a collective entity and in this capacity they had to safeguard their common interests. How far the vision corresponded to reality is debatable. The interests of the upper and the middle classes, who shared between them whatever political awareness then existed among Indians, demanded the retention of the import duties. The choice for the poor Indian could be made either way. The interests of this mute creature were pleaded both by his better placed compatriots and by Manchester, of course with almost equal unconcern for him. But while they flayed Manchester for simulating solicitude for the poor in India, these Indians managed to persuade themselves that they represented the Indian people. The simultaneity of belief in their representative character and their primary concern for personal and group interests was a striking feature of the emerging national consciousness.

III

Famines constituted another recurrent feature that added to the economic discontent and accentuated the element of national consciousness in it. Attributed by Indians to poverty and heavy taxation, famines highlighted with a touch of tragic drama the divergence between the basic requirements of the people and the priorities of the government.

The first major famine after 1858 overtook the North Western Provinces in 1861. It passed off without creating dissatisfaction. Rather, the government was praised for its 'liberality', and aid from England was gratefully acknowledged. The government was also commended for having grasped the connection between famines and 'the defects in the landed system which clogged the springs of industry and repressed energy'.[253]

But reaction was different when, disregarding the viceroy about preventive action, the lieutenant-governor of Bengal allowed scarcity in Orissa to develop into an unmanageable famine.[254] Calcutta was reported to have been infiltrated by no less than thirty thousand

253. *Hindoo Patriot*, 6 Jan. 1862.
254. Lawrence to Beadon, 29 Aug. 1866, *Lawrence Collection*, reel 8; Lawrence to Beadon, 11 Oct. 1866, *ibid.*; and Lawrence to de Grey, 16 Oct. 1866, *ibid.*

houseless strangers', with 'mothers leaving their infants by the wayside to perish and to be eaten by dogs and jackals, husbands forsaking their dying wives and leaving them to the tender mercies of the adjutants and vultures of the burning ghats.' Yet, 'dead to all feelings of humanity', the lieutenant-governor had retired to 'a luxurious and comfortable retreat in the hills, isolated from the cares of the Government entrusted to his charge'.[255] But more tormenting was his cynical observation at the Cuttack *darbar* that 'such visitations of Providence as these no Government could do much either to prevent or alleviate.' Talking glibly of food for minds when people wanted food to keep themselves breathing, this representative of Queen Victoria 'had the callousness of heart to declare that by the coming revision of settlement their rents would be increased and inferentially their condition made more miserable.'[256] The Bhutan war, which simultaneously broke out, naturally induced the reflection: 'why a war with men should be deemed more legitimate and glorious than a war with nature'? A crore of rupees was spent by the government for the recovery of prestige in Bhutan while grudging 'an outlay of fifty lakhs in order to rescue from extermination a hundred times the population of the Dooars'.[257]

Official action to deal with famines provided a measure to determine the seriousness of the government for the welfare of the people.[258] Want of forethought on the part of the authorities brought home to Indians the inequity of a system in which the consequences of official failure to prevent 'such disasters' were 'visited on the poor Indians, first by allowing famine to overtake them, and then taxing them to relieve it, and to make up deficits to revenue.'[259]

Resentment against official indifference to people's weal was increased by famine in Rajputana.[260] Prompt relief during famine in parts of the Bengal presidency, however assuaged Indian feelings. This time, however, non-official Europeans, apprehending taxation to make good the relief expenditure, and piqued by the denial of an opportunity to'profit from the miseries of the poor and the helpless', came down upon the government for wasteful relief operations.[261] Consequently, the viceroy, Northbrook, was thanked by Indians and

255. *Bengalee*, 4 Aug. 1866.
256. *Hindoo Patriot*, 5 Mar. 1866.
257. *Bengalee*, 15 Dec. 1866.
258. *Indu Prakash*, 28 Dec. 1868, *Report on Native Press, Bombay*, 2 Jan. 1869, p. 3.
259. Naoroji, 'England's Duties to India', 2 May 1867, Parekh. ed., *Essays, Speeches, Addresses and Writings of Dadabhai Naoroji*, p. 42.
260. *Indu Prakash*, 6 Mar. 1871, *Report on Native Press, Bombay*, 11 Mar. 1871, p. 3.
261. Temple to Salisbury, 14 Jul. 1874, *Salisbury Papers*, reel 818.

non-official Europeans were accused of 'heartless scepticism'.[262]

This goodwill was irrevocably lost as a result of famine administration in Bombay and Madras during 1876-77. Criticism began towards the last quarter of 1876 when the Bombay government insisted
on treating as scarcity what Indians regarded as famine. Ryots in
many villages were reported to be abandoning their homes to escape
famine and epidemics. But the Bombay governor and his councillors
were said to have been too engrossed in 'gaieties' to give much attention to 'the cries of woe' from the afflicted areas.[263]

The *Indu Prakash*, in such circumstances, stressed the need for
self-reliance and fellow-feeling, the lack of which had rendered
Indians contemptible 'in the eyes of the civilized nations'. It wanted
that instead of 'enjoying the merry festival' of *diwali*, every Indian
should 'consider it his duty to exert his power and give his help to
the sacred work of saving millions of his countrymen from starvation.'[264]

Though not much was done by Indians, and *diwali* in the unaffected areas was none the less merry, Indian feelings were ulcerat-
ed by the thought of the Delhi *darbar* which meant that the government could 'spend large sums on a *tamasha* while millions' of Indians
'were on the brink of starvation'.[265]

The ulceration deepened as it seemed that money would be preferred to men. A part of India was gripped by a famine the like of
which had not been seen 'during the past century'.[266] Yet, the government had stated that while it desired to make every effort, 'so far
as the resources of the State admit, for the prevention of deaths from
famine, it is essential in the present state of the finances that the
most severe economy should be practised.' What was worse, it had
added that 'had the finances been in a better condition than they
actually are at present, even then it would not be the duty of Government to undertake the task of preventing the sufferings or privations of the people during a famine any more than in the time of
plenty.'[267]

This departure from Northbrook's policy was viewed as 'an act
of inhuman economy and moral debasement'. The poor people, on
whom the government spent not 'a farthing' in ordinary times, expected it to 'avert the evils of its own creation'. That 'limits' were

262. *Report of an Address by the British Indian Association to Lord North-
    brook*, p. 4, Northbrook to Argyll, 1 Mar. 1875, *Argyll Papers*, reel 318.
263. *Dnyan Prakash*, 12 Oct. 1876, *Report on Native Press, Bombay*, 14 Oct.
    1876, p. 8.
264. *Indu Prakash*, 22 Oct. 1876, *ibid.*, 28 Oct. 1876, p. 7.
265. *Bengalee*, 11 Nov. 1876. The *tamasha* was the proposed Delhi *darbar*.
266. 'Poona Sarvajanik Sabha's Famine Narrative No. 1', *Quarterly Journal of
    the Poona Sarvajanik Sabha*, title page missing, p. 1.
267. *Native Opinion*, 28 Jan. 1877.

prescribed for preserving life indicated the degree of official respon-
siveness to 'the sentiments and feelings of its people'. Otherwise the
fear of its impression 'on the popular mind' would have prevented
the enunciation of such a principle in a State document.[268] Moreover,
at the same time that six and a half millions was grudged to save
2,70,00,000 souls in 21 districts of the country, the annual drain of
16 millions to England had remained quietly unaffected.[269] Napoleon,
after all, had reasons to label the English as a nation of shop-
keepers.[270]

Lytton's policy might have been economically justifiable. Its
publication was politically indefensible. If meant to be accepted by
Indians, it made a harsh demand on their tolerance. But Lytton was
helpless. His heart was not in famine administration; and he had no
appreciation of the susceptibilities of the Indian people. Above all,
he had to provide relief to Manchester. He could do no better than
land on the principle of local responsibility for famines, which had
less to do with its ostensible object than with the commitment of the
viceroy's patron.[271]

The working of economy in famine relief demonstrated its in-
humanity. There was a strike of relief workers at Sholapur against
insufficient wages. The strikers said that they would rather die at
once than of slow starvation.[272] During the Bengal famine, Temple
had, 'after due consideration and discussion', fixed the daily ration
at 3/4 seer per head on the ground that the diet of a labouring adult
was 'one seer of rice besides 1/4 seer (about 1/2 pound) of fish, pulse,
pepper or other condiments'. But the same Temple now wondered
'whether life cannot be sustained with 1 lb. of grain per diem; and
whether Government is bound to do more than sustain life'. The
answer was simple. Life could be thus sustained 'for a few days or
even weeks'. But the crucial point, which had been 'deliberately put
aside', was whether life could be 'so sustained for months together
without fatal effects'. Dr Cornish (1828-97), the sanitary commission-

---

268. *Ibid.*
269. *Rast Goftar*, 28 Jan. 1877.
270. *Indu Prakash*, 5 Feb. 1877, *Report on Native Press, Bombay*, 10 Feb.
     1877, p. 7.
271. See section II of this chapter. Lytton's policy may be contrasted with
     Wilson's answer to the demand for exemption from income tax to Mad-
     ras and Bombay as it had been occasioned by the Mutiny. Wilson said:
     '...are we one people...or are we not?...We want greater combination and
     unity....The bane of India has been these sectional principles and preten-
     sions. Let us see an end of them, and feel that we are all one for weal
     or for woe.' *Proceedings of the Legislative Council of India*, vol. VI, pt.
     I, cols 135-37. Criticising Lytton, the *Dnyan Prakash* of 8 Feb. 1877, poin-
     ted out that the principle was inconsistent with the declaration of Indian
     unity at the Delhi *darbar*, and added that Indians were united for weal
     or woe. *Report on Native Press, Bombay*, 10 Feb. 1877, p. 9.
272. *Native Opinion*, 11, 18 Feb. 1877.

er of Madras, had proved that this was not possible. He had shown that '1 lb. of rice containing from 68 to 80 grains of nitrogen and a small money payment of six pice or three farthings would not suffice to enable a labourer to provide a sufficiency of nitrogenous food to restore his daily expenditure of tissues.' When Temple suggested that 'the amount of nitrogen required by natives must be much less than that required by Europeans', Cornish had to affirm that the matter could not be 'settled on the *ipse dixit* of Sir Richard Temple'. Comparison of the average weights of prisoners under trial and of relief workers confirmed this view:

	In Jail	
Men	*Women*	*Children*
109.1 lbs.	92.3 lbs.	70 lbs.
	At Relief Works	
94.3 lbs.	77.6 lbs.	46 lbs.

Figures of mortality among workers in the Madras relief camps for ten weeks ending 31 March indicated loss of life as follows:

Mean Strength	*Total Deaths*	*Annual ratio per mile*
11,005	1,971	930.8

This enormous death rate, which meant the wiping out of 'nearly the whole of the living within a year', could be applied to relief camps all over the country. It was not due to cholera or small-pox, but to 'extreme wasting of tissue, and destruction of the living membrane of the lower bowel' as a result of underfeeding and starvation.[273]

This created 'a wide feeling of unrest and consternation'.[274] Indians wondered, by way of insinuation, if this would have been so, had 'the lives of Europeans been concerned in the matter'.[275] In one of the occasional outbursts of desperate reaction, the government was compared with monsters: like them it was destroying its own children, the subjects.[276] Most Indians, however, did not have to react so extremely to feel certain that, like them, history would not excuse Lytton 'the suffering of a million of men to be starved on financial grounds'.[277]

The uninterrupted export of foodgrains during famine years was criticised as another violation of Indian interests. It was maintained that export of foodgrains tended to diminish the population of

273. *Native Opinion*, 22 Apr. 1877.
274. *Indu Prakash*, 12 Feb. 1877, *Report on Native Press, Bombay*, 17 Feb. 1877, p. 7.
275. *Indu Prakash*, 19 Feb. 1877, *ibid.*, 24 Feb. 1877, p. 6.
276. *Hitechchhu*, 8 Apr. 1877, *ibid.*, 14 Apr. 1877, p. 8.
277. *Bengalee*, 5 Jan. 1878.

the exporting country. Embargo on such export was made all the more essential by the frequency of famines in India.[278] But whatever Indians might have felt, the needs of Britain and of Indian economy, operating as they did within the framework of the Indo-British relationship, ruled that export of raw material, including foodgrains, would continue.

A more intimate link between famines and foreign rule was established. Absence of industries and total dependence on land perpetuated the economic backwardness of the country.[279] Excessive land revenue left the poor ryot with scarcely enough to feed himself and his family.[280] What remained was partly consumed by the salt and stamp duties, and the road and education cesses. As against $8\frac{1}{2}$ per cent. in a rich country like England, which was 'not even a flea-bite or any bite' to an Englishman, an Indian paid 22 per cent. of his meagre earnings by way of taxes. This meant to nearly three-fourths of Indians 'simply "half-feeding" or starvation, or famines and disease'.[281] They could save little for the eventuality of crop failure. The Poona Sarvajanik Sabha, for example, concluded after extensive enquiries that the famine of 1876-77 was not a 'grain' but a 'money famine caused by poverty'. In 'consequence of the great facilities of communication', grain 'poured itself from other parts of India, but people had no means to buy it with'. Nor could they obtain labour as a consequence of the 'utter absence of all other industrial agencies'.[282] Increasing population, a factor emphasised by the authorities, did aggravate poverty, but without causing it. Famines, therefore, could not be attributed in any large measure to population growth.[283]

Naoroji went further in linking famines with British rule when he traced these to the 'drain' from India.[284] This made the problem of famine a part of the fundamental conflict between Indian and British economic interests.

Famines were utilised to dramatise the exploitation of India by Britain. Addressing a British audience in 1885, N.G. Chandavarkar[285] asserted that the condition of the agriculturist classes in India, who

278. *Bardwan Sanjivani*, 21 Oct. 1878; *Report on Native Press, Bengal*, 26 Oct. 1878, p. 5.
279. *Hindoo Patriot*, 6 Jan. 1862.
280. *Native Opinion*, 12 Nov. 1876.
281. Naoroji, 'Memorandum on a few Statements in the Report of the Indian Famine Commission, 1880', 4 Jan. 1880. *Poverty and Un-British Rule in India*, Delhi, 1962, pp. 195-98.
282. Poona Sarvajanik Sabha to the government of India, 1 Apr. 1878, *Quarterly Journal of the Poona Sarvajanik Sabha*, title page missing, para 7, p. 5.
283. 'Over-Population and Marriage Customs', *ibid.*, vol. I, no. 2, pp. 29-30.
284. Naoroji, *op. cit.*, pp. 193-202.
285. Chandavarkar (1855-1923) was one of the three Indian delegates sent to England in order to conduct a pre-election campaign to advance India's case.

formed three-fourths of its 200 millions, was 'worse than that of the people in the slave States of America'. He summarised the Indian view regarding famines when he said:[286]

> During the past 20 years they had had a series of famines, and the number of people who had died from want of food was 9,000,000; and their National Debt had increased from 36 millions to 214 millions sterling (shame); and yet they were told that the present Conservative Government were about to impose upon them further burdens.

IV

The 'drain' also made a powerful impact on the Indian mind. As an integral feature of the existing Indo-British relationship, it attracted Indian attention even before 1858. Rammohan Roy and his collaborators observed that the East India Company alone drew 'annually from India *four Millions sterling, in bullion*', more than half of which was 'for the payment of dividends to the share-holders, and the remainder for the expense of the Home establishment'.[287] Young Bengal, for whom British rule was a dead-weight on the economic progress of India, pointed out that if 'only a tithe' of this annual loss was spent in the country, it would derive immense advantages 'not only in the construction of public works but also in the establishment of schools and colleges for the instruction of the People'.[288] In 1839 the Bombay Chamber of Commerce reproduced a series of newspaper articles criticising 'home' remittances on government and private account.[289] The 'home' charges and transfer of capital to England 'formed the chief burden of complaint' of a small group of Indians in Bombay that 'used to meet secretly to discuss the effects of British rule upon India'.[290]

The 'drain' was viewed as tribute to England. When Wilson stated that not a rupee of tribute was taken from India, the *Rast Goftar* retorted that the 'Home charges of the Indian Government' were really a tribute under a 'more decent' description. Tribute meant 'payment made by one country to another without any equivalent, and the effect of which is to impoverish the paying and enrich the receiving country'. And India made 'such payments to England' every year[291] in the shape of 'a very large proportion of her annual ex-

286. Speech at a meeting organised by Maidstone Radical Association, 20 Oct. 1885, L. V. Kaikini, ed., *TheSpeeches & Writings of Sir Narayan G. Chandavarkar*, Bombay, 1911, pp. 262-63.
287. *Bengal Herald*, 13 Jun. 1829.
288. *Reformer*, quoted in G. Chattopadhyay, ed., *Awakening in Bengal*, Calcutta, 1965, pp. xviii-xix.
289. R.J.F. Sulivan, *One Hundred Years of Bombay. History of the Bombay Chamber of Commerce, 1836-1936*, Bombay, 1936, p. 12.
290. *Speeches and Writings of Dadabhai Naoroji*, Madras, undated, p. 33.
291. *Rast Goftar*, 11 Mar. 1860.

portations, for which not only no adequate return but no return at all was made'. The first direct effect of this was 'to deprive us of so much treasure, and thus enhance the value of money; next to depreciate the exchange by the demand for bills...to lower prices by carrying to and forcing upon foreign markets a larger quantity of our products than those markets would have taken off while commerce was in a state of equilibrium'.[292]

The matter was seriously taken up by the *Bombay Times* and by Major Wingate (1812-79) of the Bombay army.[293] Later on, Robert Knight (1826-90)[294] wrote two pamphlets on the financial relations between India and Britain. His views were avidly read and readily accepted by Indians.[295] It was with reference to these pamphlets that the *Hindoo Patriot* made a detailed study of the subject. It wrote that 'the charges paid in England by India (excluding the value of stores supplied to India) for the year ending 30th April, 1864, amount to £6,446,913,' and were mainly 'for services rendered, or as interest for money lent'. These could be split as follows:[296]

Dividends to the proprietors of India stock	£	629,970
Interest on loans contracted in England	£	1,372,599
Civil pensions and retired allowances	£	246,913
Military pensions and retired allowances	£	1,165,043
Marine pensions and retired allowances	£	53,951
Guaranteed interest on the capital of the railway and other companies after deducting net traffic receipts	£	1,669,283
Total	£	5,137,764

The five millions of 'the annual dividend due by India to England', which amounted to 'nearly one-fourth of the dividend on the National Debt of Great Britain', gave 'an inadequate idea of the flow of wealth from India to England'. The 'Home' establishment threw another four millions a year on India to provide for the following charges:[297]

Home establishments	£	171,120
Civil furlough and absentee allowances	£	72,092
Military furlough and absentee allowances	£	161,410
Marine furlough and absentee allowances	£	2,654
Total	£	407,276

292. *Proceedings of the Legislative Council of India*, vol. VI, pt. I, cols. 159-60.
293. *Bombay Times*, 25 Dec. 1860.
294. Knight succeeded Dr Buist as editor of the *Bombay Times* and later on converted it into the *Times of India*.
295. In the Holkar State, the backwater of political awakening, a Marathi version of the pamphlets was published. *Native Opinion*, 13 Jan. 1867.
296. *Hindoo Patriot*, 17 Sep. 1866.
297. *Ibid.*

India had also to pay other recurrent and non-recurrent charges like the salary of the secretary of state for India, and the cost of the office under construction in St. James' Park and of depots whenever a new regiment was ordered for service in India. In fact, everything even remotely connected with her was paid for by India. Added together, these made 'a vast amount of miscellaneous charges'. The *Patriot* estimated that the annual sum paid by India in England averaged about £ 13,000,000. This did not include the large remittances made by official and non-official Europeans in India.[298]

The *Hindoo Patriot* looked upon this annual payment as India's tribute to England 'for the blessings of civilized rule'.[299] But other Indian journals were less charitable. The *Native Opinion* found 'the price of the boon' a drawback as a result of which Indian 'art and trade languish day by day, money becomes more and more scarce, and a general feeling is generated of despondency and despair of all future prosperity for the country and the race'.[300] The *Suryodaya* alluded to the parable of a fox whose blood was being sucked by a swarm of flies as it had got entangled in some creepers. On being asked by a crow if it might drive away the flies, the fox replied, 'No, these flies are now satisfied, and if you drive them away another hungry swarm would take their place.'[301] The anticipated satiety, though, could hardly have been comforting. A Parsi gentleman, who had resided in England for eight years, bitterly complained that Englishmen 'draw millions every year from India, and in return abuse its people, caring not so much for it as for a rotten borough.'[302]

Implicit in the understanding of 'drain' was a total exposition of the Indo-British connection. The task was systematically undertaken by Dadabhai Naoroji with his characteristic statistical approach. He first referred to 'drain' in March 1866.[303] By May 1867 a tentative draft of his thesis was ready.[304]

Naoroji estimated that the 'home' charges since 1829 had caused 'a transfer of about 100 millions of pounds sterling, exclusive of interest on public debt'. Territorial charges during the same period being about 820 millions, Europeans in government service must have remitted at least one-eighth of this, or 100 millions, to England. At the ordinary interest of 5%, the principal of 200 millions amounted to 450 millions. Between 1787 and 1829 the territorial charges totalled about 600 millions, of which no less than 60 millions must have gone out of India. Adding its interest and acquisitions prior to

298. *Hindoo Patriot*, 17 Sep. 1866.
299. *Ibid.*
300. *Native Opinion*, 30 Dec. 1866; Parekh, ed., *op. cit.* p. 32.
301. *Suryodaya*, 9 Sep. 1866, in Parekh, ed., *op. cit.*, p. 33.
302. *Ibid.*, p. 17.
303. Naoroji, 'The European and Asiatic Races', 27 Mar. 1866, *ibid.*
304. Naoroji, 'England's Duties to India', 2 May 1867, *ibid.*, pp. 29 ff.

1787, the total could 'fairly be put down for 1150 millions'.[305]

Besides this cumulative drain in the past, Naoroji found a remittance of 'something like 33 millions a year, at an exceedingly low estimate', comprising 25 millions of interest and 8 millions of 'tribute in its hundred shapes'.[306] This was exclusive of commercial and manufacturing profits.

Moreover, 72,000 Englishmen were employed in India: 60,000 of these were in the lower, and 12,000 in the middle and higher grades. This meant relief to professions and industries in England, and denial, to the same extent, of employment to the sons of the soil. Also, India was burdened with nearly 100 millions of political debt. In fact, the British conquest, unlike past ones, made India lose for ever a fourth of its annual revenues.[307]

Taking up the political debt of India, Naoroji stated in 1870 that £ 2,000,000 was annually remitted to England as interest on £ 45,000,000. As Europeans in India held some £ 30,000,000 of the political debt, Naoroji 'estimated the amount of interest sent by them to England to be £ 600,000. £ 600,000 of interest on the East India Company's stock provided for total remittances of three millions of interest a year. Taking the tribute, which he was prepared to place at 8 millions in 1867, to be 10 millions in 1870, Naoroji estimated 13 millions a year as 'the price of the English rule'. To be on the safer side, he was ready to reduce it to 12 or 10 millions.[308]

During the preceding 20 years, India had also paid some £ 30,000,000 as guaranteed interest on the railways. Of this only £ 14,000,000 represented the income from the railways. Another £30,000,000 was spent, during the preceding 12 years, on building, and £ 9,000,000 on repairing public works. Naoroji complained that the whole of this £ 69,000,000 had been 'thrown upon the present generation when it could least afford to do so, for the benefit of the future'.[309]

In 1867 Naoroji had observed that no commercial return had been made by England during the preceding 50 years for above 300 millions of imports from India and China.[310] He developed the point further in 1870. Assuming the reasonable commercial profits of any country to be 10 or 15 per cent. on its exports, he showed that England had enjoyed a profit of 25 per cent. As against this, and in spite of the help of opium, railways, irrigation and other public works, and increased land under cultivation, India had obtained, during the 1860s, imports worth £ 419,000,000 for her exports of

305. *Ibid.*, p. 29.
306. *Ibid.*, p. 30.
307. *Ibid.*
308. Naoroji, *'The Wants and Means of India'*, 27 Jul. 1870, ibid., p. 98.
309. *Ibid.*, pp. 98-9.
310. Naoroji, 'England's Duties to India', *ibid.*, p. 29.

£ 456,000,000.[311]

Naoroji rejected the official claim that the great excess of Indian exports over imports was 'regularly liquidated in silver'.   During 1834-68, exports worth £ 260,000,000 and £ 90,000,000 of profits had not been paid back to India.   It was 'simply impossible' to carry on such a trade 'without being impoverished'.[312]

Naoroji worked up to the startling conclusion that despite the overall excess of exports over imports, purely commercial exports were less than commercial imports. This meant that but for non-commercial exports, necessitated by foreign subjection, India would have profited from her international commerce. Of the exports worth £ 53,700,000 in 1868-69, £ 7,000,000 accounted for the bills drawn by the secretary of state for India; £ 4,500,000 for the money sent to England by the 67,500 Englishmen employed in India; £ 500,000 for imported goods required by Europeans in India; and £ 4,000,000 for remittance of interest on loans for public works.   This left only £ 37,000,000 of exports to represent the real commerce of India. The imports for the same year totalled £ 51,000,000.   These included railway loan for the year, £ 5,000,000; state railways and other loans, £ 2,000,000; government stores £ 1,500,000; payment on account of the Abyssinian expedition, £ 1,250,000. The remaining commercial imports of £ 41,000,000 showed 'something like a national commercial profit of about £ 4,000,000'. But since India had to pay £12,000,000 for its administration, it actually suffered a loss of £ 8,000,000.[313]

About the claim of the British that India had progressed under them, Naoroji admitted that 'some progress had been made during the last fifteen years'. But this was like a strong man who, after knocking down a weakling, gave a glass of water to revive him and said, 'See how I have benefited you; I have given you a good glass of water, and now you are ever so much better.'[314]

It was difficult for India's exports of 50 millions to earn profits worth ten millions a year which had to be paid by way of 'drain'. For, besides placing a crushing demand on the resources of the country, 'drain' progressively reduced her productive capital and obliged her to exchange on less advantageous terms her products for foreign commodities.   Though seven millions was accounted for by the opium revenue from China, the remaining three millions could scarcely be spared by a poor people whose per capita income was less than 27s. a year.   Accounting for unequal incomes and for 'a large administrative and military expenditure', the 'very poor' masses, to borrow Grant Duff's expression, were left with just a 'scanty subsistence'. A contrast was provided by England, the receiver of India's 'drain',

311. 'The Wants and Means of India', Parekh, ed., op. cit., pp. 99-101.
312. 'On the Commerce of India', 15 Feb. 1871, ibid., pp. 112-14.
313. Ibid., pp. 114-16.
314. Ibid., p. 130.

where men paid 'about 48s. a head for *revenue* only'. Obviously unable to produce enough for her own wants, India was obliged to contribute regularly one-fourth of her revenues to augment the wealth of rich England.[315]

'Drain' acquired an almost hypnotic effect as a symbol of the injustice of British rule in all its manifestations. It gave an image to the multiplicity of Indian grievances. Naoroji defined its extended dimensions by spectacularly summing up the adverse effects of British rule in four words: 'material and moral drain'.[316] Not many Indians could marshal facts and figures as Naoroji did. They might not even grasp the import of 'moral drain'. But in their mental makeup 'drain' was a formative influence. Belief began to gain ground that 'drain' had brought India to the verge of insolvency. People had no food to eat, nor salt to keep them in good health; they could not clothe themselves adequately; and they were sunk in debt. Yet, they were 'required to send about fifteen or sixteen krors of rupees to England annually for the home charges', and 'about 20 krors more to the same country as the balance of trade'[317]. Accuracy of figures did not matter. The tendency, rather, was to exaggerate. What mattered was that India was being irresistibly and increasingly denuded of its resources. On this point near unanimity prevailed.

V

A kindred source of discontent was the military charges taken from India by England and regarded by Indians as inequitable and excessive. They resented paying six millions of annual interest on the expenses incurred by England on conquering India.[318] They also disliked the additional military expenditure caused after 1857 by the employment of nearly 10,000 European troops 'in excess of the number previously determined and sanctioned as the maximum European strength of the Indian Army'.[319] Considering the needs and resources of the country, expenditure on its defence was incommensurably high. It not only increased taxation, but also led to the drain of wealth in a measure that could be easily reduced.[320] The feeling of subjection that naturally followed was strengthened by the realisation that no self-governing British dominion could be deprived of its money like India was.

A constant source of conflict existed in the frequent saddling of

315. 'The Wants and Means of India', *ibid.*, pp. 101-03, 108.
316. *Ibid.*, p. 98.
317. *Indu Prakash*, 7 Aug. 1876, *Report on Native Press, Bombay*, 12 Aug. 1876, p. 3.
318. *Indu Prakash*, 7 May 1876, *ibid.*, 13 May 1876, p. 3.
319. *Hindoo Patriot*, 6 Jan. 1862.
320. *Rast Goftar*, 16 Sep. 1869.

India with the expenses of extra-Indian military undertakings. Even
non-official Europeans saw eye to eye with Indians in this respect. The
Friend of India, for instance, argued against charging to India half
the expenses of the China war: 'But the war is not ours.   We are
not more bound to pay half its expenses than Canada is, or New South
Wales, or the Red Indians of the Hudson's Bay Territory.'   Backed
'by the selfishness of a whole people', the *Friend* continued, the parliament was 'not slow to accept an excuse for shifting taxation from
itself'.   India was 'a sleeping partner' having no 'voice in the dealings
of the house', and 'snubbed if she asks for an account' before footing
the bills.[321]   The authorities in India, too, took exception to such
arbitrary demands. Denison (1804-71), governor of Madras (1861-66),
exposed the selfishness of the 'home' authorities in maintaining 'a
dozen Regiments and 20 Batteries of Artillery as a sort of reserve,
for whch they make the people of India pay'.[322] The occasion for this
charge was provided by the burden thrown on India of a part of the
Abyssinian expedition.   The viceroy also thought likewise.[323]   But
the secretary of state saw no objection to India's paying for its troops
in Abyssinia so long as these had not to be replaced with new troops
in India.   He argued that otherwise India would be making money
by the transaction.   The troops, he emphasised, had been lent, not
hired out.[324]

Apart from being fallacious, the distinction made by the secretary of state rested on double standards. England had never sent
troops to India without charging 'the whole expense'. No reason
existed to treat India differently. Moreover, it was for something
that troops were maintained in a certain number; if India lost nothing
by sending some of these abroad, 'the army should be reduced by so
much'.   The fact of the matter was that England could appropriate
Indian money 'at its own pleasure' because India was under subjection.[325]   And Indians could do nothing but remind the rulers of the
Day of Judgment when 'the Ruler of all nations' would ask how they
had 'discharged the trust reposed in them'.[326]

Another instance of the arbitrary allocation of military expendi-

321. *Friend of India*, 23 Apr. 1857.
322. Denison to Lawrence, 8 Dec. 1864, *Lawrence Collection*, reel 10.
323. Lawrence to Northcote, 4 Nov. 1867, *ibid.*, reel 3.
324. Northcote to Lawrence, 1 Oct. 1867, *ib.d.*, reel 1.
325. *Speeches and Writings of Dadabhai Naoroji*, pp. 53, 58. *Bhaskur*, 4 Jan.
   1868, *Report on Native Press, Bengal*, 11 Jan. 1868, p. 9.   The frustrating
   ludicrousness of the apportionment of these expenses was underscored
   by the imposition on India of Rs. 6,000 a year for the education of King
   Theodore's son. The *Som Prakash* bitterly observed that Indians would
   be lucky 'if the Sirdars of New Zealand being made to live at Benares,
   money is not extracted from us' *Report on Native Press, Bengal*, 25 Sep.
   1869, p. 2.
326. *Report on Native Press, Bengal*, 28 Aug. 1869, pp. 5-6.

ture was the charging to India of half the expenses of the Zanzibar mission. Indians conceded that the mission had a humane purpose. But they wanted England to bear the full cost of the credit that would redound to her. The association of a few Indian *banias* with the accursed slave trade gave no excuse for making all Indians contribute to the cost of suppressing it. Above all, it was painful to see the government simultaneously bestow 'its enthusiastic sympathies on the alien negroes of the interior of Africa' and 'coolly' allow 'its own subjects of the various parts of India to pine away and even to die for want of food, clothing, lodging and medical help.'[327]

A similar instance was the annual payment by India of £ 12,000 to maintain an English ambassador at the Persian court. Bereft of independent political existence, India was not entitled to send an ambassador in her own right. The country that enjoyed the honour must pay the price thereof.[328]

It was, however, the Afghan war that offered the most glaring example of imperial high-handedness in forcing upon 'miserable, famine-stricken India' 'the cost of a war undertaken not for her defence but in pursuit of a new imperial policy inaugurated by Lord Beaconsfield'.[329] The government was heartily assailed in spite of the Vernacular Press Act. The *Bharat Mihir* feigned ignorance about why Beaconsfield, 'who could pocket so much insult during the Russo-Turkish war and yet stand aloof from the affray, should give the order to declare war against the Amir for a slight cause.' Dropping the simulation, it concluded that the idea was to defeat Russia in Asia 'at the expense of the blood of the native troops and India's money'. Even if the plan failed, 'the damage to England by defeat in India would not be so great as by defeat in Europe'.[330]

When the Liberal government did agree to share a portion of the expenses of this war, Indians complained that the amount was inadequate. Still, the fact that 'the British taxpayer had consented to pay at all' was welcomed as the acceptance of a principle that augured well for India. Realisation of the futility of the war and of the burden imposed by it, however, continued. Nothing had been achieved except disgrace and loss of blood and treasure.[331]

What outraged Indians was the misappropriation of the famine insurance fund. They disbelieved the official explanation that the loss by exchange had absorbed the fund. The loss on this account, during 1878-79, was £ 3,400,000, only £ 400,000 in excess of the offi-

327. *Indu Prakash*, 23 Dec. 1872, *Report on Native Press, Bombay,* 28 Dec. 1872, pp. 3-4.
328. *Rast Goftar*, 29 Jun. 1873.
329. *Bengalee*, 14 Dec. 1878.
330. *Bharat Mihir*, 31 Oct. 1878, *Report on Native Press, Bengal,* 9 Nov. 1878, p. 2.
331. Home Department, Public Proceedings, B, Jun. 1882, No. 159.

cial estimate. It was 'presuming too much upon the credulity of the public' that £ 400,000 had 'virtually swept away the financial improvements arrived at with so much difficulty'. The actual extent of the liquidation of the fund was 'nothing more or less than the expenses of the Afghan War, and the gap caused by the partial repeal of the import duties for the purpose of catching the Lancashire vote'. And this had happened in the face of unequivocal assurances from the highest quarters that the fund would not be used for extraneous purposes.[332]

The satisfaction given by the sharing of the expenses of the Afghan war soon vanished after the expenses of the Egyptian campaign had been partly thrown on India. Regretting that the Liberals had done this, Indians condemned the entire Egyptian proceedings as the outcome of 'the interests of a few avaricious English bondholders'.[333]

Fixation of India's share of certain military expenses incurred in England made for chronic friction. It was this that accounted for a major portion of the increase in India's military expenditure. The inequity of the arrangement was evident from the fact that though India's burden had been increased on the pretext that England was maintaining an army costlier than before, the British exchequer was paying less on both effective and non-effective military services. In spite of a diminished gross charge on non-effective services, India's share had gone up since 1857 by 'much more than half a million sterling a year'. This meant a relief to the British exchequer at the expense of India.[334]

The effective charges, too, were similarly apportioned. Out of 68 infantry brigade depots, for instance, India's share was fixed at the cost of the staff of ten depots, making her pay perpetually what, till 1867, she had been spending sporadically on separate India depot battalions. Actually this staff involved no 'expense to the British Exchequer, additional to the expense incurred by the Exchequer, on account of officers before the formation of the depots.' Moreover, these depots were maintained primarily for 'the more efficient organisation and training of the Militia'; recruitment for India was an incidental duty. Since no extra expenditure was being incurred for India, nothing was justly chargeable to her. The debit to India on account of artillery depot brigades and military educational institutions, too, was of a similar nature.[335] This was the Indian version

332. 'The Broken Pledge and its Consequenses', *Quarterly Journal of the Poona Sarvajanik Sabha*, vol. II, no. 1, p. 40.
333. Home Department, Public Proceedings, B, Aug. 1883, Nos. 95-6; B, Feb. 1883, Nos. 187-88; B, May 1884, Nos. 194-95; and B, Jun. 1885, Nos. 269-72.
334. 'Memo. for the Committee of the British Indian Association', 28 Feb 1878, Palit, ed., *Speeches and Minutes of Kristo Das Pal*, pp. 362-63.
335. *Ibid.*, pp. 363-67.

of Northcote's objection to making money from the Indian troops serving in Abyssinia.

Increase in separate items of the 'home' military charges was equally extravagant. These consisted of recruiting charges, marching money and cost of conveyance, transport service and pensions. The first of these charges under the East India Company for the average ten years ending 1859 had been £19-10½d. per head. By 1877-78 it had risen to £136-13-11d. for cavalry; £63-8-5d. for infantry; £78-14-8d. for Royal Horse Artillery; £59-2-8d. for Royal Artillery mounted; and £58-9-3d. for Royal Artillery. It was an 'unreasonable, illegal, inequitable, unrighteous increase of charges'.[336]

The charge for marching money and conveyance during 1865-70 had been 15s. 6d. per recruit. In 1877-78 this had shot up to £3-8-11d. for cavalry and £1-19-9d. for infantry. Moreover, the transport charges could be reduced by 1/5 million if the merchant vessels of the P. & O. Co. were employed for the purpose; more so as these vessels 'lay idle for no less than five months in the year, and the pay of the officers and men during this time was a mere waste of money.' Pension charges revealed the same 'high-handed adjustment of accounts'. These were £ 939,000 in 1860-61. In 1877-78, in spite of reduction in the number of troops in India, the charges had gone up to £ 1,331,000.[337]

India lay helpless. 'England supplied the troops, and India was bound to pay whatever the conscience of the War Office demanded.' Britain was not 'as just to her other colonies'. Unlike the India Office and European troops for India, the Colonial Office and garrisons were charged to the British treasury. Insurrectionary movements in the colonies were suppressed at the cost of the imperial exchequer. But while 'the Indian army served as a most efficient reserve for England' and India provided a school for British soldiers, Britain even refused to guarantee Indian loans. The whole basis on which the War Office moved in relation to India was opposed to morality, equity and the law laid down by parliament. Successive viceroys and secretaries of state had vainly sought justice for India. The utmost that Indians could do was to 'petition Parliament and leave the rest to Providence'.[338]

Indians might feel helpless for the time being. But inherent in the cumulation of discontent against the persistent appropriation of their resources was a clearer perception of their political situation. Constant references to the difference in Britain's dealings with subject India and self-reliant dominions constituted a refrain to hold together the different notes and patterns of Indian grievances. Every year of military expenditure with its upward tendency and pattern

336. Pal's speech, 2 Mar. 1878, *ibid.*, pp. 289-90.
337. *Ibid.*, p. 290.
338. *Ibid.*

of apportionment made Indians apprehend that one day not even all the diamonds of Golconda would suffice to meet it.[339] The rhetoric of this apprehension threatened to come true. For neither petitions to parliament nor trust in providence seemed to check India's military expenditure. Though the expenditure managed by the government of India had stood at £ 2,500,000 since 1874-75, that controlled by the War Office had 'risen since that year from £ 800,000 to about £ 1,400,000' in 1885; and there could be 'no saying how rapidly it may swell to £ 2,000,000.' Illustrative of the 'appalling enormity' of this increase was the fact that 'one year's growth of military expenditure absorbs the growth of the net land revenue for nearly $2\frac{3}{4}$ years.'[340]

In 1857 Indian military expenditure was £ 11,463,000. In 1862 Laing had assured that this could be maintained at £ 12,000,000. But it continued to increase in spite of internal peace, improved locomotion and loyalty of the people.[341] Neither was the government deterred by Indian criticism. Thus while Indians found the 17 millions of military expenditure, in 1884, too much for poor India, the government decided, in 1885, to increase it by another two millions.[342] No wonder that even sober Congressmen moaned that 'India existed for the army and not the army for India'.[343] The army, and India, they knew, existed for Britain.

VI

Alongside of economic discontent, and also as a consequence of it, emerged a concern for the country's trade and industry. Possessing 'all the requisites of a manufacturing people', Indians had abandoned 'the impossible race of the human hand against a machine driven by a powerful and subtle element' to feed 'the looms of Manchester and Paisley'.[344] Continuance of such backwardness was sure to reduce them 'to the condition of the helots of old'.[345]

The degree of Indian dependence on foreign manufactures justified the pessimism. Barring food, very few things used by Indians

339. Palit, ed., *Speeches and Minutes of Kristo Das Pal*, p. 289.
340. D. E. Wacha at the first Congress session. *Proceedings of the First Indian National Congress*, p. 60. Wacha showed that the military expenditure amounted to $30\frac{1}{4}$ per cent. of the net Indian revenues of 43 millions, or 'the whole of the net land revenue save a million'. The military expenditure increased by £ 150,000 and land revenue by £ 57,000.
341. *Ibid.*, p. 52; *Rast Goftar*, 13 Nov. 1870.
342. *Manuscript Minute Book* (Bombay Presidency Association), vol. I, p. 47; *Proceedings of the First Indian National Congress*, p. 52.
343. Chandavarkar's speech at Newcastle, Nov. 1885, Kaikini, ed., *op. cit.*, p. 266.
344. *Hindoo Patriot*, 27 Nov. 1856.
345. Letter by 'A Creeper', *ibid.*, 24 Feb. 1858.

were indigenous. Coats, paper, ink, pens, knives, walking sticks, shoes, turbans, *dhoties*, *cholies* 'and a thousand other things' were imported from abroad. It seemed that even the sacred threads of the Hindus would 'some days hence' be imported from 'some celebrated London shop of some Tom & Co.' Establishment of a variety of local industries was required to 'supply a perennial source of employment' and 'prevent our national wealth from going in such large quantities to foreign countries.' True, cotton had enabled the country to sustain the outward flow of wealth; but its capacity, after all, was not unlimited.[346]

The revival of trades and industries alone could arrest the 'rapidly increasing impoverishment' of India.[347] Land tenure having inhibited industrialisation on the part of Bengalis, they could at best derive vicarious pleasure from the achievements of the Bombay *entrepreneurs* and treat their interests as common national interests.[348] In western India, however, besides industrialisation, a movement was started to encourage the use of indigenous manufactures. Some inhabitants of Poona 'determined to wear no cotton fabrics but those of home production'.[349] A *Nischaya Patrika* was circulated for signatures. Publishing a Gujarati translation of the original public resolution in Marathi, the *Rast Goftar* urged the people to patronise indigenous articles 'in the interests of their country and countrymen'.[350] About the same time, at Nagpur, a journal was launched with the same end in view; and a group of blacksmiths was 'induced to turn out knives and scissors which were purchased with the help of a fund specially raised for the purpose and then sent out for sale in different parts of the country.' Efforts were also made 'to improve the rude implements used by our weavers with a view to cheapen the production of their looms'.[351] *Swadeshi* companies were formed at Bombay, Ahmedabad, Surat, Satara, Sholapur, Nagpur and other places.[352]

The propagation of Indian products was undertaken in an orga-

346. *Native Opinion*, 6 Jun. 1869.
347. 'A Voice for the Commerce and Manufactures of India', *Mookerjee's Magazine*, vol. V, Nos. XXXVI-XL, p. 2.
348. Sir Jamsetji Jijibhai came to be regarded as a national hero and it began to be hoped that 'at no distant date such men would be common in Bombay'. *Hindoo Patriot*, 27 Feb. 1858. Even the financial disaster that overtook Bombay after the American Civil War could not damp the spirits in Bengal, for 'such vicissitudes of fortune through which their Bombay brethren have passed is far better than the listless kiranee life' of Bengalis. *Ibid.*, 24 Sep. 1866.
349. *Native Opinion*, 29 Jun. 1873.
350. *Rast Goftar*, 13 Jul. 1873.
351. B. K. Bose, *Stray Thoughts on Some Incidents in My Life*, Madras, 1923, pp. 51-2.
352. *Native Opinion*, 1 Aug. 1880.

nised manner by the Ahmedabad Swadesh Udyam Vardhak Mandali. Founded in December 1875, it decided in the following March to raise money for *swadeshi* stores by issuing 400 shares of Rs. 25 each. After half the shares had been subscribed to, the company was registered.   Members of the Mandali pledged themselves to purchase for two years goods from the proposed stores.[353]   Thinking that 'united efforts' would have greater chances of success, the Mandali issued a circular letter to individuals and institutions all over the country 'to save our dear country from further ruin'.   It also sought information about 'the arts and manufactures that formerly flourished in the various cities and provinces of India', 'the foreign goods that now supply their places, and the manufactures that flourish at present'. Though the information was not procured, the appeal did   induce some thought on the subject.   At Surat a public meeing to establish a similar organisation was attended by 1,000 persons including almost all the notable inhabitants of the city. It led to the formation of the 'Company for the encouragement of Native Arts and Manufactures Ltd.' with an object to 'cause articles of native manufacture to be made, to buy and sell such articles, or to keep them for sale on commission'.[354]

Besides leaving an impression on a few individuals, the efforts to encourage Indian products failed to make much headway as organised movements.   The problem, however, was focused,   ensuring that more people would give it a thought.   Appeals to patriotism at the cost of one's material interests often elicit a lean response.   But the only tactics the promoters of *swadeshi* could employ was to exhort their compatriots to make some initial sacrifice for the country by purchasing indigenous goods even if these were, in the beginning, coarser and costlier.[355]   Also, educated young men were advised to look beyond government service and take to trades not only for their own sake but also for the sake of the country.[356]   Every pioneering venture was publicly commended.   Messrs. Ratnagar & Co., for instance, were praised for inaugurating a new branch of indigenous industry in the form of their pottery work at Dadar after having studied this minor art in America, England and China.   The venture was important because India lost three to four lakhs of rupees a year by importing earthen ware.   It was hoped that other small scale industries like soap-boiling, candle and glass manufacture would

353. First Annual Report of the Mandali in *Bombay History of the Freedom Movement Papers*, pp. 874-77. I am indebted to Shri B. N. Phatak for information about the Mandali.
354. *Native Opinion*, 18 Jun. 1876.
355. *Ibid.*, 3 Jul. 1870.
356. *Dnyan Prakash*, 21 Nov. 1870, *Report on Native Press, Bombay*, 26 Nov. 1870, p. 11.

also be taken up by Indians.[357] The need for independence in technical know-how was also realised. When the Bombay Hemp and Jute Co. put Bombay on the map of jute manufacture, it was a matter of added joy that the engines of the mill had been made by a Hindu engineer and were operated by a Parsi.[358] As Gopalrao Hari Deshmukh argued, the acceptance of Europeans as superiors caused loss of money and stifling of indigenous intelligence.[359] The Bombay Mill-Owners' Association even established a technical and experimental factory at the joint expense of the members in order 'to impart a theoretical knowledge of the art of spinning and weaving, and to enable the work people to carry out the theory in practice.'[360]

Further, it was felt that Indians should conduct their own commerce as a means to augment the country's wealth and enhance its political consequence.[361] Damodar Thakarsi (1847-93), an industrialist, suggested that the Bombay Mill-Owners' Association should send an agent to study prospects of trade in Burma, Siam, China, Japan, Mozambique and other countries. But the *Native Opinion* favoured permanent agencies. In fact, a sort of agency was actually established in Australia where Indian hosiery and shirtings were likely to find a market. At an exhibition there, specimens sent by the Morarji Goculdas Mill even won an award.[362]

The inchoate *swadeshi* movement was politically tinged. It contained in embryo the idea of boycott. Since Britain's strength lay in trade, her trade had to be attacked. The idea was expected to sap the foundations of British rule; for by British interests was understood and in the protection of British commerce was seen 'the continuation of British rule in India'.[363] Its practical implementation was suggested by Gopalrao Deshmukh: if India could not manufacture certain articles, these should be imported from countries other than Britain, failing which Indians should do without them.[364]

Besides providing employment, augmenting national wealth and checking 'drain', *swadeshi* was thus expected to prepare the country for independence. Songs were spreading about this time 'among the people of Western India, against the destruction of Indian industry and arts'. These were then directed against British wares only; but if by its selfish policy the government made the people 'despair for

357. *Native Opinion*, 11 Mar. 1877.
358. *Ibid.*, 5 Aug. 1877.
359. N. R. Phatak, 'Gopalrao Deshmukh "Lokhitwadi"', *Rationalists of Maharashtra*, Dehradun, 1962, p. 10.
360. *Native Opinion*, 8 Oct. 1882.
361. 'A Voice for the Commerce and Manufactures of India', *Mookerjee's Magazine*, vol. III, Nos. XXI and XXII, p. 310.
362. *Native Opinion*, 8 Oct. 1882.
363. *Sadharani*, 10 Feb. 1878, *Report on Native Press, Bengal*, 23 Feb. 1878 p. 2.
364. *Rationalists of Maharashtra*, p. 10.

any amelioration', the songs could be turned against British rule as well.[365] Despair had begun to gather momentum since Lytton's tariff administration.

With or without aspirations of political independence, more and more Indians were beginning to realise that 'the cultivation of industrial arts was the best and the only remedy for the regeneration of India'. Encouragement to mechanical industries was essential for the material, intellectual and moral advancement of India to the level of European nations.[366] That 'our raw produce and stuffs are exported for manufacture and imported back for our consumption' no longer remained merely a question of material ruin; it also became 'a standing shame to the nation'.[367]

365. Naoróji, 'The Moral Poverty of India, and Native Thoughts on the Present British Indian Policy', Parekh, ed., *op. cit.*, pp. 468-69.
366. M. M. Kunte, quoted in *Native Opinion*, 8 Jun. 1884.
367. 'Employment of Educated Indians', 6 Jun. 1879, *Selections from the Writings and Speeches of Peary Mohan Mukherjee*, p. 33.

4   The Political Aspect

CONFLICT with educated Indians was inherent in the character of British rule. Pragmatic and liberal so far as imperialism permitted, it granted equality and freedom of thought, speech and association. Moreover, since non-official Englishmen in India retained their notions of free Press and civil liberties, it would have been inconsistent to allow certain rights to them and deny the same to Indians. By the time Indians could make sufficient educational progress to claim in practice what they had obtained in principle, the natural proclivity of rulers to resist devolution of power had found in 1857 a justification for suspending the implementation of these concessions. Initially the claims of Indians were ignored. But when their agitation became too strong to be safely neglected, the authorities devised stratagems to make a show of concession without conceding much in substance. The disenchantment produced by official circumvention and the resolve of a growing body of Indians to obtain their rights expanded the scope of national consciousness.

I

One of the cherished rights of Indians related to their eligibility for appointment to high offices. It rested on the provision, in section 87 of the Charter Act of 1833, that 'no native of the said territories, nor any natural-born subject of His Majesty resident therein, shall, by reason only of his religion, place of birth, descent, colour, or any of them, be disabled from holding any place, or employment under the said Company.'[1]

Indians, however, discovered that the removal of legal disabilities *ipso facto* conferred no advantages on them. They took up the question on the eve of the renewal of the East India Company's Char-

---

1. Government of India Act, 1833 (3 & 4 Will. 4, c. 85), section LXXXVII, Keith, *op. cit.*, vol. I, pp. 272-73.

ter in 1853, arguing that the condition of compulsory training at Haileybury and Addiscombe made the 87th section a dead letter and preserved the exclusiveness of the civil service. As long as these institutions continued, 'so long would the whole one hundred and fifty millions of this country be shut from the advantages' offered by the Charter. The risks involved in sending a young boy 'to a clime not congenial to his constitution and among strangers' rendered this policy 'an anomaly in itself, and a cruelty' to Indians. It was designed to educate them 'in as high a degree as they could be educated, and at the same time' exclude them 'from the higher-prizes of the public service'.[2] As requisite education could be provided in India also, parliament was petitioned to remove the Haileybury College.[3]

The distinction between the covenanted and the uncovenanted services was also resented as an injustice to Indians. Believed to have been based on race so that Europeans could be favoured, the distinction was supposed to violate 'the letter and spirit of the 87th section' by excluding even the most qualified Indians from 'the higher grade of judicial and revenue situations and from the regular Medical service'. As a proof was adduced the case of Dr D. S. Chuckerburty (1827-74) who, in spite of a distinguished academic career in England, had been 'refused admission into the covenanted Medical Service by the Court of Directors collectively and individually.' This refusal was attributed to the fact that Dr Chuckerburty was an Indian.[4]

The system offered no prospects for Indians. The court of directors, it was alleged, had a conscience the blunt side of which was turned towards those not belonging to 'the guild which constitutes the governing classes, and the delicate side towards those who are of it.' Even the covenanted revenue officer was treated as 'a pet' and the uncovenanted deputy collector deemed 'sufficiently rewarded for a lifelong service amidst privations and dangers ... of the Soonderbuns and the marshes of Chittagong...by the acme of prosperity represented by an income of Rs. 700 a month.' In the whole of Bengal only three Indians had risen above this limit: one 'to the Clerk Assistantship of the Legislative Council on a salary of Rs. 1,200 a month,

2. *Report of the Proceedings of a Public Meeting of the Native Community held in the Town Hall on Friday, the 29th July, 1853*, Calcutta, 1853, pp. 10-11, 15.
3. *Ibid.*, p. 46.
4. Petition of the Bombay Association to British parliament, May 1853, *Minutes of Proceedings of the Bombay Association*, vol. I. The feeling had been gaining strength for quite some time. See *Calcutta Review*, vol. IV, Jul.-Dec. 1845, p. 364. It is interesting that Chuckerburty himself was out to test a point while proceeding to England. He wrote: 'If I fail it will be a satisfaction to me that I have used my best efforts in the service of my country, and that it is only physical difficulties thrown in our way by the Legislature which have been the cause of my disappointment and loss.' *Times*, 13 Feb. 1855, quoted in *Native Opinion*, 18 Oct. 1874.

another to the 3rd Judgeship of the Court of Small Causes on 12,000
a year, and a third to the Junior Police Magistracy on 9,500 per annum.' This 'tardy liberality' was 'but a mean acknowledgment of the
very important aid rendered by the uncovenanted men in the administration of the country.' Justice demanded that the authorities
should 'remunerate with an even hand an equal amount of service'
irrespective of 'the creed, caste, color or necessities of its servants.'[5]

There was thus resentment against the employment policy of the
government and the problem was viewed in the context of India as
a whole when the covenanted civil service was opened to competition in 1855. Indians quickly realised that the new scheme was 'calculated to virtually exclude' them from the civil service. A 'perpetuation of the non-operative' 87th section of the Charter Act of 1833,
it was 'highly unjust to them in point of principle, and unjust to this
country in point of utility and economy'.[6] This was so because the
civil service examination would be held in London and the syllabus
for it had been devised to benefit British public schools. The British
Indian Association, therefore, urged for a modification of 'the merely
literary tests' in accordance with the education provided in India,
and for simultaneous examinations in the presidency towns.[7] This
was construed by the authorities as a request for admission to the
civil service, every year, of a certain number of Indians 'without
competition with other classes of the Queen's subjects, and under a
lower standard of qualification than that required from others.' The
Association rightly protested that this conclusion rested 'on a mis-
representation' of its views.[8]

The rejection of this petition and opposition to it by non-official
Europeans foreboded the formidableness of the problem. Referring
to the attacks of the *Bengal Hurkaru* on the petition, the *Hindoo Patriot* wrote that these only contributed 'to heighten the baseness of
the deception' of which the Indian Acts of 1833 and 1853 were the
recorded proofs. The 'dodges' of 'the contumacious executive' to nul-
lify the declaration of 1833 had convinced Indians that 'vigilant, per-
tinacious and unyielding endeavours must be made by the political
leaders of the Indian people to ensure them a fair share of those offices in which their right to participate had been admitted.'[9]

The *Patriot* argued that in the existing circumstances the exclusion of Indians from high offices was detrimental to British rule.
Such a policy was probably justified when the British were establish-
ing their power in the country. But appreciation of British rule had
since then confirmed the loyalty of Indians; and increase of wealth

5. *Hindoo Patriot*, 27 Jul. 1854.
6. *Pamphlet of the Bengal British Indian Association*, Calcutta, undated, p. 21.
7. *Hindoo Patriot*, 22 Jan. 1857.
8. *Englishman*, 9 Jun. 1857.
9. *Hindoo Patriot*, 5 Feb. 1857.

and intelligence among them had produced 'a strong desire for direct political power.' The dissociation of wealth, intelligence and social influence from power having made them 'sources of disorder', their reunion had become 'a measure of urgent necessity'.[10]

By 1858 the question of employment to high offices had thus begun to agitate educated Indians. Basing their case on the growth of education and loyalty, they were demanding fair facilities for themselves as a matter of right. Their main demand was for simultaneous examinations in England and India.[11] They also complained that the syllabus suited the British students. The main features of the civil service agitation were soon to crystallise with the first reduction in the upper age limit for the civil service examination.

The intensification of racialism in 1857 also impelled Indians to insist on their right to high offices because by occupying offices with jurisdiction over Europeans they hoped to be able to check the growing European insolence and violence. But while demanding this, Indians had to rebut the charge that they were unfit for high offices. They attributed this charge to the jealousy of the bureaucrats who discredited Indians because they had found 'in the growth of intelligence and property among the natives of the country the greatest danger to their absurd claims to social pre-eminence.'[12]

Moreover, unfitness could be shown only when Indians had got the chance to exhibit their worth and had failed. There was no reason why 'the sons of aristocracy and gentry of the land, when allowed the same advantages of education', should not do as well, if not better, as 'the nephews and sons of Directors palmed off so unscrupulously to feed upon the resources of India.' It was contended that the civil administration was really conducted by 'that unpresuming man who, sitting on a mattress with a knot of mohurirs drawn around him, keeps pulling the wire while his white-faced automaton is waltzing to a tune.' Yet, this man was 'jealously excluded from participation in the loaves and fishes of the land'.[13]

Figures were pressed into service to prove the superiority of Indian officials: during 1845-51 'omitting fractions, 19 per cent. of the decisions of the European Judges appealed from are confirmed, and 80 per cent. reversed by the superior court, but ... 25 per cent. of the decisions of the Native Judges of the higher grade appealed from are confirmed, and 74 per cent. reversed'.[14]

The experience of 25 years made Indians take with a grain of

10. *Hindoo Patriot*, 12 Feb. 1857.
11. H. L. Singh writes, however, that by 1860 there was no Indian demand for simultaneous examination and that Indians began agitating on this question around 1867; *op. cit.*, pp. 17, 21.
12. *Hindoo Patriot*, 4 Jun. 1857.
13. *Ibid.*, 30 Sep. 1858.
14. *Pamphlet of the Bengal British Indian Association*, pp. 22-3.

salt the promise renewed in the Queen's proclamation about the opening of all offices without consideration of colour and creed. They could consider it seriously if the examination was 'ere long' held in India, and 'the defects attending the system' were removed.[15] Rather, their faith was further shaken by a series of events.

The first of these was the dismissal of Kissory Chand Mitra, magistrate of Calcutta, after a trial on charges preferred against him by the commissioner of police. The distrust of educated Indians in the authorities is revealed by their imputation of racialism. It was believed that the discrepancies in the commissioner's depositions were startling enough to break the case down had the accused been a European. Even otherwise, the punishment, involving 'disgrace and utter ruin', was disproportionate to the actual guilt. Penalties 'ranging from undesired promotion to degradation' had been awarded earlier for 'numberless acts of the most serious misconduct'. But the penalty of dismissal was reserved for an Indian. Mitra's case did not concern an individual alone. The interests of an important and large class, and through it of the people, were involved.[16]

Opposed to the employment of Indians in offices of responsibility, Europeans, on the contrary, quoted this case 'as a proof of the utter unfitness of natives for judicial employ'. For them the 'true lesson of the affair' was 'the utter worthlessness of our education as a moral agent'. Though Kissory Chand belonged to an enlightened family, neither knowledge nor high position had 'availed to give him a moral sense'. If this was so in Calcutta 'in the presence of a strong and critical community', Indian moral stature could be improved nowhere by English education.[17]

Another incident to sap confidence in the sincerity of the rulers related to the fate of Rustomjee Hirjeebhoy Wadia. Studying in the University College, London, with a view to competing for the civil service examination in 1860, Wadia found his plan baffled by a sudden reduction of the upper age limit from 23 to 22. His petition to Stanley elicited the laconic reply that the secretary of state saw no reason for granting any 'further relaxation'. The *Rast Goftar* appealed to the Indian political associations to take up this matter if they were 'good for anything'.[18] But the Bombay Association to which the appeal was really addressed was too lackadaisical to move. However, the case marked the beginning of Dadabhai Naoroji's campaign 'concerning the injustice inherent in the system of recruiting the Indian Civil Service'.[19]

The treatment meted out to Muncherjee Beramjee Colah further

15. *Hindoo Patriot*, 2 Dec. 1858.
16. *Ibid.*, 11 Nov., 9 Dec. 1858.
17. *Friend of India*, 4 Nov. 1858.
18. *Rast Goftar*, 14 Aug. 1859.
19. R. P. Masani, *Dadabhai Naoroji*, London, 1939, pp. 81-2.

exacerbated educated Indians. Resigning as sub-assistant surgeon, Colah had gone to England to qualify for the Indian army medical service. By the time he became a Member of the Royal College of Surgeons and Licentiate of Mid-wifery and Doctor of Medicine, the Indian army medical service had lost its separate existence. So Colah offered himself for the general military service. On being asked if he could serve on the West Coast of Africa, he replied:[20]

> I am prepared to serve in any part of the world, to which in the course of my duty I may be sent, yet I feel that any submission to the special terms now proposed would not only be prejudicial to myself, but would imply an acquiescence in what I cannot but regard as an injustice to my countrymen.

Colah's petition to the secretary of state for India was rejected on the ground of the 'constitutional unfitness of the native and mixed races of India and tropical countries, to sustain for any length of time the climate of our northern regions'. The Parsis in England met this objection by gathering convincing professional evidence to the contrary.[21] Later on Colah petitioned the War Office and the two houses of parliament separately. By the time his petition was accepted, he had crossed the upper age limit. He was, therefore, disqualified.[22]

Though Colah was eventually employed, his case was treated as a national grievance. If the royal promises were to be relied upon, demanded the *Hindoo Patriot*, 'Ministers must not be allowed to decree our countrymen proscribed from Her Majesty's General Medical Service.'[23] Public awareness born of individual grievances thus transcended differences of region and religion.

Meanwhile, following the impetus given to higher education by the universities, Indians could not be satisfied with the offices of moonsif, principal sadar ameen and deputy collector which had been designed to satisfy a generation that had not made such educational progress. As more Indians were receiving higher education 'proportionately freer scope' was claimed for 'the irrepressible yearnings of national ambition'.[24]

The economic aspect of the question, though tending to become secondary, was never neglected. This was natural in view of increasing taxation and unemployment. Expenditure could be reduced and more jobs offered to Indians by employing, as far as possible, Indian rather than European agency in the administration. Economic and political considerations thus pressed alike 'for a solution of the question [as to] how far our public schools are to be the feeders of

20. *Hindoo Patriot*, 5 Sep. 1861.
21. *Ibid.*
22. Masani, op. cit., pp. 83-4.
23. *Hindoo Patriot*, 5 Sep. 1861.
24. *Ibid.*, 5 Dec. 1860.

our public services'.[25]

Tantalised for 30 years, Indians were thirsting for some success. The departure of every young Indian to England was publicly discussed and viewed as a prospective harbinger of national glory. The activities of those in England were watched with eager expectancy.

In such a state of anxious anticipation was reported the departure, in 1862, of two young men to compete for the civil service examination. As a proof of their accomplishments, it was stated that one of them had been in charge of the *Tattvabodhini Patrika*, and the other had conducted the *Indian Mirror* till the day of his departure.[26] The two young men, Satyendranath Tagore (1842-1923) and Manmohan Ghosh (1844-96) were destined to become national heroes.

Tagore's success produced a triumphant and vindictive jubilation in India. The frustrations and bitter experiences of earlier years were recounted in a spirit of exultant satisfaction that flows from success after incessant hardships and failures. The *Bengalee* recalled the inherent handicaps of the system— 'the enormous distance, the enormous expense, the enormous danger to life, and the enormous disappointment of failure—all were befittingly crowned by the insuperable difficulty of the Hindoo religion—that ubiquitous blight ever and anon pursuing a Hindoo and blasting his happiness'. Vain had been 'the articles written and agitations made and memorials to the Secretary of State and petitions to Parliament'. The device of the London competition had kept the covenanted civil service 'sacred from Indian intrusion'. But 'the spirited grandson of Babu Dwarka Nath Tagore' had included it 'amongst the national conquests'. It seemed so pleasant to speculate on 'the feelings of all monopolists, when monopolies expire'.[27]

This maiden success lent greater plausibility to the Indian refutation of the charge of intellectual inferiority. So far Indians had agitated for better facilities without making successful use of the existing ones. But now one of them had succeeded against the pick of the English youth in the face of stupendous odds. They could argue that if these impediments were removed, and a fair chance was given to them, Indians would show their real worth.

Instead, these difficulties were increased by a further reduction of the upper age limit for the London competition from 22 to 21 years, and of the marks for Sanskrit and Arabic. Manmohan Ghosh, still in England, was thus robbed of a chance to try for the service. He immediately corresponded with the British Indian Association and advised it to communicate on the matter with the London Indian Society. The Association felt that for Indians the reduction was 'calculated to have the effect of a prohibitory order'. It proposed that the

25. *Ibid.*, 12 Dec. 1860.
26. *Ibid.*, 7 Jul. 1862.
27. *Bengalee*, 16 Sep. 1863.

age limit should be 21-25 years. However, before addressing the secretary of state for India, the Association decided to confer with the London Indian Society.[28]

The London Indian Society met twice before advising the Association. There was a division of opinion among the members. The majority, however, favoured a trial of the new regulation before petitioning the secretary of state. Dadabhai Naoroji went to the extent of observing that a petition for raising the limit of age would be a 'humiliating admission of the inferiority of Indians to English youth'. If Indians were incapable of competing at 21, they did not 'deserve entrance into the service'.[29]

The moderation of the London Indian Society irritated the *Hindoo Patriot*. It hoped that the advice, coming from expert men of business who had 'generally speaking little intellectuality' and who were 'altogether isolated' from the Indian society, would not be accepted. Particular exception was taken to Naoroji's remark. The Indian youth was willing to compete at 21 or even at 20 for that matter. But he wanted the same facilities which had been given to his British coeval. He did not mind the disadvantage of being examined in a foreign language. But it was invidious to allow European classical languages 'exactly double the preference in number of marks' as compared to the Oriental classics. Moreover, the rules of the Indian universities precluded graduation before the age of 20. An Indian graduate was left with little chance of success if the maximum age was 21. However, these disadvantages could be removed by holding the examination in India also. The Indian youth thus wanted not 'special favours' but equal facilities.[30] The British Indian Association ignored the advice of the London Indian Society and decided to petition the secretary of state.

The official justification that, if sent out after 23 or 24, the English civilians would not be able to stand the climate of India, received little credence from Indians. Manmohan Ghosh exposed its fallacy by pointing out that according to the new regulations the successful candidates had to spend two instead of one year in England. This meant that the age of departure from England had remained 23. In any case, supposing that training for two years in England was desirable, the retention of the old age limit would make a difference of only one year. As a single year hardly mattered, the question of health was 'an absurd one'. The new limit would not only deter 'well

28. *Report of the Fourteenth Annual General Meeting of the British Indian Association held on 14 February 1866*, p. 7. The London Indian Society had been recently formed and its honorary secretary, W. C. Bannerjee, had, in a letter dated 18 Aug. 1865, sought the co-operation of the British Indian Association; *ibid.*, pp. 22-3.
29. *Hindoo Patriot*, 7 May 1866.
30. *Ibid.*

educated young men' and result in the recruitment of 'a parcel of school boys', but also 'practically prevent our countrymen from entering the Civil Service'. Ghosh expected a similar effect from the 'capricious and arbitrary distribution' of marks unless Indians decided to 'come to Europe very young, and learn thoroughly the Latin and Greek languages'.[31] Even Dadabhai Naoroji and the London Indian Society protested to the secretary of state on the subject of marks.[32]

While the agitation was going on, news was received that Khettar Mohan Dutt had stood first in the medical service competition in England. It is indicative of the avidity with which such successes were broadcast all over the country that the *Native Opinion* immediately reported the news without ascertaining Dutt's name. It wrote Woomesh Chandra and was corrected by the *Hindoo Patriot*.[33] What mattered was not a name but the fact that an Indian had established his superiority in England.

By 1867 educated Indian opinion on the question of employment in higher offices had become sufficiently articulate to oblige the authorities to attend to it. In the absence of an efficacious political association, the Indian Press in Bombay was showing keen interest in the matter. In Bengal the Press and the British Indian Association had kept up a sustained agitation. Indians in England were also alive to the problem.

A significant move was made when Dadabhai Naoroji proposed, on 13 August 1867, for adoption by the East India Association a memorial to Northcote, submitting that it was time 'to admit the natives of India to a larger share in the administration of India than hitherto'. Naoroji argued that the spread of education had effected a marked improvement in the character and administrative capacity of Indians. Moreover, increasing employment of Indians was needed for the better administration of India. For, unable to 'understand the natives of India as a body', Anglo-Indian administrators 'taxed in vain' their energies to solve the problems of the country.[34]

Naoroji used a new argument in pleading for simultaneous examinations. Encouraging the wealthiest and not the most talented Indians, the existing system was designed to produce 'only a body of independent educated natives' without providing a counterpoise to their agitation. If not appointed to high offices, they would not realise the difficulties of administration.[35]

A week later a deputation of the East India Association waited on Northcote and asked for simultaneous examinations and state

31. *Ibid.*, 29 Jan. 1866.
32. Masani, *op. cit.*, p. 98.
33. *Hindoo Patriot*, 19 Nov. 1866.
34. Parekh, ed., *op. cit.*, pp. 345, 348.
35. *Ibid.*, pp. 349, 352.

scholarships for enabling deserving Indians to study in England.[36]

The exertions of the East India Association were backed by the Indian Press and political associations. People were exhorted to 'stir themselves up in the matter, and by dint of repeated attempts and anxious movements show that their claims should be complied with in this particular'.[37] When the British Indian Association appointed a committee to prepare a memorial, the *Native Opinion* appealed to the people of Bombay to strengthen Naoroji's hands even if the effete Bombay Association remained inactive.[38] While the petition of the British Indian Association was about to be transmitted to England,[39] the revived Bombay Association organised a public meeting at which a memorial to the secretary of state was adopted.[40] This was for the *Hindoo Patriot* a matter of special rejoicing.[41] But in the midst of general effort to have this grievance redressed, there lurked an apprehension that it might yield nothing.[42]

Resident Europeans, on the other hand, were alarmed by these activities. Anglo-Indian journals, from the anti-Indian *Bombay Gazette* to the sympathetic *Times of India,* denounced simultaneous examinations.[43] It began to be openly written:[44]

It affects every Englishman in the country. The civilian sees his service deprived of its peculiar character and value. The non-official must be prepared for the Black Act in its worst form, that is, he will be liable to be tried, or at least committed for trial, by native civilians of an alien faith and a radically different civilisation.

Vainly did Indians hope that even though every 'feeling of pride, prejudice and interest' among resident Europeans might be 'arrayed against the liberal measure', England would live upto the 'progressive conception of its duties towards India'.[45] European opposition was to be utilised by the authorities to resist the liberalisation of the employment of Indians.

However, the authorities were, for the first time since 1833, obliged to recognise the 'urgent political necessity' of attending to the problem of higher employment for Indians.[46] Lawrence noticed with

36. Parekh, ed., *op. cit.,* p. 346. In 1860 Hodgson Pratt of the Bengal civil service had suggested annual scholarships for Indians in his *University Education in England for Natives of India;* see *Times of India,* 2 Nov. 1860.
37. *Suryodaya,* quoted in *Native Opinion,* 29 Sep. 1867.
38. *Ibid.,* 13 Oct. 1867.
39. Memorial of the British Indian Association to Northcote, 16 Mar. 1868.
40. *Native Opinion,* 8 Mar. 1868.
41. *Hindoo Patriot,* 16 Mar. 1868.
42. *Mitrodaya,* quoted in *Native Opinion,* 10 Nov. 1867.
43. *Ibid.,* 20 Oct., 3 Nov. 1867.
44. *Ibid.,* 20 Oct. 1867.
45. *Ibid.*
46. Government of India's Resolution, 19 Aug. 1867, Philips, ed., *op. cit.,* p. 536.

anxiety the propensity of the growing European community in India to be 'more and more against the employment of natives in offices of much importance'. This, he felt, had 'a strong tendency to render our rule unpopular'. But instead of abrupt changes, he favoured the gradual elevation of Indian officials. An Indian sitting as a judge with one or more European judges in the high court was 'no doubt of value'; but it was a different thing to have him as the chief judge of a district.[47]

But Northcote preferred concrete steps 'for rendering it easier than at present for natives to gain appointments in the covenanted service.' Having no definite scheme in mind, he asked Lawrence if the Gilchrist foundation could be utilised to enable young and competent Indians to visit and compete in England. He also suggested that a few Indians could be selected after competitive examination in India to be trained in England. The latter plan especially appealed to him.[48] Later on he specified that five or ten Indians could thus be selected every year.[49]

Lawrence refused to go so far. He agreed that the existing arrangements were a check on the employment of Indians. But such had been 'the intention of the framers of the law'. Apart from the opposition of resident Europeans to such a change, it was likely to affect the foundation of British rule in India. Lawrence opposed the system of competitive examination in India because this would virtually mean the appointment of Bengalis and create resentment among the Panjabis and other vigorous races of India. He agreed, however, to introduce some cautious measures.[50]

Lawrence was faced with a dilemma. Anglo-Indian officials were opposed to the more extensive employment of Indians.[51] They looked on jobs in India as the preserve of their sons and dependents. But the rapidly growing class of educated Indians had 'even greater claims on the Government of India'. Competitors 'in every grade for the appointments to which the sons of officers aspire', they were sure to 'become more and more successful in this competition'. Whomsoever the authorities might favour, there was bound to be a 'large body of discontented men'.[52]

Finally, Lawrence managed to convert Northcote into a confirm-

47. Lawrence to de Grey, 4 May 1866, *Lawrence Collection*, reel 2.
48. Northcote to Lawrence, 24 Jun. 1867, *ibid.*, reel 1.
49. Northcote to Lawrence, 15 Aug. 1867, *ibid.*
50. Lawrence to Northcote, 17 Aug. 1867, *ibid.*, reel 3. There was some substance in this assertion. The Panjab Anjuman, which supported simultaneous examinations, insisted that 'a certain number be reserved for India, that of that number, a few appointments be allotted to each Province, to be competed for at the most central or convenient City, in such Province'. *Hindoo Patriot*, quoted in *Native Opinion*, 8 Dec. 1867.
51. Lawrence to Northcote, 4 Nov. 1867, *Lawrence Collection*, reel 3.
52. Lawrence to Northcote, 28 Dec. 1867, *ibid.*

ed opponent of competitive examinations in India. His original scheme of selecting five or ten Indians in India ultimately dwindled into the acceptance of the 'preferential claim' of Indians to lucrative and honourable appointments in the uncovenanted service. It was declared that though so far 'too exclusively conferred upon Europeans', these would henceforth be filled 'by Natives of ability and high character'.[53]

This declaration betrayed total incomprehension of the aspirations of educated Indians. They did want better employment facilities, and to that extent this proposal was calculated to satisfy them. But their agitation had a moral aspect also. Bubbling with enthusiasm born of the nascent national pride, they were anxious to enter the highest branches of the Indian administration. It was with this end in view that they had been agitating for fair conditions to enter the covenanted civil service. But nothing was done to meet this demand.

Even the institution of nine annual scholarships for study in England failed to satisfy Indians. These were dismissed as 'a poor gift in return for the boon solicited'.[54]

The measures intended to satisfy Indians stimulated their agitation. The British were asked not to tantalise the people if they had private objections to the entry of Indians to the covenanted service.[55] The rulers, it was claimed, were afraid that the employment of Indians in offices of trust would diffuse and dissipate their dominance.[56] This reminded Indians of their subjection. High appointments were held back because 'we are black, Europeans are white; they have political power which we have not; we are supplicants, they are claimants'.[57] Besides producing dissatisfaction,[58] such conduct damaged faith in the rulers who began to be stigmatised as 'very sweet in talk, and quite otherwise in action'.[59] This logically led to the suspicion that when Indians had qualified themselves for self-government, the British would not accept their claim to independence.[60]

Meanwhile, the petition of the East India Association having been abortive, Dadabhai Naoroji had persuaded Fawcett (1833-84),

53. Secretary of state to the government of India, 8 Feb. 1868, Philips, ed., op. cit., p. 537.
54. Native Opinion, 3 Jan. 1869.
55. Amrita Bazar Patrika, Report on Native Press, Bengal, 28 Mar. 1868, p. 10.
56. Som Prakash, ibid., 15 Feb. 1868, p. 3.
57. Vritta Waibhawa, 24 May 1868, Report on Native Press, Bombay, 30 May 1868, p. 7.
58. See Naoroji's paper on 'Admission of Natives into the Indian Civil Service', 17 Apr. 1868, Parekh, ed., op. cit., p. 95.
59. Indu Prakash, 25 May 1868, Report on Native Press, Bombay, 30 May 1868, p. 3.
60. Som Prakash, Report on Native Press, Bengal, 3 Feb. 1868, p. 3.

'the Member for India', to give notice of a motion asking that the examinations for the covenanted civil service should be held simultaneously in London, Bombay, Calcutta and Madras.[61] Naoroji also called upon the East India Association to support this motion.[62] A petition favouring the motion was sent to the secretary of state by the inhabitants of Bombay.[63]

Northcote, however, induced Fawcett to withdraw his motion by promising that the government of India would be empowered to appoint men to posts reserved for covenanted civilians. Northcote further added insult to injury by declaring in parliament that competition was not 'at all suitable to the condition of India'.[61]

The very nature of the plan provoked Indians. Having no confidence in the government of India, they were convinced that even the most liberal measure 'for improving their status in the public service' would not benefit them if its execution was 'left entirely to the local authorities'. The latter even earlier had opportunities to employ Indians in responsible posts. But this had not been done. The bar, as Frere had pointed out, was as often 'social or sentimental as legal', and it could be neutralised only 'if there were a real anxiety to overcome it'. The anxiety, as figures showed, was not there. The revenue survey department had 68 Europeans and only one Indian who held a superior post. In the public works department there was only one Indian as against 105 Europeans. In fact, some of the best Indians had to leave this department 'whereas if they had merely the skin of a Jones or a Smith' they would have topped the list. The police department had 46 Europeans and no Indian. The Indian employee of the government was like a Hindu widow whose rights were 'rampantly trampled down' and whose 'length of service, superior ability and unflinching integrity' proved 'of no avail when opposed to prejudice and interest'.[65] It was only after having despaired of making the government of India listen to their grievances that Indians had appealed to parliament. But the secretary of state had thought it prudent to win over those Englishmen who treated the Indian civil service 'as their own patrimony'.[66]

More significant than this, Northcote's profession regarding the unsuitability of competition to the Indian conditions was for Indians 'tantamount to a denial of the national right, for the recognition of which we have been contending'. They did not crave for 'the extension of the privilege of admission into the Civil Service' as a fav-

61. Masani, op. cit., p. 104.
62. Parekh, ed., op. cit., p. 96.
63. Northcote to Lawrence, 13 Aug. 1868, Lawrence Collection, reel 2.
64. Native Opinion, 21 Jun. 1868.
65. Ibid., 24 May 1868.
66. Jame Jamsed, 19 May 1868, Report on Native Press, Bombay, 23 May 1868, p. 11.

our; they demanded it 'as a matter of right'.[67]   In any case, coming 'in the thirty-fifth year of a statute and tenth year of a Royal Proclamation', the declaration confirmed the apprehension that these statutory and royal promises were 'never intended to be fulfilled'.[68]

Already touchy about the imputation of inferior moral character, Indians resisted a different mode of selection as an aspersion on their character . If the 'various other qualifications' alluded to by Northcote could not be tested through competition in India, neither could that be done in England.   The few Indians who had been entrusted earlier with responsible offices had shown that they were endowed with these 'other qualifications' also.   Given the opportunity, they had 'in them elements of success and greatness'.[69]

The strength of Indian misgivings about the official policy is revealed by the fact that even Naoroji, sober and reluctant to suspect motives, viewed Northcote's 'other qualifications' as a subterfuge. Chagrined, he asked the secretary of state to lay down once and for all the test that he thought best for Indians so that they might prepare accordingly.[70]   The *Hindoo Patriot* repeated the suggestion, and hoped that Naoroji's pamphlet, answering all the objections to the system of competition in India, would be a strong weapon in the hands of Indians.[71]

Naoroji advised the authorities that educated Indians represented the rising power in the country.   The government could still enlist them by redressing their grievances. But this certainly could not be done by making them realise 'the humiliation of a conquered people'. They claimed equality with the British and 'a proper share in the administration'.[72] But they would have it 'as men', not 'as grown up boys' through the 'back door' of seasonal manoeuvres at the viceregal court.[73]   They scorned away what Northcote had given as a 'morsel flung at a starving people'.[74]   Their gaze was fixed at simultaneous examinations.

The civil service agitation weakened the moral basis of British rule and led to the enunciation of a fundamental postulate of Indian nationalism.   The official objection to competitive examination in India, that this would throw up Bengalis and arouse other vigorous races against them, implied British claim to act as mediators among the discordant communities of India.   There were Indians who counter-claimed that the British had no inherent right or qualifications

67. *Hindoo Patriot*, 8 Jun. 1868.
68. Naoroji's Memo. to the secretary of state for India, 2 May 1868, Parekh, ed., *op. cit.*, p. 491.
69. *Ibid.*, pp. 491-93.
70. Naoroji's Memo. of 2 May 1868, Parekh, ed., *op. cit.*, p. 492.
71. *Hindoo Patriot*, 8 Jun. 1868.
72. Naoroji's Memo. of 2 May 1868, Parekh, ed., *op. cit.*, p. 498.
73. *Native Opinion*, 16 May 1869.
74. *Rast Goftar*, 7 Jun. 1868.

to be the guardians of particular Indian communities. The Bengalis were Indians and at least knew 'the requirements of India in the same manner as the Europeans'.[75] Implicit in this was the idea of a united India that was better understood by its own people than by the foreign rulers. Indians also made light of the repugnance of Europeans to being administered by Indians. Those who scrupled to submit to Indian officials 'had better leave the country'.[76]

Criticism of the secretary of state's despatch and parliamentary pronouncement indicated that the loss of faith in the government of India was complete. Indians, therefore, decided to 'rouse and enlighten the generous and philanthropic portion of the English public on the subject of our grievances'.[77] Even the creation of a fund was suggested to enable eloquent and patriotic Indians to carry on agitation in England.[78] Though no fund was created till the late 1870s, the strategy of agitation in England was separately adopted by the British Indian Association, the Bombay Association and the Bombay Branch of the East India Association.

Indians also came to realise the efficacy of agitation. They thought that it was constant exertions by them that had obliged the authorities to change their attitude of negligence. The petitions of public bodies in India and of the East India Association, it was argued, had convinced the secretary of state 'that the subject was sure to come before Parliament' which had 'several sincere and true friends of India'. He had instructed the government of India to provide better employment to Indians in order to forestall discussion in parliament by being able to say that 'as he had already anticipated the petitioners' wishes,...there was no need to discuss the subject at all'. But because the assurances given by Northcote were not sincere, it was prudent for Indians to continue their agitation.[79] The idea that the secretary of state was afraid of parliament and that he could be pressurised to make concessions sustained faith in agitation in England. It was, however, felt that the agitation in England could not succeed without backing from the people in India. It was, therefore, necessary that the educated youth should 'bestir themselves in this matter, if for no other reason at least for their own interest, and prove by acts that they possess a true public spirit and interest in the welfare of their country'.[80]

Even the Liberal secretary of state for India, the Duke of Argyll, only favoured freer employment of Indians 'in the uncovenanted ser-

75. *Som Prakash, Report on Native Press, Bengal*, 1 Aug. 1868, p. 1.
76. *Ibid.*, 26 Apr.—9 May 1868, p. 4.
77. *Indu Prakash*, 25 May 1868, *Report on Native Press, Bombay*, 30 May 1868, p. 3.
78. *Arunodaya*, 10 May 1868, *ibid.*, 16 May 1868, p. 5.
79. *Arunodaya*, 17 May 1868, *ibid.*, 23 May 1868, pp. 5-6.
80. *Indu Prakash*, 25 May 1868, *ibid.*, 30 May 1868, p. 3.

vice and promotion according to tried ability from that service to the covenanted service'.[81]   The Bill introduced by him for the purpose became Act on 25 March 1870.   Its sixth clause empowered the authorities in India to appoint 'any native of India' who had not passed the London examination to any office in the covenanted civil service. This was subject to such rules as might be prescribed from time to time by the governor general in council and sanctioned by the secretary of state in council.[82]

From the moment of its introduction in parliament, the measure was condemned by Indians.   They expected it to be little more than another addition to the magnanimous but broken promises they had received in abundance.[83] Even Naoroji, himself disposed to give the measure a trial, admitted that Indians' incredulity was 'based on past experience'.[84] Besides the fear of its becoming 'a dead letter like the Charter provisions of 1833', there was also the risk of the proposed scheme being 'converted into a source of jobbery'.[85] Feelings against it were so strong that in spite of advocacy by its founder, Dadabhai Naoroji, the Bombay Branch of the East India Association passed a resolution against this humiliating measure.[86]

Pherozeshah Mehta summed up the Indian point of view by listing four fundamental objections against the measure.   It struck a fatal blow to the principle of competition; it facilitated 'the promotion of political jobbery'; it destroyed 'the unity and *esprit de corps* of the service'; and it was 'unjust and demoralizing to the natives themselves'.[87] By remaining a dead letter for a decade, the measure disillusioned even those whose initial response to it was favourable.

In the midst of general disappointment a fillip was given to the agitation by the success of four Indians at the London examination in 1869. The joy, pride and vindictive triumph produced by Satyendranath Tagore's success were once again manifest.   But this jubilation was marred by the news that two of the four candidates, S. N. Banerji and S. B. Thakur, had been disqualified on the ground of exceeding the upper age limit.   Though they were ultimately taken in, Indians imputed motives to the authorities. So long as Indians had shut themselves at home, the authorities had bragged about opening the highest offices to Indians.   But once the Indian youth had

81. Educational Despatch to India. No. 3, 8 Apr. 1869, *Argyll Papers*, reel 315.
82. 33 Vict. c.3, s.6, Philips, ed., *op. cit.*, pp. 541-42.
83. *Rast Goftar*, 11 Apr. 1869.
84. Naoroji's paper to the East India Association, 7 Jul. 1869, Masani, *op. cit.*, pp. 108-09.
85. *Hindoo Patriot*, 21 Mar. 1870.
86. *Native Opinion*, 26 Jun. 1870.
87. 'On Cl. 6 of the East India Bill', 27 Apr. 1870, C.Y. Chintamani, ed., *Speeches and Writings of the Honourable Sir Pherozeshah M. Mehta*, Allahabad, 1905, p. 56.

shown their mettle, efforts were being made to keep them away.[88]
Even those who did not suspect foul play in the rejection of Banerji
and Thakur, adduced this as a proof of 'what the natives have to expect from the goodwill of those who have the portals of the civil
service in their hands.'[89]

Resident Europeans, on the contrary, advanced the rejection of
Banerji and Thakur as an argument against higher employment for
Indians. It showed how Indians could forge ahead educationally
'without getting beyond falsehood and deception'. This observation
of the *Indian Examiner* received wide publicity from the *Englishman*
with the additional charge that Indians did not possess that whole-
some terror of litigation which Englishmen did.[90] This referred to
the legal proceedings instituted by S. N. Banerji against his rejection
Such was the prejudice against the employment of Indians that even
honest efforts by a young man to avert disaster to his career were
construed as national addiction to litigation.

Indian faith was shaken also by the abolition, in 1870, of the
scholarship scheme. The *Maharashtra Mitra* insinuated that while
this small concession to the long, loud complaints of Indians had been
withdrawn, education allowance to the European and Eurasian children would continue.[91] The Liberals as a whole were criticised for
withdrawing such a scanty allowance.[92] The East India Association
was urged to take up the matter in England.[93] For a while some
Indians advised patience in view of the official explanation that the
abolition was in anticipation of a bigger scheme.[94] But the reception
given to Argyll's scheme, which followed in the wake of the abolition, showed that the hectic activities since 1867 had left them more
disillusioned than ever. The opening of the Cooper's Hill College
about the same time further discredited the authorities, this time for
blighting the future of engineers produced in India.[95]

But Indians were handicapped by the stage of their political
development. In spite of the realisation of the national character of
the question, there was no national organisation to take it up at the
national level. Meanwhile dissatisfaction continued to mount. By the
time Lytton was obliged, less than a decade later, by the deteriorat-

88. Cf. *Report on Native Press, Bombay*, 10 Jul. 1869, p. 6; *ibid.*, 17 Jul 1869,
    pp. 7-8.
89. *Native Opinion*, 27 Jun. 1869.
90. *Bengalee*, 17 Jul. 1869.
91. *Maharashtra Mitra*, 27 Jan. 1870, *Report on Native Press, Bombay*, 5 Feb.
    1870, p. 4. Since its institution, this allowance had been a sore to Indians; cf.
    Native Opinion, 3, 17 Mar. 1868.
92. *Indu Prakash*, 10 Jan. 1870, *Report on Native Press, Bombay*, 15 Jan. 1870,
    p. 3.
93. *Rast Goftar*, 13 Feb. 1870.
94. *Native Opinion*, 30 Jan. 1870; *Bengalee*, 19 Feb. 1870.
95. *Native Opinion*, 9 Jul. 1870.

ing political climate in the country to attend to the question of employing Indians, political awakening had taken rapid strides. A political association also had been founded that was capable of reaching the length and breadth of India.

For seven years practically nothing, barring correspondence between Calcutta and London, was done towards framing rules for implementing Argyll's scheme. Obstruction to better employment of Indians pervaded 'the whole administrative atmosphere'. Since what was 'for the good of the Blacks' curtailed the 'prospects and privileges' of Anglo-Indians, they, as Mayo put it, resisted all attempts to save Indians from being robbed.[96]

The exasperating suspicion caused by official procrastination was aggravated by S. N. Banerji's dismissal from service. Indians were frankly sceptical about the enquiry into Banerji's case. They asked if there existed 'one scale of justice for the White, and another for the Black civilian.'[97]   That the enquiry concluded much as they had apprehended naturally prompted the query 'if a European in Mr. Banerjea's position has ever or would have ever been treated similarly.'[98]   Examples were recalled.   J. H. Rivett-Carnac, the cotton commissioner, was suspended for one year on a charge of peculation. The result of enquiry in his case was never known.[99]   The same thing had happened in Crawford's case.[100] The *Hindoo Patriot* traced Banerji's dismissal to his independent disposition and the circumstances of his entry in the service. 'Transplanted in early youth to England and nurtured in the atmosphere of freedom which he had breathed there, he forgot that in India he should follow Indian obeisance, and the free easy manner, with which he conducted himself, apparently worked to his prejudice.'   Thus was antagonised his immediate boss, H. C. Sutherland, the disrict magistrate.   On the other hand, the lieutenant-governor was disinclined, as a result of Banerji's litigation, to deal leniently with him.[101]

The dismissal hammered into Banerji's consciousness the abject state of his country. He felt that he had suffered because he was an Indian, 'a member of a community that lay disorganized, and had no public opinion, and no voice in the counsels of their Government.' Mere 'helots, hewers of wood and drawers of water' in their own land, Indians would continue to suffer individually and collectively until they became strong and organised.[102] Out of personal suffering was

96. Mayo to Argyll, 1 Sep. 1871, *Argyll Papers*, reel 314.
97. *Native Opinion*, 17 Aug. 1873.
98. *Ibid.*, 17 May 1874.
99. *Ibid.*, 24 May 1874
100. *Hindoo Patriot*, 11 May 1874.
101. *Ibid.*
102. Banerjea, *op. cit.*, pp. 32-3.

born a sense of dedication to the country.

In this realisation, Banerji was not alone. There were many more for whom the triumphs and tribulations of one of their country-men were their own triumphs and tribulations. His dismissal was not forgotten by Indians even afterwards. It continued to be cited as a flagrant instance of the government's race partiality.

Ever since the recognition of their right to higher employment, Indians had thus been disillusioned, irritated and impelled to fight for their cause by a series of official measures. One such act converted the civil service agitation into a national movement. This was the order of the secretary of state, in defiance of the advice of the authorities he had consulted, reducing the upper limit of age for the civil service examination in London from 21 to 19 years.[103]

Official papers do not prove that the secretary of state was motivated by a desire to diminish the prospects of the Indian candidates. Yet evidence exists to show that he wanted to deter Indians from competing in London. He confessed to having always dreaded the possibility of Indians taking greater advantage of the London examination than they had hitherto done. He could imagine 'no more terrible future for India than that of being governed by Competition-Baboos'. If the number of Indians succeeding at the London competition ever became sizable, 'it would be absolutely necessary to stop the avenue: which would be an indecent and embarrassing necessity'. He would rather get rid of them through 'a more respectable excuse'.[104] The new age limit was perhaps the respectable excuse designed to obviate, or at least minimise, the possibility of that indecent and embarrassing necessity.

Indians, who had seen in the earlier reduction from 22 to 21 years a contrivance to exclude them from the covenanted civil service, naturally assailed this drastic reduction as a deliberate, more efficacious move to effect the same end. The earlier limit had at least left the Indian graduate with a year to compete in London; but the proposed measure made it impossible for him to compete at all. It was the 'crowning blow at the fair and regular admission of natives to the Civil Service.' The path of an Indian to the covenanted service was already littered with obstacles. Since the introduction of the competitive examination, only nine Indians had achieved success. But the proposed reduction would take away 'all chance from Indian candidates of ever being successfully able to compete with English candidates in England'. As for the avenue opened in 1870, the misgivings of Indians had been justified by the performance of the autho-

103. Secretary of state to the government of India, 24 Feb. 1876, Philips, ed., op. cit., pp. 543-45.
104. Salisbury to Lytton, 13 Apr. 1877, Salisbury Papers, reel 822.

rities: during the ensuing period only one Indian from an aristocratic family had been appointed.[105]

It was realised to be the time for 'all parts of India' to 'send forth an united and energetic appeal before the people of England in Parliament assembled'.[106] Initiative in this regard was taken by the Indian Association. On 24 March 1877 it called a meeting at the Calcutta Town Hall. The gathering, exceeding 3,000, comprised 'all sections of the native community'. There were present 'Rajas, Zemin-dars, lawyers, members of the judicial and executive service, medical men and representatives of the education department'; Muslims, Parsis and Maharashtrians also attended the meeting. Dr Mahendra Lal Sarkar (1833-1904), the founder of the Indian Association for the Cultivation of Science, spoke in spite of a severe ailment. Keshab Chandra Sen, essentially a religious leader, was also present. Mess-ages of support were received from 'all the leading associations in the country, and from many gentlemen of acknowledged position and eminence in different parts of India'. Significantly, these included Mohamed Ali Rogay and Syed Ahmad Khan.[107]

Having decided 'to organize a national movement in connection with the Civil Service Question', the Indian Association deputed S. N. Banerji to tour the North Western Provinces, Panjab, Bombay and Madras. This was a unique phenomenon.   Apart from its direct, limited objective, the agitation was calculated 'to unite in a bond of common sympathy and common action the different peoples of India' by 'evoking the sentiment of a common and united nationality'.[108] It represented a conscious effort to shape into a national movement the dissatisfaction caused by a major grievance.

During May-July 1877 Banerji visited Lahore, Amritsar, Mee-rut, Delhi, Aligarh, Agra, Lucknow, Kanpur and Bankipur during his northern India tour. Everywhere he received ready co-opera-tion from the local leaders who included Dyal Singh (1848-98), a philanthropic zemindar, Syed Ahmad Khan, Raja Amir Husain Khan, Munshi Nawal Kishore (1836-95), a leading journalist and publisher, Syed Mahmud (1850-1903), barrister, Pandit Ajodhyanath (1840-92), advocate, and Bharatendu Harish Chandra (1850-85), journalist and litterateur. The memorial prepared on behalf of the Indian Associa-tion was translated into Urdu, circulated widely and adopted at public meetings in all these places. Branches of the Indian Association or in-

105. Chintamani, ed., *Speeches and Writings of P. M. Mehta*, pp. 130, 133-34.
106. *Ibid.*, p. 130.
107. *Proceedings of the Public Meeting on the Civil Service Question*, Calcutta, 1879, pp. 1-7, 26.
108. General Report by A. M. Bose, Honorary Secretary, Indian Association, *The First Annual Report of the Indian Association, 1876-77*, Calcutta, 1877, pp. vi-vii.

dependent political associations were also started in some of these places.[109]

In November Banerji proceeded to complete his all-India tour. In Bombay he elicited the support of prominent leaders like V. N. Mandlik, K. T. Telang, P. M. Mehta and M. G. Ranade. His visit to Bombay and the petition he had brought with him were given considerable publicity. It was admitted that Bombay had not suffered any 'trying affliction' in this regard. Yet Bombayites were exhorted to join in 'the national demand about to be made to the British Parliament'.[110] A largely attended public meeting was held on 15 December 1877 under the auspices of the Bombay Association. Meanwhile, Poona, Surat and Ahmedabad also had adopted similar petitions.[111] In Madras, however, Banerji did not meet with encouraging response and found the presidency politically backward.[112]

After this expression of sympathy for the civil service movement by 'the whole of India',[113] Lal Mohan Ghosh (1849-1909), barrister, was entrusted with the task of taking the petition to England. He addressed a meeting at Willis' Room in London with John Bright in the chair. 'Within twenty-four hours of it there were laid on the table of the House of Commons, the Rules creating what was subsequently known as the Statutory Civil Service'.[114]

The support given to the Indian Association revealed the national consciousness that was being generated by identical aspirations and frustrations. It strengthened 'the hopes of an Indian union upon the common platform of loyal and constitutional action for the redress of our grievances and the assertion of our rights and privileges'.[115] Even in the North Western Provinces and Panjab, the backwaters of political awakening in India, 'a hidden but deep under-current of political feeling' flowed beneath the surface of apathy and despair.[116]

The imperialistic claim to rule different regions according to the peculiar temperaments of their inhabitants had been verbally repudiated in 1868. A decade later, the 'unanimous response' to the appeal of the Indian Association was offered as practical refutation of the official claim that Indians of one region did not wish to be administered by Indians of other regions.[117]

109. 'Special Report on the Civil Service Question' by S. N. Banerjea, 17 Sep. 1877, *ibid*.
110. *Native Opinion*, 2 Dec. 1877.
111. *Ibid*., 23 Dec. 1877; Bagal, *op. cit*., pp. 30-1.
112. Banerjea, *op. cit*., pp. 49-50.
113. *Native Opinion*, 23 Dec. 1877.
114. Banerjea, *op. cit*., p. 54.
115. General Report by A.M. Bose, *The First Annual Report of the Indian Association*, p. vii.
116. 'Special Report on the Civil Service Question' by S. N. Banerjea, *ibid*., p. 14.
117. *Ibid*.

Rising unrest made Lytton admit that the problem had become 'vast and vexatious', requiring an 'early settlement on some definite and comprehensive principle'.[118] But the conflicting considerations imposed by the safety of the empire and by the statutory promises to Indians had created a dilemma. On the one hand was 'a national pledge to redeem, on the other a national danger to avoid'.[119] It was impossible to employ Indians safely in important administrative posts. At the same time, 'the gratuitous public pledges of a great Govt. (to any class of its subjects) have a strong & valid claim on its own character to the reasonable fulfilment of them.'[120]

To remove what he thought was a 'scandal and a weakness to the Govt.',[121] Lytton suggested that instead of being tantalised, Indians should be 'plainly and publicly' told that they 'must never aspire' to important administrative posts. They should be asked to confine their vision to 'judicial, medical, and public works function—with perhaps a certain class of minor administrative posts'. But to these Lytton wanted the best available Indians to be appointed in the largest number and at the earliest opportunity.[122]

The problem, however, was not so simple. The solution suggested by Lytton as decisive and final was neither. Agonised by 'the disappearance of each successive morsel of promotion',[123] Anglo-Indian administrators were antipathetic to the scheme; and Indians would not take it as final. So Salisbury favoured 'a gentle and tentative application of the dreaded measure'. If it failed, there would be an answer for Indians; if it succeeded, even the prejudice of the Anglo-Indian mind would be overcome.[124]

This was unlikely to succeed. Indians would not be satisfied with minor concessions. Simultaneous examinations had become for them a matter of prestige. But the authorities would not accede to this demand; because if the competitive examination ceased 'to be a farce it will become a serious danger.'[125] Nor was the Anglo-Indian prejudice likely to subside with the success of the scheme. The prejudice, having deep racial and material roots, was only superficially related to the performance of Indian officers.

The principle of Lytton's policy was laid down by James Stephen, who exercised considerable influence on the viceroy in Indian matters. Stephen felt that on 'the general principle of the way in which nat-

118. Lytton to Salisbury, 9 Feb. 1877, *Salisbury Papers*, reel 815.
119. *Ibid.*
120. Lytton to Salisbury, 10 May 1877, *ibid.*
121. Lytton to Salisbury, 16 Mar. 1877, *ibid.*
122. Lytton to Salisbury, 9 Feb. 1877, *ibid.*
123. Salisbury to Lytton, 19 Jul. 1876, *ibid.*, reel 822.
124. Salisbury to Lytton, 9 Mar. 1877, *ibid.*
125. Lytton to Salisbury, 10 May 1877, *ibid.*, reel 815.

ives should be employed' lay 'practically the fate of the empire'. It could be safeguarded to a great extent by getting 'hold of the better class of natives, by giving them plenty of places, both civil and military, thoroughly well paid according to their standard'. But inspection and superintendence had to remain 'the special function of a smaller, more highly paid and better class of Europeans'.[126]

Lytton responded faithfully. He suggested the creation of a close native service, organised on a footing entirely distinct' from the covenanted service, which was to be reserved 'exclusively for Europeans'. Scions of good families were to be attracted to it in order to secure for the government 'all the members, and all the influence of their families'.[127] It was finally decided that in the recruitment to the proposed service promotion from the uncovenanted service would be an exception, the rule being the nomination of 'young men of good family and social position, possessed of fair abilities and education'.[128] The proposal to exclude Indians from the London competition, supported by Salisbury, was negatived by Cranbrook, the new secretary of state, who had no mind to carry 'an application to Parliament, which would have no prospect of success'.[129]

Thus was fashioned into existence Lytton's brain child, the statutory civil service. Despite the support given by stray leaders like Naoroji, the Indian reaction to it was inimical. Within three days, the committee of the Indian Association had condemned the new service rules for encroaching upon the right of Indians to hold all offices, and for militating 'against the principle of admission into the Covenanted Civil Service by Open Competition, and upon equal terms with Her Majesty's British-born subjects.' The committee also corresponded with different public bodies. Messages of support were received from all over the country for its public meeting on 3 September 1879.[130] Even in the relatively placid upper India, excepting the *Aligarh Institute Gazette*, the entire Indian Press assailed the proposed rules.[131] The scheme was completely discredited as a result of the official interpretation that those nominated 'under the new rules would form a Native Civil Service' instead of being inducted to the covenanted civil service. Which meant that they would be 'kept at a distance like Pariah dogs obliged to fawn upon their master for his caresses or to crouch under his frowns.' They would never be *sahebs*,

126. Stephen to Lytton, 6 Jul. 1876, *Stephen Papers*, reel 1.
127. Lytton to Salisbury, 10 May 1877, *Salisbury Papers*, reel 815.
128. Lytton's Minute, 12 Nov. 1879, Home Department, Public Proceedings, A. Dec. 1879, Nos. 361-72.
129. Secretary of state to the government of India, 7 Nov. 1878, Philips, ed., *op. cit.*, p. 549.
130. *The Third Annual Report of the Indian Association*, Calcutta, 1880, pp. 7-11.
131. Memo. on the Vernacular Press of Upper India, Home Department, Public Proceedings, B, Apr. 1881, No. 98.

but 'sink into Rav Sahebs and Khan Bahadcors'. They would be detested by subordinates as creatures of fortune and unacceptable to
superiors as men belonging to the same class. If uncovenanted civilians were to be rarely upgraded and educated Indians nominated only
when possessing blue blood, the question arose, 'why are then our
universities established'?[132] Even the Bombay government conceded
that the scheme, while pleasing a few individuals, had disappointed
and affronted 'the general body of educated Natives'. It saw 'justice
in their dissatisfaction with a plan' which ignored their 'ambition
and aspirations'.[133]

The statutory civil service was introduced at a time when the
Arms Act, Vernacular Press Act, License Act, enhanced salt duty in
Bombay and Madras in the wake of famine. Afghan war and the remission of the import duties on cotton goods had released a flood of
feelings against the government. In the political awakening that followed, isolated grievances lost their separate character and came to
be seen as part of a national movement directed to promote the rights
and interests of Indians.

The nominations made by the government to the new service
gave rise to the complaint that the nominees normally belonged to
such families as happened 'to enjoy the favours of some elevated
official'. They represented neither the aristocracy nor the intelligence
of the country. Educated young men of independent bearing, with
no social influence to propel them, but unwilling to enter service
through the back-door of favour, were left with little chance of entering this service.[134] The Bombay government even complained that
not many candidates combining social influence with educational
qualifications were available.[135] The government of Bengal on its
own introduced the system of competition to select its nominees.[136]
Yet no change was introduced for the whole country.

Ripon perceived the danger of keeping up the discontent produced by this question among people from whom came 'the writers in
the press, the speakers at public meetings, the pleaders before our
courts, and not unfrequently the officials of Native States'.[137] He suggested a few reforms to satisfy Indians, but was overruled by the
secretary of state.[138] His efforts, embodied in his minutes of 26 Sept-

132. *Native Opinion*, 4 Jan. 1880.
133. Bombay government to the government of India, 15 Sep. 1880, Home
     Department, Public Proceedings, A, Nov. 1880 No. 49.
134. Wordsworth's letter to the *Pall Mall Gazette*, 16 Jun. 1884, in Chintamani,
     ed., *Speeches and Writings of P. M. Mehta*, pp. 207-08.
135. Bombay government to the government of India, 15 Sep. 1880, Home De-
     partment, Public Proceedings, A, Nov. 1880, No. 49.
136. *Calcutta Review*, vol. LXXVIII, pp. 228-29.
137. Ripon's Minute, 10 Sep. 1884, Philips, ed., *op. cit.*, p, 554.
138. Notes to Home Department, Public Proceedings, A, Jun. 1885, Nos. 202-
     04.

ember 1883 and 10 September 1884, impelled Indians to strengthen their agitation and convinced them of the justice of their demands.

Meanwhile, the intention of Lytton to debar Indians from the covenanted service and Cranbrook's refusal to do so had become public knowledge. The ensuing dissatisfaction was aggravated by the refusal of Kimberley, the secretary of state, to raise the upper age limit for the civil service examination when a delegation of Indians waited on him on 3 April 1884.[139]

Indians felt that there was little for them to choose in practice between the Liberals and the Conservatives;[140] more so as the Gladstone ministry had made it clear that no reliance could be placed on 'the pledges given by English politicians, not at least while they are out of power.'[141] Irrespective of party affiliations, official policy had been aimed from the outset at keeping Indians out of the civil service. However, in order to be able 'to keep a show of justice and fair play', the authorities had taken years to execute the design. But the 'effrontery' of Lytton in having recommended the segregation of Indians from the covenanted service had lifted 'the veil of secrecy'. Salisbury also, it was now evident, had been motivated likewise in his decision to reduce the age limit.[142]

Renewed activity followed the confirmation of Indian suspicion by documentary evidence. Public organs suggested that agitation should be continued till the demands were conceded.[143] Meeting followed meeting in every part of the country. Never before had so many public meetings been held to press for the same demand.[144] In 1878 the same petition had been sent on behalf of the people of India; this time the secretary of state was deluged with separate but similar petitions from all over the country.

An upper age limit of 23 years and simultaneous examinations were demanded as 'the minimum change necessary' to belie the criticism that the rules for the civil service had been framed 'if not deliberately against the just claims of the Natives of this country, at least in flagrant disregard of those claims.' What Indians asked for, the secretary of state was told, was 'strict justice'; but the distrust

139. *Ibid.*, A, Jun. 1884, No. 184.
140. *Voice of India*, 30 Apr. 1884, pp. 263-64.
141. *Ibid.*, 31 May 1884, p. 328.
142. *Bengalee*, 17 May 1884.
143. *Voice of India*, 31 May 1884, p.359.
144. Among others public meetings were organised by the Indian Association, Burdwan Association, Sadharan Hitashadini Sabha, Anjuman-i-Islam, Sind Sabha, Vengurla Hitchintak Sabha, Nasik Sarvajanik Sabha, Poona Sarvajanik Sabha and the Literary Association of Coconada; meetings were held at places like Calcutta, Tarash, Burdwan, Bombay, Poona, Satara Belgaum, Aligarh, Kanpur, Lucknow, Bangalore, and several districts of the Panjab etc. See Home Department, Public Proceedings, A, Jun. 1884, No. 184; A, Oct. 1884, No. 36; A, Mar. 1885, No. 168.

reared by periodical reductions of the age limit had made them despair of obtaining even that.[145] The frustration of educated Indians was increasing.

The civil service question was peculiarly suited to expose the incompatibility of imperial and Indian interests. The educated middle classes, who first imbibed and transmitted ideas of nationalism, had a material stake in the settlement of this question. But the circumstances essential to a foreign rule imposed limits beyond which concessions could not be given; and Indians could not submit for ever to voluntary or compulsive controls over their aspirations. The basic irritant remained imbedded in the imperial structure. Anglo-Indian administrators treated the Indian civil service as their 'personal prey'.[146] Also, the safety of the empire required that trustworthy Indians should be gradually appointed 'only in such offices and in such places as, in the actual condition of things, the Government of India may determine to be really suited to them.'[147] Open competition could however, offer no test of trustworthiness. In view of the loyalty of contemporary educated Indians to British rule, the wisdom of this suspicion may be doubted. But the official policy was to make just as much, or as little, concession as was necessary to prevent Indians from losing faith in the efficacy of constitutional agitation. Open competition was also ruled out by the authorities on the ground of the conditions prevailing in India. Some races, though educationally backward, it was argued, possessed greater vigour, courage and administrative ability. There also existed, in many parts of the country, a strong influence of social rank and caste. These were elements 'altogether alien to the system of competitive examination', and necessitated that 'each Province and Race should be treated by itself'.[148]

Educated Indians tried to rebut these arguments by pointing to their loyalty, educational advance, moral improvement and the untenabiliy of the claim that Indians preferred to be administered by foreigners as compared to their own countrymen. Condemned before it was created,[149] the statutory civil service, had made its members 'the laughing stock of all India'.[150] By artifices like this the authorities had kept Indians virtually out of high offices. In 1885, out of 909 covenanted civilians only 20 were Indians. In the uncovenanted service there existed whole departments without an Indian getting Rs. 200 or more a month. The opium department had 125 such European officers and no Indian; the marine department had 30 Europeans and

145. Memorial of the Bombay Branch of the East India Association to Kimberley, Home Department, Public Proceedings, B, Oct. 1884, Nos. 185-87.
146. Lytton to Salisbury, 28 Sep. 1876, *Salisbury Papers*, reel 814.
147. Educational Despatch to India, No. 3, 8 Apr. 1869, *Argyll Papers*, reel 315.
148. *Ibid.*
149. *Indu Prakash*, 5 May 1884.
150. *Native Opinion*, 21 Oct. 1883.

no Indian; the salt and customs departments had a solitary Indian out of 178 officers; the medical department had 27 Indians out of 188 officers; and the police department had 60 Indians out of 425 officers.

In terms of emoluments, the disparity was more glaring—in Bengal, out of Rs. 2, 14,803, Indians got Rs. 34,883; in Bombay, Rs. 22,178 out of Rs. 2,37,540; in all India, about 70,000 out of about 800,000. In fact Europeans got 91½ per cent. of the total emoluments paid to the uncovenanted service.[151]

The civil service question naturally became for Indians 'the most important key to our material and moral advancement'.[152] Employment of foreign agency meant a constant material and moral drain from India. This could not be minimised without transferring to India 'examinations for all the higher services in all the civil departments'.[153] Without 'this reform of all reforms', all 'other political reforms' would be of little avail. It was not simply a question of satisfying the aspirations of educated Indians, but one of 'poverty or prosperity', 'life and death to India'.[154]

The views of the authorities and educated Indians thus ran on parallel lines which promised to meet nowhere. Here was a question which could exasperate Indians and strengthen their resolve to fight, but a satisfactory solution of which was precluded by the circumstances of British rule. In 1885 Indians stood on the verge of this realisation. They had lost faith in the secretary of state and the government of India, 'the active obstacles' in their way.[155] But faith in the people and parliament of Britain still lingered. Maybe this was due to the absence of an alternative course of action in the existing state of the country. Even this vestige of faith was bound to give way.

II

Freedom of the Press was another privilege which brought educated Indians and the authorities into conflict. Before its grant in 1835, Indians had discovered in this concept a safeguard against executive absolutism in the absence of representative institutions.[156] Realisation of its importance increased proportionately with education and public awakening.

151. *Indu Prakash,* 12 Oct. 1885.
152. *Proceedings of the First Indian National Congress,* p. 41.
153. Naoroji, 'The Indian Civil Service', 1884. Parekh, ed., *op. cit.* pp. 500-03.
154. *Proceedings of the First Indian National Congress,* p. 41.
155. *Native Opinion,* 31 Aug. 1879.
156. See the memorials against Adam's Press Regulation of 14 Mar. 1823, to the Calcutta supreme court and the King in council. J. C. Ghose, ed., *The English Works of Raja Rammohun Roy,* vol. II, Calcutta, 1901, pp. 278-319.

The crisis of 1857 necessitated a temporary curb on the Press. The indiscriminate attacks of the Anglo-Indian journals made Indians welcome the curb as a measure of relief. The *Hindoo Patriot* found in the action taken against the *Dacca News*, the *Bengal Hurkaru* and the *Friend of India* an answer to the demand of the Anglo-Indian Press that its Indian counterpart should be manacled.[157]

For a decade, in spite of its growth after 1857, the Indian Press gave the authorities no reason to move against it.[158] But the defiance of the Anglo-Indian Press induced them to propose an official organ as a counterpoise;[159] though the idea was finally dropped after four years of discussion.[160] The Anglo-Indian Press, however, apprehending the signs of maturity and independence exhibited by its Indian counterpart, demanded measures to curb it. The latter reacted sharply to such suggestions. Claiming to be the only interpreter between the rulers and the ruled, it warned that a revolt would ensue from restrictions on its freedom.[161] A boiler had to be provided with a valve.[162] Moreover, it was the Anglo-Indian Press which had been sowing the seeds of revolution by creating misunderstanding between the government and the people.[163]

While antipathy developed between the Indian and the Anglo-Indian Press, the authorities were realising the inadequacy of the existing law to deal with objectionable articles. Nothing short of 'waging war against the Queen' or abetment thereof was legally punishable. A section in the original draft of the Penal Code had made it an offence to excite feelings of disaffection towards the government.[164] This was incorporated in 1870 by amending section 5 of the Indian Penal Code which now became section 124A of the Code.[165]

Progressing intellectually and 'day by day attaching very high value to the liberty of speech and writing', Indians protested the moment this amendment was proposed. If the section was deleted when the legislature 'had before its mind's eye the most vivid recollections of the political events of 1857', the 'profound peace' of 1870 was no justification for its insertion.[166] Even 'though intended to apply to "attempts to excite feelings of disaffection to the Government"', the revived clause would 'in practice seriously interfere with

157. *Hindoo Patriot*, 24 Sep. 1857.
158. Lawrence to Cranborne, 8 Nov. 1866, *Lawrence Collection*, reel 2.
159. Lawrence to Wood, 21 Dec. 1865, *ibid.*
160. Mayo to Argyll, 14 Mar. 1869, *Argyll Papers*, reel 311.
161. *Amrita Bazar Patrika, Report on Native Press, Bengal*, 20 Feb. 1869, p. 5.
162. *Som Prakash, ibid.*, 8 Aug. 1868, p. 2.
163. *Amrita Bazar Patrika, ibid.*, 20 Feb. 1869, p. 5.
164. Strachey to Lawrence, 28 Jul. 1868, *Lawrence Collection*, reel 5.
165. M. Barns, *The Indian Press*, London, 1940, p. 269.
166. Memorial of the Poona Sarvajanik Sabha to the government of India, 9 Sep. 1870, *Native Opinion*, 18 Sep. 1870. *Rast Goftar* was an exception and gave the amendment a qualified support, 4 Dec. 1870.

the liberty of speech and writing'. More particularly, it 'would in times of political excitement be a source of serious mischief and liable to great abuse.' Also objectionable, apart from the unnecessary haste in the proceedings, was the fact that 'nothing analogous to the proposed measure' existed in the English law.[167] It was no satisfaction to be assured by Strachey that the law would take cognizance of the motive of the accused, and that nobody would be punished unless he incited opposition to the government. There could be no guarantee that people would not be called upon too often to prove their intentions. The modified law would silence them just as they had started speaking freely, and benefit neither the government nor the people.[168] The move seemed especially alarming because it was seen as a part of the increasing executive severity towards the people. They had been disarmed and the expenditure on their education curtailed; now their voice was being muzzled.[169]

The amended law was not enforced; and it was not powerful enough to exercise a deterrent effect. Feelings against the government—flowing from numerous directions—continued to find manifestation in the Indian Press with increasing force and freedom. Mainly because it required proof of the seditious intention of the writer, the authorities in India started doubting whether even section 124A of the Indian Penal Code was enough to cope with the Press.

Requesting the government of India for modification of the law, the lieutenant-governor of Bengal referred, in 1873, to the difficulty of proving seditious motives on the part of 'wretched Bengali scribblers' whom no one credited with 'the courage to do anything else than to render obedience' to the government. Further, the 'amount of litigation and scandal' involved in prosecution 'would make the cure worse than the disease'. The authorities, consequently, could do nothing beyond issuing warnings that invariably proved ineffectual, thus making the matter 'worse and worse'. But publications which meant nothing in Bengal could, when read and copied in other parts of the country, become 'highly inflammatory and dangerous'. The lieutenant-governor favoured 'a law to punish summarily and severely, without all the eclat of a long prosecution for sedition, those who write and publish mischievous and seditious libels on the Government, and to shut up newspapers which are the vehicles of this language.'[170]

167. *Report of a General Meeting of the British Indian Association held on 22 September 1870*, p. 1.
168. *Bombay Samachar*, 13 Sep. 1870, *Report on Native Press, Bombay*, 17 Sep. 1870, p. 9.
169. *Indu Prakash*, 26 Sep. 1870, *Report on Native Press*, I Oct. 1870, p. 9.
170. Government of Bengal to Government of India 2 Aug. 1873, Home Department, Judicial Proceedings, A, May 1878, No. 96.

The following year, F. P. Lely (1846-?) I.C.S., condemned, in the *Indian Economist*, the objectionable nature of writings in the Indian Press. The Baroda affair further excited the Indian Press, and two articles on the subject were reproduced from the *Amrita Bazar Patrika* by the *Pall Mall Gazette*. This obliged the secretary of state to enquire of the government of India if any action was being contemplated against the *Patrika*.[171] The government of India did not favour prosecution 'except in the case of systematic attempts to excite hostility against the Government', because failure to obtain conviction would be 'most damaging', and 'a prosecution, even if successful, would probably occasion greater public excitement than the occasional publication of such attacks'.[172]

A formidable difficulty, which was emphasised by Hobhouse but deliberately not conveyed to the secretary of state, was the habitual use of improper language by 'some of the Anglo-Indian papers'. It was 'calculated greatly to encourage the Native Press in their hostility to the Government'. One Anglo-Indian journal or another was 'perpetually' denouncing the administrators as 'blockheads and blunderers' and 'oppressors of the country'. The tariff of 1875, for instance, was condemned 'as a wicked betrayal of the interests of India to the interests of the English traders'. There was, Hobhouse asserted, 'no substantial difference between such sentiments and those of the *Patrika* to the effect that we poison one nation with opium and emasculate another by stopping education.' Neither meant 'anything beyond noisy bluster intended to sell the paper'. But even if it did, it was prudent to let discontent find expression. Indian newspapers supplied to some extent the lack of other systematic expression of sentiments which it concerned the rulers to know.[173]

Though the authorities were in a state of irresolution, the attention bestowed upon the Press appeared portentous to Indians. They justified their Press, explained its difficulties, reiterated its loyalty and argued for the retention of its freedom.[174] Yet they anticipated the 'forfeiture of the boon secured to us by the exertions of Metcalfe, Bentinck and Macaulay'. 'In the boasted land of liberty', foreboded the *Bengalee*, 'the Parliament has gagged the Irish Press, and in India the Government which passed Act XV of 1857 is not likely to be oversqueamish in dealing with the Native Press.'[175]

It was, however, through theatrical representations that restric-

171. Secretary of state to the government of India, 16 May 1875, Home Department, Judicial Proceedings, A, Apr. 1878, No. 202.
172. Government of India to the secretary of state, 6 Sep. 1875, *ibid.*, 206.
173. Note by Hobhouse, 18 Aug. 1875, *ibid.* Arthur Hobhouse (1819-1904) was the legal member of the supreme council, 1872-77.
174. *Native Opinion*, 2 Aug. 1874, 20 Jun. 1875; *Bengalee*, 2 Jan. 1875.
175. *Bengalee*, 30 Jan. 1875.

tion was first imposed on the freedom of expression. The lieutenant-governor of Bengal having complained that the Bengali drama had become intolerably insolent, an ordinance was issued empowering him to prohibit objectionable dramatic performances. On 14 March 1876 was introduced a Bill to invest the government with the power to prevent the staging of a play of defamatory, obscene or seditious character.[176]

This was immediately attacked by Indians as a prelude to the contraction of the freedom of the Press.[177] This premonition was confirmed by the report of the London correspondent of the *Bombay Gazette* that 'the Government contemplate shortly issuing an important regulation affecting the Indian newspapers'.[178] A meeting was held, on 4 April 1876 at Bhawanipur, Calcutta, to protest against the ordinance and the proposed legislation. It was attended by about 'two hundred gentlemen belonging to the respectable classes, principally pleaders of the High Court and the Judge's Court, Alipore, and independent gentlemen of property'.[179] Similar meetings were held at Kanpur, Lucknow and Allahabad also.[180]

The protest marked a distinct advance in the political awakening of Indians. It indicated, as the *Englishman* observed, that Indians were being agitated by 'abstract questions'. It was not a matter like taxation or conservancy that touched their pockets. Awareness 'of the importance of the principle involved, rather than a loving enthusiasm for the drama' or 'mere factiousness' had given birth to the agitation.[181] Though the question was not purely abstract, it is remarkable that only its political aspect excited Indians. While admitting the necessity of control over immoral or libellous plays, they wanted freedom for performances which expressed 'appropriate sentiments on political matters'.[182]

In this state of apprehensiveness, representatives of many Indian newspapers were invited to the Delhi *darbar*. They waited on the viceroy with an address praying that 'the rights and privileges' enjoyed by them as a body 'may be continued and extended both for

176. Temple to Salisbury, 29 Aug. 1875, *Salisbury Papers*, reel 818; and 3 Mar 1876, ibid., reel 819; *Abstract of the Proceedings of the Council of the Governor-General of India*, vol. XV, pp. 73 ff.
177. For a detailed criticism of the ordinance and the proposed Bill, see *Mookerjee's Magazine*, Jan.-Jun. 1876, pp. 125-67. Also see *Report of a General Meeting of the British Indian Association held on 15 September 1875*, p. 2, and *Report of the 25th Annual General Meeting of the British Indian Association held on 12 May 1877*, pp. 2-3.
178. *Native Opinion*, 5 Mar. 1876.
179. *Bengalee*, 8 Apr. 1876.
180. *Ibid.*, 20 May 1876.
181. *Englishman*, 9 May 1876.
182. *Bombay Samachar*, 6 Mar. 1876, *Report on Native Press, Bombay*, 11 Mar. 1876, p. 9.

the benefit of British rule and the promotion of the best interests of
the people at large.' The viceroy was silent about the continuance
and extension of their rights. But there was an ominous note in his
expression of the confidence that 'the privileges enjoyed by you will
not be abused.'[183] Treating the 'baboos' as of 'no importance', Lytton
actually hoped to overawe 'some of their most ambitious and noisy
representatives, such as the Editors of the Calcutta Native Press' by
confronting them 'with the powerful representatives of other native
races—who would grind them and theirs into powder' in case the
British were to withdraw their protection.[184]

Adherence to the policy of winning over the aristocratic classes
had incapacitated Lytton from perceiving the transformation within
the Indian society that involved a shift in leadership. Deriving his
lessons from the study of European history, he failed to discern the
history that was being enacted in India in his own time and, to a degree, through his own instrumentality. The experience at the *darbar*,
far from demoralising the baboos, inspired the fruition of the idea of
a Press Association and Press Conference to be held 'at some central
place once or twice a year for discussing and adopting measures, if
possible, for protecting the interests of the Press and of the country
at large'.[185]

It was Ashley Eden who gave a clear warning to the Indian Press
by referring to its 'growing tendency to criticise the work of Government and the intentions and actions of public officers in a spirit
which was distinctly disloyal, and sometimes seditious'.[186] But neither Lytton nor Eden could induce a change of tone beyond adding
to the bitterness of Indians. 'When a Government is determined on
finding sedition, there will be little difficulty in finding it.'[187] But determined to resist 'wicked tyrants', Indians would not be awed even
by British bayonets to 'call oppression by the misnomer of kind treatment'.[188]

This intrepidity was symptomatic of the growth of national consciousness during the preceding 20 years. No longer could the rulers

183. *Native Opinion*, 14 Jan. 1877.
184. Lytton to Salisbury, 19 Jan. 1877, *Salisbury Papers*, reel 815.
185. *Native Opinion*, 31 Dec. 1877. For the early history of the idea, see *Indian
    Daily News*, 11 Oct. 1873; *Native Opinion*, 4, 11 Jan. 1874. The first con-
    ference was held in Calcutta on 14 Jan. 1878 with about 300 delegates from
    Bengal. The Poona Sarvajanik Sabha sent a letter of support. *Native
    Opinion*, 27 Jan. 1878. On 29 Mar. 1878 another Native Press Conference
    was held in Bombay with representatives from Bombay, Poona, Surat,
    Nasik, Thana, Ratnagiri and Dhulia; *ibid.*, 31 Mar. 1878.
186. Home Department, Judicial Proceedings, A, Apr. 1878, No. 229. Sir Ashley
    Eden (1831-87) was the lieutenant-governor of Bengal, 1877-82.
187. *Bengalee*, 1 Sep. 1877.
188. *Bharat Sanskarak*, 31 Dec. 1877, *Report on Native Press, Bengal*, 12 Jan.
    1878, pp. 4-5.

'take account of local nationalities and particular races'. They had to deal 'with 200 millions of people united by sympathies and intercourse'. The Indian Press had begun to 'appeal to the whole native population of India against their foreign rulers'.[189] But Lytton, contemptuous of the educated middle classes, could not gauge the efficacy of the new spirit. He hoped to crush it by the exhibition and, if necessary, use of force.

But legislation about the Press was a delicate matter on which hinged the character of the British Indian government. Salisbury anticipated 'the obloquy which any such legislation will provoke in England', though he admitted that this would have 'to be done some day'.[190] More important, however, was the 'deeper and wider question' that restrictive legislation involved. It was whether Indians were to be educated or kept ignorant. For, as Hobhouse argued, acquisition of knowledge and freedom of speech inevitably produced 'some unpleasant excesses'. The British had chosen the generous and wise policy of encouraging both. Increasing knowledge was making Indians impatient to obtain power and liable 'to use their tongues without discretion'. But these drawbacks were the essential price of having 'a more intelligent and less reticent people in India'.[191]

Hobhouse further maintained that a measure affecting the vernacular Press alone would be 'class legislation of the most striking and invidious description, at variance with the whole tenor of our policy, and only to be justified by the most cogent proofs of danger from the maltreated class'. The government could hardly lay down that the same thing would be innocent if said by an English newspaper, and criminal if said by a Native one'.[192] Even Lytton attributed 'the extravagant improprieties of the vernacular Press largely, if not mainly, to the bad example set to Native journalists by their English contemporaries in India'. He went to the extent of saying that only European journalism in India could 'seriously embarrass or weaken the Government'.[193]

But the fundamental difficulty of the government arose from the fact that the grievances—the expression of which in the vernacular Press had instigated Lytton to embark on legislation—contained 'an unfortunate element of truth'. Restrictive enactment might bring about external decency of expression; but not without generating 'an

189. Memo. by W. B. Jones, 28 Feb. 1878, Home Department, Judicial Proceedings, A, Apr. 1878, No. 216.
190. Salisbury to Lytton, 30 Aug. 1877, *Salisbury Papers*, reel 822.
191. Minute by Hobhouse, 10 Aug. 1876, Home Department, Judicial Proceedings, A, Apr. 1878, No. 215. The whole of this minute was reproduced in *Supplement to the Bengalee*, 3 Aug. 1878, as an indictment of Lytton's policy.
192. Minute by Hobhouse, 10 Aug. 1876, quoted above.
193. Circular of 20 Dec. 1877, Home Department, Public Proceedings, A, Oct. 1878, Nos. 127-29, K.W.

amount of smouldering impatience, dissatisfaction, possibly disaffection, which would only gain strength and consistency by repression
of its blaze'. Under the existing law, the government could know the
worst that was said of it, if not also the worst that was thought about
it. But 'this immense advantage' would be lost by curtailing the freedom of expression.[194]

There also loomed the danger of distrust and hostile feelings
being implanted in the minds of those who were 'best affected towards Government'. No measure was 'more likely to confirm' the impression that the British were untrue to their 'pledges and principles'
than the withdrawal of what Indians had 'come to look on as a constitutional privilege'.[195]

But Lytton had made up his mind.[196] He decided to use the Russo-
Turkish war as a justification for urgent action. This war, he persuaded Salisbury, had produced among Indians an 'undisguised disbelief
in the British Power', leaving the authorities to depend on their
actual force unaided by the power which they had hitherto been
supposed to possess. The British 'hold upon India was perhaps never
more uncertain'. The year 1878 being feared to be 'a very critical and
anxious one', repressive legislation was 'urgently called for'.[197]

With his usual penchant for rationalisation and self-delusion,
Lytton predicted that the contemplated legislation would occasion
but 'a short sharp shriek at the first blow'.[198] The merit of his pre-
diction apart, he overlooked the fact that his action was not designed
to solve the problem. Having admitted that the vernacular Press
would be greatly improved by the injection of a more loyal spirit in
the Anglo-Indian Press, Lytton should have understood that no measure that left the Anglo-Indian Press alone could have been effective.
But he lacked the courage to follow the logic of his analysis, and
risk, soon after the Fuller controversy, another spurt of European
hostility. Unable to meet Hobhouse's serious objections, Lytton followed, perhaps against his own better judgment, the line of least
resistance.[199] By his timidity in relation to the Anglo-Indian Press,
Lytton not only exposed the government to the charge of racial discrimination, but also nullified considerably whatever advantages
might have accrued from restrictive legislation.

The Indian reaction to the Vernacular Press Act vindicated Lyt-

194. Minute by Hudleston, 25 Feb. 1878, Home Department, Judicial Proceed-
     ings, A, Apr. 1878, No. 218.
195. Minute by Robinson, 28 Jan. 1878, ibid.
196. Minute by Lytton, 28 Oct. 1877, ibid., Nos. 211, 216.
197. Lytton to Salisbury, 15 Feb. 1878, Salisbury Papers, reel 816.
198. Lytton to Salisbury, 1 Mar. 1878, ibid.
199. It is interesting to note that Lytton looked upon Hobhouse as 'the Evil
     genius of Northbrook's administration'. Lytton to Salisbury, 21 Nov. 1876,
     ibid., reel 815. Indians, on the other hand, respected Hobhouse as 'an Eng-
     lishman to the core'; Bengalee 27 Jul. 1878.

ton's critics inside the administration. In certain respects it virtually re-echoed them. In spite of their presentient fears, the Act shocked and agitated Indians. In the constriction of the freedom of the Press they visualised a diminution of the possibilities of constitutional agitation. The vernacular Press had criticised misrule and conveyed to the rulers 'the feelings and the wants of the people'. The suppression of its freedom was 'highly mischievous in its tendencies and fraught with consequences prejudicial to the best interests of the people'. With Damocles' sword hanging over his head, no man could write fearlessly, more so as absolute power, as given by this Act, would exercise a deleterious effect on the rulers.[200]

The *Hitechchhu* symbolised the Indian reaction by inserting a paragraph within black borders lamenting that 'on the 14th March, 1878, in the 41st year of the reign of Her Majesty the Queen of England and the Empress of India, the Vernacular Press of India was cruelly massacred by the hands of Lord Lytton.'[201]

The protest meeting organised by the Indian Association, on 17 April 1878, demonstrated the strength of educated Indian opinion against this measure. Neither the dissociation of the British Indian Association from the projected protest nor the fear of being considered disloyal could deter the leaders of the Indian Association.[202] Messages from numerous associations, leaders and journalists in different parts of the country expressed their 'feeling of dismay and consternation'. The Town Hall was packed with people, and hundreds of persons had to go back for lack of even standing accommodation. The proceedings lasted four hours and great enthusiasm prevailed throughout.[203]

Lytton might persist in his contempt for the baboos. But the baboos in Bengal emerged from the agitation against his Press Act as the political leaders of society, and discredited the classes courted by him. The claim of the middle class leadership to represent the people was put forth rather pompously at the Calcutta meeting against the

200. 'Censorship of the Vernacular Press', *Quarterly Journal of the Poona Sarvajanik Sabha,* vol. I, No. 1, pp. 15-6.

201. *Hitechchhu,* 28 Mar. 1878, *Report on Native Press, Bombay,* 6 Apr. 1878, pp. 9-10.

202. News reached Calcutta on the day fixed for this meeting that Disraeli had directed the despatch of 6,000 Indian troops to Malta. The lawyer friends of Ananda Mohan Bose warned him of serious consequences if the meeting took place in spite of the uncertain European situation. But S. N. Banerji insisted that 'it was one of the first great demonstrations of the Indian Association and of the middle class party in Bengal, and that, if it were to be postponed, it would never again be held'. This would discredit the new party, and 'mean the beginning of the end.' Banerjea, *op. cit.,* pp. 61-2.

203. *Report of the Proceedings of a Public Meeting on the Vernacular Press Act held in the Town Hall on Wednesday, the 17th of April 1878,* Calcutta, 1878, col. i, p. 1.

Act. Referring to the leaders of the British Indian Association, Rash Behary Ghosh (1845-1921), a lawyer, said that the 'Maharajas and Rajas' and the 'Nawabs and Khan Bahadurs' were 'only the Corinthian capitals of Society', who could 'add grace and beauty to the structure' without constituting 'the structure itself'.[204] The leadership of the British Indian Association was censured in the Press and on the platform. The vote of its honorary secretary, Jotindra Mohan Tagore, in favour of the Act was regarded as a betrayal of national interests, and his effigy was burnt by students in Dacca. It was publicly talked about that the viceroy had sent for Tagore before the Vernacular Press Bill was rushed through.[205] The deliberate quiet of the Association was also attributed to the reluctance of its leaders to displease Eden. Being the lieutenant-governor's 'friends and favourites', the few individuals who managed the Association 'did not wish to attack his favourite Press Act'.[206]

The Poona Sarvajanik Sabha also organised a protest meeting, on 2 May, at which animated speeches were delivered to condemn the Act.[207] This, too, provided a sharp contrast to the lukewarm stand of the Bombay and the British Indian Associations. The Bombay Association, it may be added, decided to postpone a petition to parliament for fear of embarrassing the government.[208]

The elaborate official justification of this measure carried no conviction with Indians, who subjected it to close scrutiny and incisive reasoning. Glaring inconsistencies in the debate on the Bill were pointed out. Arbuthnot had stressed the desirability of introducing the measure at a time of peace rather than one of political disturbance, 'when it would be attributed to panic'.[209] But Evans had found 'special urgency' for the measure in 'the disturbed state of the political horizon and the agitation of men's minds by wars and rumours of wars'.[210] Neither of these contradictory assertions explained official motivation, which actually was to arm the government to deal with cases 'in which a criminal prosecution would simply be ridiculous'.[211] Indians made light of the three reasons advanced by the govern-

204. Speech at the Calcutta meeting of 17 Apr. 1878, quoted above, col. i, p. 4.
205. Banerjea, *op. cit.*, pp. 59-60.
206. *Sahachar*, 26 Aug. 1878, *Report on Native Press, Bengal*, 31 Aug. 1878, pp. 6-7.
207. *Quarterly Journal of the Poona Sarvajanik Sabha*, vol. I, No. 2, pp. 1 ff.
208. *Native Opinion*, 31 Mar. 1878.
209. Legislative Department Proceedings, A, Mar. 1878, Nos. 143-47, p. 8. Sir Alexander John Arbuthnot (1822-1907) served the Madras government in various capacities before becoming a member of the supreme council, 1875-80; the Bill was piloted by him.
210. *Ibid.*, p. 13. G.H.P. Evans (1840-1902), barrister, was a member of the supreme legislative council.
211. Speech by H.R. Fink at the Calcutta meeting, 17 Apr. 1878, quoted above, col. ii, p. 11.

ment for this measure. The official contention about the evil effect of seditious writings on the unenlightened masses was countered by the assertion that they did not read newspapers, as hardly one per cent. of them were literate.[212] India had 'not yet reached that state of blessedness', quipped Banerji, when her peasants might be seen 'ploughing with the one hand, and holding the *Sulav Samachar* in the other.'[213] Moreover, as even the British Indian Association was constrained to observe, the vernacular Press could not be regarded as a public danger insomuch as it was neither disloyal nor seditious.[214] In selecting some excerpts to justify restrictions, the government had taken into consideration only what could be interpreted as seditious. This was in keeping with the viceroy's habit of seeing just what he wanted to see.[215]

In any case, if a stray paper tended to be disloyal, it was not good policy 'to place restrictions on the whole body for the sake of certain wild members'. 'The British Lion should not have been thrown into excitement by the buzzing of a few gnats.'[216] Should it, however, become necessary to punish a guilty editor, the existing law was sufficiently effective. Surely, it had not been proved otherwise.[217] Supposing that the government had found it inadequate, the right course would have been to modify the Indian Penal Code.[218] Instead, a vague and arbitrary measure had been imposed, making it dangerous to conduct a newspaper.[219]

Granting, the argument proceeded, that the vernacular Press was seditious, the Act could not convert seditious men into loyal subjects.[220] No effect could be 'guarded against without removing the cause'. It was a poor physician who promised 'to effect a cure simply by suppressing the symptoms of a disease without taking any steps for rendering its cause or causes inoperative.'[221] There were in India certain patent sources of complaint like increasing taxation, impo-

212. *Kiran*, 17 Mar. 1878, *Report on Native Press, Bombay*, 23 Mar. 1878, p. 8.
213. Banerji's speech at the Calcutta meeting, 17 Apr. 1878, quoted above, col. i, p. 8.
214. Petition of the British Indian Association to the governor-general in council, 20 Sep. 1878. Home Department. Judicial Proceedings, B, Oct. 1878, Nos. 165-69.
215. *Indu Prakash*, 25 Mar. 1878, *Report on Native Press, Bombay*, 30 Mar. 1878, pp. 6-7.
216. *Bengalee*, 16 Mar. 1878.
217. Petition of the British Indian Association, 20 Sep. 1878, quoted above.
218. *Jame Jamsed*, 19 Mar. 1878, *Report on Native Press, Bombay*, 23 Mar. 1878, p. 11.
219. *Arunodaya*, 24 Mar. 1878, *ibid.*, 30 Mar. 1878, p. 9.
220. *Native Opinion*, 17 Mar. 1878.
221. 'Censorship of the Vernacular Press', *Quarterly Journal of the Poona Sarvajanik Sabha*, vol. I, No. 1, p. 13.

verishment of the country and the drain on its resources.[222] Discontent could not be removed so long as these causes remained.[223] The only remedy lay in representative government without which discontent would continue, the Vernacular Press Act notwithstanding.[224] A quasi-philosophical note was struck by the *Sadharani* which viewed discontent as the essence of body politic. Dissatisfaction with the present bred the urge for a better lot. If fear of government deterred newspapers from fostering this feeling, it was better for them to cease to exist.[225]

The second reason officially furnished for the Act was that the vernacular Press had been engendering racial antipathies. Even if this were so, the Anglo-Indian Press had been no innocent lamb in this respect; and to gag one party while leaving the other free was 'eminently calculated to increase and perpetuate the very evil sought to be removed.'[226] The *Gujarat Mitra*, two articles of which on racialism had been pronounced seditious by the government, put the issue bluntly:[227]

> If the officers of Government, sitting on the sacred seat of justice, deal out justice to two persons in two different ways: have one law for punishing Europeans and another law for punishing Natives; punish a Native murderer with death by hanging, but punish a European murderer with two years' imprisonment; if cases of diseased spleen frequently arise; if numerous Natives lost their lives every year, and if Government was slandered for it uselessly, are we, public writers, to see these things mutely? By the publication of such matters in newspapers it is true that hostility arises among the people, but is it right to exercise control over writers writing on such subjects; or is it not rather right to adopt measures to prevent causes for such writings?

Sensitive to discrimination, Indians reacted sharply to this 'altogether unusual and unjustifiable' distinction.[228] No vernacular paper ever wrote as pungently as the *Statesman* and other Anglo-Indian journals did.[229] It was difficult to understand how similar matter be-

222. Petition of the Bombay Branch of the East India Association to the House of Commons, 18 Aug. 1878, Home Department, Judicial Proceedings, B, Oct. 1878, No. 161.
223. Speech by Fink at the Calcutta meeting, 17 Apr. 1878, quoted above, col. ii, p. 12.
224. *Sahachar*, 18 Mar. 1878, *Report on Native Press, Bengal*, 30 Mar. 1878, pp. 4-5.
225. *Sadharani*, 17 Mar. 1878, *ibid.*, 23 Mar. 1878, p. 8
226. K. L. Nulkar's speech at the Poona meeting of 2 May 1878, *Quarterly Journal of the Poona Sarvajanik Sabha*, vol. I, No. 2, p. 17.
227. *Gujarat Mitra*, 31 Mar. 1878, *Report on Native Press, Bombay*, 6 Apr. 1878, pp. 10-1.
228. Petition of the Bombay Branch of the East India Association, 18 Aug. 1878, quoted above.
229. *Som Prakash*, 18 Mar. 1878, *Report on Native Press, Bengal*, 23 Mar. 1878, p. 9.

came treasonable in a vernacular paper though it remained justifiable so long as published in the English papers.[230] Rev. K. S. Macdonald (1832-1903), a missionary of the United Free Church Mission and widely respected in Bengal, felt that this 'invidious distinction' had put a sting into the Act which would 'inevitably cause discontent and disaffection, and will tend also to create disloyalty and sedition if anything will.'[231]

Indians dismissed as a mere pretence the third reason for the Act. This pertained to the intimidation of and annoyance to Indian officials and princes. Indian officers of the government were educated and could be 'safely trusted to take the ample remedies provided by the existing law against the alleged injuries.' The princes had 'long since learnt to bear with equanimity, if not stolid indifference, such newspaper criticism as may reach their ears.' However, if the government was really so anxious to spare their feelings, there existed 'a vast field' in the 'political department for sowing contentment broadcast without any sacrifice of principle, much less of such a great principle as that of the Liberty of the Press.'[232]

Even the haste with which the Act was passed could not impress its urgency upon Indians. Kali Charan Banerji exposed its true character by distinguishing between a haste that was 'the outcome of objective pressure—uncontrollable objective pressure', and one that was 'the outcome of deliberation'. This was actually a 'most objectionable law' enacted in a 'most objectionable haste'.[233]

The official reasons having been dismissed as 'illogical and without any foundation in fact',[234] the Act was represented as 'the crowning-piece'[235] of a class of legislation which the government, by abusing its legislative authority, had of late been passing to aggrandise 'the Executive in India at the expense of the Judiciary'. This had weakened the rule of law and deprived the people of a privilege which had 'in a very great degree made up for some of the inevitable disadvantages of dependence on a foreign power'. It would also arrest 'the political and intellectual progress of the country'.[236] The tendency of the Act was clear from the absence of the provision of judicial

230. *Kiran*, 24 Mar. 1878, *Report on Native Press, Bombay*, 30 Mar. 1878, p. 9.
231. Macdonald's speech at the Calcutta meeting, 17 Apr. 1878, quoted above, col. i, p. 4.
232. K. L. Nulkar's speech at the Poona meeting, 2 May 1878, quoted above, p. 17.
233. K. C. Banerji's speech at the Calcutta meeting, 17 Apr. 1878, quoted above, col. ii, p. 13.
234. K. L. Nulkar's speech at the Poona meeting, 2 May 1878, quoted above. p. 18.
235. *Poona Herald*, 20 Mar. 1878, *Report on Native Press, Bombay*, 23 Mar. 1878, p. 9.
236. Petition of the Bombay Branch of the East India Association, 18 Aug. 1873, quoted above.

trial, permitted even under the Irish Peace Preservation Act, which made the government judge, prosecutor and witness at the same time. So unanimous was the feeling on this point that when the Act was about to be amended, all the political associations petitioned for the provision of judicial trial.[237]

Equally obnoxious was the application of the Act to Oriental literature. No nation could rise without developing its literature. Vernacular literature had not been shown to have betrayed 'the same mischievous tendencies that had been alleged against some of the Vernacular newspapers'.[238] Yet, the Act had been applied to it with immediate detrimental effect. In Bengal, for instance, no printer was prepared to undertake 'so important and valuable a work as a Bengali History of the Mutiny of 1857'.[239]

Like Lytton's other measures, the Vernacular Press Act contributed to the erosion of faith in the government of India. But it also strengthened the hope of Indians that redress could be obtained from England, which was looked upon as the home of freedom and the hope of the down-trodden.[240] The criticism of the Act in parliament led Surendranath Banerji to remark that 'before a word of protest was publicly raised in this country, those ardent advocates of human freedom and of liberty of speech, had already called in question, in the House of Commons, the wisdom, the policy and the justice of this most objectionable law.'[241] This faith was confirmed by the repeal of the Act.

The Vernacular Press Act quickened political life in the country. Agitation against it was kept up till its repeal, and carried from important towns to the interior by the Indian Association and the Sarvajanik Sabha.[242] The placid regions of the mofussil were animated politically, and a larger flow of people was drawn into the vortex of national politics.

The Vernacular Press Act was eventually admitted to have been a mistake. While violating the principle of equality before the law,

237. Telegram from the Indian Association to the government of India, 5 Sep. 1878, Home Department, Judicial Proceedings, B, Oct. 1878, Nos. 161, 165-69.

238. Petition of the British Indian Association, 20 Sep. 1878, quoted above.

239. Petition of the Bombay Branch of the East India Association, 18 Aug. 1878, quoted above; Home Department, Judicial Proceedings, B, Oct. 1878, Nos. 165-69. This related to the third part of a work by Rajni Kanta Gupta, a Bengali author of considerable repute.

240. Speech by Rash Behary Ghosh at the Calcutta meeting, 17 Apr. 1878, quoted above, col. i, p. 5.

241. Speech by S. N. Banerji at the Calcutta meeting, 17 Apr. 1878, quoted above, col. i-ii, p. 11. The Calcutta public meeting thanked those members of parliament who had spoken 'on behalf of the unrepresented millions of India', ibid; col. ii, p. 14.

242. See Home Department, Public Proceedings, B, Apr. 1881, Nos. 12-3.

and provoking 'strong feelings of discontent and resentment', it had
made little impression on the vernacular Press in regard to the use of
language inimical to British rule.[243] It was, consequently, repealed
not long after Lytton's departure.

The repeal dissolved the agitation. But the breach between the
claims of the ruled and the constraints of the rulers continued as better understanding by Indians of their collective interests and progressive disenchantment with the authorities worked towards a major
confrontation between them. In this struggle, Indians would utilise
the Press, as they had hitherto done; and the authorities would attempt to enfeeble it as much as was possible in the circumstances of
British rule. The problem, as the *Statesman and Friend of India* put
it, was that 'the outspokenness of the Vernacular papers is a real danger because they approximately state truths as to the shortcomings
of our administration.'[244] The shortcomings, indeed, were endemic in
the administration.

III

Another aspect of the divergence between the principles and the
practice of British rule referred to the jurisdiction of Indian officials
over European British subjects in criminal cases. Equality before the
law, as contained in the Charter Act of 1833, had been negated, in this
as in other respects, by the requirements of foreign rule and by the
sense of superiority betrayed by the members of the ruling community. For years, as we have seen,[245] Indians had agitated for the removal of this discrimination without succeeding in the face of European
antagonism.

The matter came to a head when Ripon decided to do away with
this discriminative privilege. He was first drawn to it by the recom-
mendation of the Bengal government to appoint some Europeans to
the subordinate executive service. This contravention of the official
resolution to appoint only Indians to the uncovenanted service, except in certain specified departments, was necessitated by the settlement of Europeans in certain parts of the mofussil and the ineligibility
of Indians to try them outside the presidency towns. Instead, in accordance with the tenor of his Indian policy, Ripon directed the legislative department to reconsider if Indian magistrates could rather not
be 'invested with the powers of a Justice of the Peace'.[246]

Less than two years later, Behari Lal Gupta (1849-1916), one of

243. Secretary of state to the governor-general, 28 Jan. 1881, in Philips, ed., *op. cit.*, p. 116. The governor-general also thought likewise; see Home Department, Public Proceedings, B, Jun. 1885, Nos. 269-72, K.W.
244. Home Department, Judicial Proceedings, B, Oct. 1878, Nos. 161-69.
245. See chapter 2.
246. Home Department, Establishment Proceedings, A, Aug. 1880, No. 44.

the four Indians who had qualified for the covenanted civil service in 1869, represented to the government that the existing law would 'give rise to an invidious distinction and to many practical inconveniences' after Indians had become district magistrates and sessions judges. He proposed the extension of criminal jurisdiction over Europeans to Indians holding either of these offices. Fowarding this note, Eden recommended necessary alterations in the law.[247]

The reactions of the local administrations to the proposed change contained sufficient warning against disturbing the *status quo*.[248] D.F. Carmichael (1830-1903), of the Madras council, recalled how practically nothing had been done in this connection because 'the British Lion, a vulgar brute, no doubt, has wagged his tail and roared'. If disturbed again, the lion would act similarly. The Indian covenanted civilian was received cordially by his European colleagues, but not by the European 'Society'. They proposed him at the 'Club' but the 'Society' blackballed him. The lower orders of Britons in India would not trust him in regard to their personal liberty. The surrender of this privilege would 'cause great exasperation, perhaps accompanied with much political mischief', among 'the privileged class' of European British subjects.[249] Like his colleague, W. Hudleston (?-1894) also anticipated 'an outcry that would aggravate race friction far more than the removal of the *already existing* disability attaching to a small number of officials would allay it'.[250] The chief commissioner of Coorg favoured the existing jurisdiction for political reasons.[251]

Within the viceroy's own council, James Gibbs (1825-86), though inclined to favour the proposed alteration, predicted that 'it would raise a great "howl" amongst the planters of Bengal especially, as also from many Europeans in private positions scattered about the country, and the result might be too strong for the Government to resist.' General J. F. Wilson (1820-86) and Hope opposed any change. Ilbert (1841-1924) alone agreed with Ripon that perpetual 'tinkering at these race questions' being unwise, the subject, 'if dealt with at all, ought to be dealt with in a final manner.'[252]

Eventually, sanction was obtained from the secretary of state for legislation to empower the local governments to confer the power of trying, even outside the presidency towns, European British sub-

247. Note by Gupta, 30 Jan. 1882, Home Department, Judicial Proceedings, A, Sep. 1882, Nos. 221-22.
248. The claim of Wolf, *op. cit.*, vol. II, pp. 119-20, and S. Gopal, *The Viceroyalty of Lord Ripon*, Oxford, 1953, p. 129, that Ripon was given little warning of hostile reaction to the proposed change is untenable.
249. Minute by Carmichael, 15 May 1882, Home Department, Judicial Proceedings, A, Sep. 1882, No. 224. This minute is noticed by Gopal, *op. cit.*, p. 129.
250. Minute by Hudleston, 16 May 1882, Home Department, Judicial Proceedings, A, Sep. 1882, No. 224.
251. *Ibid.*, No. 235.
252. *Ibid.*, K.W

jects upon any member of the covenanted and statutory civil service and also of the Non-Regulation Commissions provided he was already exercising first class magisterial powers.[253]

The European community in India was meanwhile getting uncomfortable owing to what it regarded as Ripon's policy of placing 'the native on the *Gaddi'*.[254] The bond that united all classes of resident Europeans was their 'absolute unwillingness' 'to be tried by persons not of their own race'. The prejudice, though unreasonable, was real, and its disregard liable to produce perpetual disturbance.[255]

Already in a contumacious frame of mind, resident Europeans condemned the Bill moved by Ilbert as 'an unexpected and apparently unnecessary piece of legislation'.[256] Their latent passions erupted in violent eloquence and rabid racialism that reminded of 1857. Reason was transfused to the passionate tirades that came spontaneously to a community which felt outraged by an attack on its cherished interests and sentiments. Involving 'momentous interests', the matter was 'not one in respect of which Englishmen will be content to accept arguments based on mere convenience, or references to a policy of factitious equality'.[257] Even the *Indian Daily News,* which, rising above 'class questions and race questions', had found the measure inevitable, sympathised with the fear of Europeans about the failure of justice, and with their pride which would submit to being tried by nobody but Europeans.[258]

Even the sound official logic that the Bill proposed to do away with a chronic anomaly which had all this while characterised British rule did not cut much ice with non-official Europeans. It was countered by reference to the underlying illogicality of British imperialism. The raj was 'an anomaly in itself, not in this or that point of detail, but in every point'. Refusal to face this fact logically implied the abandonment of India.[259]

Europeans saw in the proposed measure 'but the thin end of the wedge' which would lead to the acceptance of 'the Indian demand for the grant of jurisdiction to all judicial officers'.[260] To avert the eventuality, an Anglo-Indian and European Defence Association was founded,[261] and a movement initiated to convene a protest meeting

253. Government of India to the secretary of state, 9 Sep. 1882, *ibid.,* No. 239; secretary of state to the government of India, 7 Dec. 1882, *ibid.,* A, Jan. 1883, No. 27.
254. Gibbs to Ripon, 17 Apr. 1883, in Wolf, *op. cit.* vol. II, p. 129.
255. C. Gonne to Tyabji, 25 Apr. 1883, *Tyabji Papers.*
256. *Englishman,* 6 Feb. 1883.
257. *Ibid.,* 10 Feb. 1883.
258. *Indian Daily News,* 5 Feb. 1883.
259. *Times,* 5 Feb. 1883, in *The Criminal Procedure Code Amendment Bill,* Calcutta, 1883, p. 109.
260. *Englishman,* 23 Feb. 1883.
261. *Ibid.,* 30 Mar. 1883.

against the Bill. The meeting, held in the Calcutta Town Hall on 28 February 1883, set the tone for the European agitation. 'The great Hall, the aisles, the ante-room, and even the gallery and platform were densely crowded.' The meeting was representative 'of all European nationalities, and of all walks and conditions of life'; in fact, of the whole Christian community 'united in an eager and determined opposition'. It symbolised 'the great opening of a revolution' 'when men would go any length for their rights, and dare and do anything for principle.'[262] Appeals were made simultaneously to the purse and the honour of Europeans, especially the honour of their wives and sisters, some of whom were present at the meeting. Distortion and exaggeration were employed to draw a monstrous picture of Indian character. Contrast between the two 'races' was magnified at the expense of Indians to ensure a powerful effect.

At this meeting, notorious for vitriolic ebullition, the most ebullient tirade came from Branson, a Eurasian barrister. Mixing rabid rhetoric with a modicum of reason, the Calcutta barrister evinced a keen perception of the psychology of his audience. Deprivation of liberty, he said, affected everyone; but it affected those more who had an innate love of freedom. Reputation, too, was dear to everyone; but it was dearer to an Englishman, who belonged to a free-born nation 'glorying in the tradition of conquerors', than to an Indian whose grovelling nation was 'steeped in the traditions of the conquered'. The Muslim hated the Englishman, and Branson would not talk of him. But if the Hindu claimed equal privileges and possessed any love for his country or freedom or any attribute which the Englishman honoured, he must hate his foreign rulers. Branson rounded off his argument with the question:[263]

> Under these circumstances, is it wonderful that we should protest, that we should say these men are not fit to rule over us; these men cannot judge us, and we will not be judged by them? (Loud cheering and waving of hats for some minutes.)

The way Branson was 'cheered and recheered and again cheered and still cheered' was for Europeans 'such a reply as no Governor-General has yet received.'[264]

Being 'the first note of indiscriminate abuse and vilification' against Indians,[265] the Town Hall assault on the Bill forced upon them the compulsion of organising a counter-agitation. On the passage of the Bill depended not only the redress of a particular grievance, but also the general drift of British Indian policy. If this 'keystone' of

262. *Supplement to Indian Daily News*, 1 Mar. 1883.
263. *Supplement to Englishman*, 1 Mar. 1883.
264. *Supplement to Indian Daily News*, 1 Mar. 1883.
265. *Indian Mirror*, 17 Jun. 1883.

India's 'further political progress' was destroyed, 'the scheme of local self-government, and all the other measures for improvement, based on liberal principles, must find their way to the limbo of the world.'[266] Its opponents, under the ideological leadership of James Stephen, had dismissed the royal proclamation of 1858 as irrelevant to practical politics and advocated the policy of might.[267] 'Sheer self-defence',[268] therefore, demanded that Indians should throw in all their weight behind Ripon to prevent the miscarriage of his liberal policy.[269] At the instance of the Bombay leaders,[270] meetings were held all over the country to support Ripon's policy and to memorialise the Empress for the extension of his viceroyalty. It was known that such an extension would not be possible; but the agitation was designed to impart 'a great degree of moral support to the policy with which the present viceroy is identified.'[271]

Though the Indian Press wrote strongly, and at least one Indian, Lal Mohan Ghosh, returned the charges of Branson with interest,[272] it was from the beginning a defensive and losing battle for Indians. It was inevitably so in view of the existing state of national development and the superior organisation of resident Europeans, including most of the civilians. Even Thompson, the successor of Eden, who had recommended the proposed alteration, opposed the Bill. It was publicly alleged that the editor of the *Englishman* had become 'a member of the Lt. Governor of Bengal's inner cabinet'.[273]

The initial reaction of Indians was one of disappointment. They resented that the Bill was 'a small measure'[274] that stopped short of putting 'the two races on a footing of perfect equality'.[275] But soon, when even this small advance seemed to be threatened, they had to defend it against 'the senseless storm' raised by the Chambers of

266. *Native Opinion*, 15 Jul. 1883.
267. *Ibid.*, 18 Nov. 1883; *Indian Spectator*, 9, 16, 23 Dec. 1883; *Hindoo Patriot*, 17 Dec. 1883; *Indian Mirror*, 30 Mar. 1883, found Stephen's views narrow and illiberal, not unexpected in a man who could betray 'extreme perversion of the moral sense'.
268. *Indian Mirror*, 17 Jun. 1883.
269. See speech by P. M. Mehta, 28 Apr. 1883, Chintamani ed., *Speeches and writings of P. M. Mehta*, pp. 158-63.
270. Naoroji to Tyabji, 8 Feb. 1883, *Tyabji Papers*.
271. *Indian Mirror*, 29 Apr. 1883.
272. See Ghosh's Dacca speech, 29 Mar. 1883, *ibid.*, 3 Apr. 1883. Ghosh stung the European community with his speech; after this were 'drawn down on his head the abuse and ridicule which were so lavishly bestowed before upon Mr. Gupta'; *ibid.*, 29 Apr. 1883.
273. *Ibid.*, 17 Jun. 1883. For an exploitation of the case against the Bill, see government of Bengal to the government of India, 22 Jun. 1883, Buckland, *op. cit.*, vol. II, pp. 776-87. Sir Augustus Rivers Thompson (1829-90) was lieutenant-governor of Bengal from 1882 to 1887.
274. *Hindoo Patriot*, 12 Feb. 1883.
275. *Native Opinion*, 18 Feb. 1883.

Commerce, English and Anglo-Indian journals and 'unprincipled men like Messrs. Branson, Keswick and Company'.[276] In England also somebody or the other was every week 'taking up the cudgels against Lord Ripon'.[277] Crowded meetings were, therefore, held in Calcutta, Bombay, Poona and other cities to support the Bill.[278] The leaders of Bengal and Bombay established regular communications between themselves in order to present a united front. Manmohan Ghosh wrote to Mehta, Naoroji, Mandlik and Tyabji that he was sending copies of a 'memorial which it has become absolutely necessary for us to submit to the Viceroy in connection with the Ilbert Bill'. He added that the 'Government would like to have the memorial very *influentially* signed' by 4 January 1884.[279]

But the pressure on the viceroy was mounting, and a compromise seemed imminent. Indians naturally disliked this. Even to the *Indian Spectator*, with its advocacy of a sober approach to the problem, compromise was inconceivable.[280] But Indians could do little beyond hoping that the viceroy would 'persevere in protecting the rights of natives'.[281] This was not to be. While the *Indu Prakash* was complaining of delay in passing the Bill,[282] an agreement was being worked out through Auckland Colvin's mediation. It was decided that though no distinction would be made between European and Indian district magistrates and sessions judges, European British subjects would be entitled to claim a jury at least half of which consisted of Europeans.[283]

The first Indian reaction to this 'peace with dishonour'[284] was that 'a political blunder of a very grave character',[285] it was 'like a sudden rebound on the part of Lord Ripon'.[286] Surendranath Banerji even 'let slip the *gros mot* of "revolution" in regard to it'.[287] In spite of this humiliation, however, Indians were obliged by their helplessness to take a realistic view and make the best of a lost case. The telegram sent by Manmohan Ghosh to seek the advice of the Bombay leaders sums up the Indian attitude. It read:[288]

276. *Native Opinion*, 25 Feb., 4, 11, 18, 25 Mar. 1883; *Indu Prakash*, every issue from 19 Feb. to 19 Mar. 1883.
277. *Ibid.*, 8 Jul. 1883.
278. *Ibid.*, 29 Apr., 20 May, 9 Sep. 1883.
279. Ghosh to Mehta, 21 Dec. 1883, *Mehta Papers*, reel I.
280. *Indian Spectator*, 8 Jul. 1883.
281. *Native Opinion*, 29 Jul. 1883.
282. *Indu Prakash*, 17 Dec. 1883.
283. Buckland, *op. cit.*, vol. II, pp. 788-89. Sir Auckland Colvin (1838-1908) had come back from Egypt where he had been comptroller-general, 1880-82, to be finance member in the supreme council.
284. *Hindoo Patriot*, 24 Dec. 1883.
285. *Native Opinion*, 23 Dec. 1883.
286. *Indu Prakash*, 24 Dec. 1883.
287. Blunt, *op. cit.*, p. 109.
288. Telegram from Ghosh to Mandlik, 25 Dec. 1883, *Mehta Papers*, reel I.

Concordat made under extraordinary pressure. Disapproved strongly; but if we assume hostile attiude, Viceroy surely resigns and Liberals damaged. Think consequences and telegraph advice.

Nor could the Bombay leaders offer any alternative to this contrast between private feelings and public conduct. They immediately wired back the advice 'to uphold Lord Ripon in any course he deems proper to follow.'[289] The *Mahratta* and the *Indian Spectator* pathetically attempted to glean from the wreck of the Ilbert Bill its basic principle and argued that this was a great victory.[290]

The make-believe apart, Indians in reality felt angry and let down. They had not given up the idea of protesting against the way the controversy had been resolved. They would hit the others hardest without deserting the viceroy.[291] Always endeavouring to do them justice, he had been 'much disheartened by the feebleness of his own Councillors' and pressurised, among others, by that 'frigid half-hearted creature', Kimberley.[292] But Indians were powerless where the well-meaning proconsul had submitted.

The controversy was for Indians a painful but significant eye-opener. It imposed upon them new political necessities. After the promise of a substantial reform, they had gained 'nothing except abuse maintained for a whole year'.[293] What they had lost was 'due to the European agitation'. What they needed was an organisation like the Anglo-Indian and European Defence Association.[294] Though the agitation which had given birth to it was over, the Defence Association continued 'with its vast organisation' and Rs. 1,50,000. It was meant to promote 'the interests of the Anglo-Indian community which might often conflict with' Indian interests. Instead of trusting to spasmodic efforts, it became more than ever necessary to consistently look after Indian interests both in India and in England. Even the willing co-operation of the viceroy was in itself of little avail. However well-meaning and highly placed, no individual could overpower the existing set-up on the perpetuation of which depended the safety of vested Anglo-Indian interests. Nothing short of united action by a strong national organisation could help Indians. The idea had long been in the air. Its materialisation could be postponed no further. The campaign for a National Fund was accordingly started by the Indian As-

289. Telegram from Mandlik to Ghosh, 25 Dec. 1893, *ibid.*
290. *Indian Spectator* and *Mahratta*, 30 Dec. 1883, *Voice of India*, 15 Jan. 1884, pp. 17-8.
291. Mandlik to Mehta, 27 Dec. 1883, *Mehta Papers*, reel 1.
292. Malabari to Mehta, 5 Jan. 1884, *ibid.* Slowly the entire Indian Press veered round to this view; see *Voice of India*, 31 Jan. 1884, p. 44; 15 Feb. 1884, p. 86; 29 Feb. 1884, p. 122. Kimberley (1826-1902) was at the time serving the first of his three terms at the Indian Office, 1882-85.
293. Speech by R.L. Mitra, 7 May 1884, quoted in Bagal, *op cit.*, p.69.
294. *Native Opinion*, 20 Jan., 3 Feb. 1884.

sociation,[295] and, with certain suggestions, supported in Bombay.[296] Nor was it an accident that the first National Conference was organised in the year of the Ilbert Bill controversy. It was intended to be 'the reply of educated India' to the European agitation.[297]

295. *Seventh Annual Report of the Indian Association, 1883*, pp. 4-5.
296. *Native Opinion*, 3 Feb. 1884.
297. Banerjea, *op. cit.*, p. 86.

5   Dependence and Disillusionment

A subjective phenomenon produced by objective factors, national consciousness emerged primarily in response to a process of social cohesion that cut across traditional solidarities within Indian society. The new social groupings that came into being represented the conjunction of perceived material interests. They appealed to the egoism of the individual which simultaneously performed a cohesive and a disruptive social role. It not only facilitated the formation of new groups, but also introduced inter-group tensions within Indian society. At the same time, material group interests, whether large or narrow, were also adversely affected by British rule. These were rationalised as national interests and contradistinguished from what came to be looked upon as British or imperial interests. Gradually, and irrevocably, these clashes of interests tended to be viewed as the manifestation of a fundamental dichotomy between Indian aspirations and imperial designs.

That the first loyalty of at least the politically awakening Indians was egoistic is evidenced by the fact that their discovery of a fundamental conflict between Indian and British interests received its initial impetus from the taxation measures of the government. Of the two contradictions that taxation brought to the surface, one was between different groups within Indian society, and the other between the rulers and the ruled. It was after the post-1857 financial exigencies had occasioned direct taxation that the natural human aversion to material deprivation prompted those Indians who felt threatened by it to examine the mechanism of British Indian administration. But they also felt tempted to seek relief at the expense of other sections in the society. Reactions to the income, the license, and the salt taxes testify that alliances emereged with a fluid membership which swelled or shrank as individuals freely chose sides depending upon which tax had to be defended or decried in consonance with their self-interest.

But those Indians who felt threatened by taxation not only tried to pass the burden on to other sections, they also undertook to scrutinise the sources of expenditure which had necessitated additional burdens. Rightly or wrongly, but naturally, they found the expenditure excessive, and beyond the needs and resources of their country. It was only natural that they should, as a sequel, realise the necessity of sharing control of the exchequer. First-hand experience of how the shoe pinched, and not mere treatises on political economy or the American War of Independence, brought home to them the lesson of no taxation without representation.

Implicit in the scrutiny of taxation and expenditure was some recognition of the kind of relationship obtaining between India and Britain. This was the genesis of 'drain' which, by symbolising subjection, shaped generations of Indian thinking. Feelings were further exacerbated by the imperial scheme of priorities as revealed by the contrast between official stinginess and vacillation during frequent visitations of famine, and the heaviness—that is how contemporary Indians viewed it — of expenditure, particularly the military expenditure and the unjust apportionment of part of it between India and Britain. Whatever doubts lingered were set at rest by the official tariff policy. Never, perhaps, had the politically conscious Indians felt the rub of dependence with such painful helplessness as at the time of the repeal of the import duties.

As the clash between Indian and British interests evolved in the economic sphere, the irreconcilability of Indian aspirations and imperial exigencies emerged from the working of official policy in regard to the employment of Indians, their legal equality with the European British subjects—especially the anti-climactic Ilbert Bill concordat—, and the freedom of expression.

Material self-interest did bring people together. But the alliances it produced were rather uncertain and unstable. Individuals freely gravitated towards and away from them. The very force responsible for the formation of new social unities also restricted their cohesiveness. For if self-interest could impel a person into a group, so could it also impel him out of the same group. So strong, in fact, could be adherence to personal interests that while most Indians welcomed the enhanced import duties of 1859 as the redress of an old injustice, Ram Gopal Ghosh, hailed as the Demosthenese of India but a businessman none the less, lent his powerful voice to the resident Europeans' opposition to the enhancement.[1]

Social unities based on economic ties were yet nascent. They lacked the external compulsion and the internal authority necessary

1. *Bengal Hurkaru.* 30 Mar. 1859.

for enforcing the requisite measure of conformism. This was natural. Material interests by themselves could not have immediately provided stable alternative units of social cohesion. Complementally, they could also not have performed a speedy disruptive role in regard to the traditional units of social cohesion. In so far as they affected but a part of an Indian's life and left untouched some of his vital psychosocial needs, material interests could have been completely effective neither in their cohesive nor in their disruptive role.

Though deriving substantially from material self-interest, national consciousness was deprived, at least during the early years of its emergence, of a strong organisational base by the fissiparous motivation provided by self-interest. This is evident from the fact that contemporary political associations, which had a causal relationship with national consciousness and acted as somewhat formal bases for interest articulation, possessed little power to discipline their members. Their weakness was symptomatic of the weakness of new social unities.

However material self-interest, in its cohesive role, was curbing its own freedom of motivation. The conjunction of interests it brought about also tended to induce a none too vague unity of sentiment, especially as greater awareness of the conflict between Indian and British interests invested the growing public opinion with a moral influence which it became progressively difficult to disregard. Thus the British Indian Association, even though its members were likely to benefit from the scheme, decided to oppose the statutory civil service. Similarly, unlike the late 1850s, the late 1870s had no Ram Gopal Ghosh who could, in order to promote his own interests, strike a discordant note on the tariff issue. It is a measure of the growing strength of public opinion that by the 1870s, instead of openly flouting it, people had to devise ways to circumvent it in order to be able to advance their own interests surreptitiously. An inexpensive, and effective, method of advocating nationalist views without forsaking self-interest was to draw an unobtrusive line between one's profession and practice. Thus Bharatendu Harish Chandra, to cite an example, could simultaneously preach *swadeshi* and promote the sales of his firm by advertising in his own *Magazine* that Messrs Harish Chandra and Brother had 'received various fresh goods direct from England per steamer *Cathay,* consisting of new and choicest novelties of the season that are not to be had in the Indian markets'.[2]

Traditional solidarities, on the contrary, possessed the advantage of external compulsion which rested on minatory sanctions, and of the suitably internalised responses of their members which ensured

2. *Haris Chandra Magazine.* 15 Jan. 1874.

that these sanctions were not too frequently resorted to. These responses, indeed, were being slowly dulled by the superimposition of a new kind of consciousness on the traditional thought processes as an inevitable result of the exposure of a growing number of Indians to a different cultural system; as also by the emergence of new social unities. But the non-availability of alternative arrangements which could cater to the totality of social needs perpetuated the hold of traditional unities. The facility of the hold, though, was gone. A variety of psycho-intellectual tensions followed, and the individual had to evolve a pattern of loyalties, and extend them, depending upon the issue at stake, to conflicting values, ideas and social unities. While his British mentors were moving towards intellectual certainty with the help of their faith in progress, the educated Indian was being overpowered by a schizophrenia that he barely understood.

In so far as it provided the bedrock of conservatism to hold Indian society together in the midst of disruptive forces, the traditional social anastomosis strengthened the emerging national consciousness. It gave the kind of emotional and psychological strength which, though indispensable, could not have come from mere conjunction of perceived material interests. It also enabled Indians to avoid being overwhelmed by a pervasive sense of inferiority which had followed in the wake of British claims of intellectual and racial superiority.

But the continuing importance of traditional unities in the life of the individual also weakened the secular potential of the emerging national consciousness, especially by constricting the area of operation of the organizations that provided an institutional base to this consciousness. A delicate situation was developing. While the projection of religious and sectional loyalties pertaining to the majority community would pass for culturally oriented national consciousness, that relating to the minority communities would be resented. The prejudice, too deep-rooted to operate at the conscious plane, eluded the grasp of even the most westernised Indians and coloured their vision.

The gradual unfolding of the fundamental contradiction between what were represented as Indian and British interests, of which national consciousness was a manifestation, seems to have acquired clarity by 1885. The conviction, at least on the plane of ideas, had crystallised that 'when opposed to purely British interests, Indian interests will always give way.'[3] There were dangerous moments of realisation that the redress of Indian grievances really implied the liquidation of alien rule.

3. *Proceedings of the First Indian National Congress*, p. 23.

But the logic of this realisation was not pressed, and national consciousness coexisted with loyalty to British rule. That the contrariety inherent in this coexistence was ignored even though the incompatibility of Indian and British interests had been laid bare reflected the predicament of politically articulate Indians. Disillusionment with British rule was complete. But dependence could not be dispensed with.

Keenly felt sense of dependence was not enough to lead to a demand for independence. A realistic appraisal of the Indian situation counselled continued British tutelage while efforts were afoot for facilitating a phased transition towards independence. The experience of 1857 had clearly ruled out an armed trial of strength with the British. Moreover, the immediate personal interests of the educated and politically conscious Indians were linked with British rule. The logic of the understanding of the reality of foreign rule was thus partially, and temporarily, neutralised. The march from the distant periphery to the centre of power had of necessity to be long.

The acceptance of this counsel was also made possible by the persistence of faith in the British. It was chiefly due to English education and to the structure of British control over India that this faith survived in spite of progressive disillusionment with the British during the quarter century preceding 1885. By making its Indian recipients psychologically and intellectually dependent upon itself, and by projecting an ideal image of British character — howsoever it might get sullied as a result of stay in India —, English education blurred the perception of the reality of British imperialism. And the structure of British control delayed the consummation of the perception by dangling the prospect of justice from British parliament and electorate even after faith in the Anglo-Indian authorities had been destroyed.

Maybe Indians needed faith in the British for sheer psychological survival. Facing squarely the contrariety between national consciousness and aspirations on the one hand and loyalism on the other would have meant confrontation with dependence in its utter nakedness with little hope of emancipation in the foreseeable future. It might have also heightened their awareness of their own petty selfishness. Ambivalence at least permitted the anticipation of a passage from a benevolent tutelage to self-dependence. Hence the tardiness of loss of faith in the British.

The first to be witten off were the Anglo-Indian civilians. They were described as 'the Praetorian guards of Imperial Rome, too strong for the Government which they serve'.[4] Whatever trust the exalted

4. *Bengalee*, 5 Jan. 1878.

office of the viceroy could command was destroyed by Lytton's sub-servience to a political party and by Ripon's inability to carry through his reforms. Yet, Indians hoped for sympathy from the British in Britain.

But imperialism is corrosive of faith in it. The Conservatives, owing to their fortuitous association with the proclamation of 1858, were initially trusted; and the Liberals generally condemned as be-longing to 'the annexationist school'.[5] The Tory image, however, was tarnished by the way Salisbury and his protege, Lytton, implement-ed policies that rode roughshod over Indian feelings and interests. At this stage was produced a swift change in favour of the Liberals as a consequence of their attitude towards the Vernacular Press Act and the Afghan war. It was in a state of disappointment, agitation and expectancy that Indians welcomed the Liberal accession to power in 1880 and looked forward to the reversal of the Lyttonian regime.[6] The performance of the Liberals disillusioned even their best Indian ad-mirers. The Arms Act stayed on to 'disfigure the Statute Book'. The civil service rules remained unaltered. An invidious distinction was created by reducing the salaries of Indian judges; which meant that 'for doing the same sort of work with equal ability and efficiency, the Native of India is to get only two-thirds of the pay of the European. In spite of being 'a barefaced subordination of Indian interests to those of Manchester', the cotton duties were altogether abolished. The gov-ernment, moreover, was disinclined to concede to Indians the right of representation in the councils.[7] The saddling of India with the par-tial cost of the Egyptian campaign further added to the disenchant-ment with the Liberals.[8]

It was clear that in the event of a clash between Indian and Bri-tish interests Indians had little to choose between the Conservatives and the Liberals. Justice could be expected of neither of the British parties. Nor had either of them done total good or total harm to India. In the face of this dilemma even the benefits accruing from the Liberals and the damage done by the Conservatives offered little ground for believing that alliance with the Liberals would be entire-ly beneficial.

5. *Native Opinion*, 17 Mar. 1876.
6. For instance, on 5 May 1880 a public meeting, organised by the Indian As-sociation, expressed 'the rejoicings of the Indian community at the result of the elections', and petitioned parliament for the repeal of Lytton's 're-pressive measures' and for 'the removal of the grievances of the people'. *Fourth Annual Report of the Indian Association, 1879-80*, pp. 1-2, 14-32.
7. A. Banerji, ed., *op. cit.*, pp. 109-12.
8. Even Jotendra Mohan Tagore, the cautious zemindar who had been gene-rously patronised by the British rulers, lamented Gladstone's apostasy and wondered that 'any man should be so base'. Blunt, *op. cit.*, p. 96.

Serious division of opinion existed among Indians about the wisdom of making India a party question in England. As the general election of 1880 approached, the Sarvajanik Sabha, feeling that on 'no previous occasion was the welfare and progress of India so dependent upon the choice of the electors of Great Britain and Ireland', canvassed for the Liberals in the name of 'the unrepresented millions of the inhabitants of India'.[9] This was understandable in view of the experience of Lytton's viceroyalty. And yet the Indian Association, which sent Lal Mohan Ghosh to present Indian grievances before the British electors and later on welcomed the Liberal return to power, played safe and supported candidates who had been interested in Indian affairs.[10] Speaking from personal experience after his return from England, Ghosh advocated alliance with the Liberals. But disagreement on the issue continued.[11]

The choice, difficult enough for Indians in 1880, was further complicated as a result of disillusionment with the Liberals during Ripon's viceroyalty. Though aware that it was 'in Parliament that our chief battles have to be fought',[12] on the eve of the 1885 general election, Indians were sceptical of alignment with a particular party. In vain did Pherozeshah Mehta plead that the 'only salvation' lay in bringing all Indian questions to the 'searching criticism of party warfare in England.'[13] Eventually a compromise was evolved that irrespective of party affiliations candidates in Britain should be supported or op-

9. *Quarterly Journal of the Poona Sarvajanik Sabha*, vol. II, no. 4, pp. 132-33.
10. *Third Annual Report of the Indian Association*, pp. 16-8.
11. Ghosh said: 'You condemn the Afghan war; you disapprove of the Vernacular Press Act; you object to repressive legislation, and to a policy of tawdry Imperialism which begins in fireworks and ends in burdensome taxation (cheers); and do you think you can possibly make the slightest impression upon the thick phalanx of ministerialists, who have over and over again supported the action of the Government in these respects?' Ghosh added that the Liberal party had 'ever stood up for justice, and advocated the right of the weak and the oppressed'. It seemed to him logical that having abolished the slave trade, emancipated the Roman Catholics and disestablished the Irish Church, 'this great party should be the first to extend us the right hand of fellowship and to plead our cause.' But welcoming Ghosh on behalf of the people of western India, Nanabhai Byramji Jijibhai said: 'The cause of India is the cause of principles and not of parties. It is to the Conservative Liberals as much as to the Liberal Conservatives that India must look and does look for the advancement of her interests'. A. Banerji, *op. cit.*, pp. 39-41, 73.
12. Naoroji's speech at the Bombay Presidency Association, 29 Sep. 1885, Parekh, ed., *op. cit.*, p. 293.
13. *Manuscript Minute Book* (Bombay Presidency Association), vol. I, p. 202.

posed by Indians on the basis of their known views on Indian affairs.[11]

The compromise, inasmuch as it disregarded the mechanism of British political life, betrayed the paradoxicality of the Indian political situation. In spite of disillusionment with the centres and wielders of power, the lack of alternatives consequent upon the prematurity of direct action prolonged Indian dependence on British parliament. But historical experience dissuaded Indians from burning their boats to cast in their lot with one party. In the event, they hoped for the impossible; their understanding of the meaning of Indo-British connection notwithstanding, they expected the British voters to cut across party affiliations for the sake of India. The verdict of the electorate exposed the futility of the expectation.

Along with, and as a result of, these experiences grew the need for participation in the governance of the country. Early in the 1850s, the *Hindoo Patriot* had written: 'What we want is not the introduction of a small independent element in the existing Council, but an Indian Parliament.'[15] In the circumstances then prevailing, this was crying for the moon. Even the small independent element was not granted. Rather, the system of nomination was so used by the government as to allow Indians 'only a farce of a voice',[16] and fill the councils with 'magnificent nobodies'.[17] These 'native non-representatives'[18] demonstrated that in 'the utter absence of any system of popular representation in the Government of India' lay 'the very origin and fountainhead of all our grievances'.[19] No administrative reform, moreover, could be real without admitting Indians to the executive councils also.[20]

The matter, which had been earlier pressed spasmodically, was seriously taken up by the Indian Association. Affirming that representative government constituted the 'great question of the future', it decided to appeal to 'public opinion in the country and to the enlightened sentiments of our rulers in England.' It also resolved   to

14. The compromise, suggested by Dadabhai Naoroji, was accepted by the Indian political associations which decided to join hands to issue a number of appeals to the British electors on behalf of India. See *Indian Association Annual Reports and Leaflets, 1882-86.* The volume contains 14 leaflets. Also see *Manuscript Minute Book* (Bombay Presidency Association), vol. I. pp. 21, 34-5, 37-8, 40-1, 44-5. For Naoroji's argument and the list of candidates proposed to be supported and opposed by Indians, see Parekh, ed., *op. cit.,* pp. 292-301.

15. Sen-Gupta, ed., *op. cit.,* p. 215.

16. Naoroji, 'On the Commerce of India', 15 Feb. 1871, Parekh, ed., *op. cit.,* p. 119.

17. A. Banerji, ed., *op. cit.,* p. 83.

18. *Native Opinion,* 24 Jan. 1869.

19. A. Banerji, ed., *op. cit.,* p. 12.

20. *Hindoo Patriot,* 16 Mar. 1868.

'raise a fund for purposes of agitation' which was bound to 'extend over years'.[21]

Nothing, however, could be obtained beyond some liberalisation of the mode of nomination during Ripon's tenure. This could not satisfy Indian aspirations. The Indian National Congress demanded that the 'first reform should be to have the power to tax ourselves.' This meant that Indians wished 'to have the actual government of India transferred from England to India under the simple controlling power of the Secretary of State and of Parliament'.[22] This government, it was clarified, would not be the autocracy of the Anglo-Indian civilians. It would be conducted by representative councils with control over taxation and legislation.[23]

Here was a realisation, even if inchoate, that the interests of the rulers and the ruled were so divergent that self-government alone could remedy the ills of the existing system. The rudimentary stage of national development, however, ruled out immediate severance of the British connection. A distant reality as yet, experience had taught those Indians who cared for these matters to aim at the control of their government. The beginning of the crystallisation of goal in the midst of an apparently hopeless situation, which seemed to elude the search for effective means, represented the growth of national consciousness between 1858 and 1885.

The search for means, however, was on. Perception of the identity of grievances and disappointment with those of whom justice had been expected underscored the need for combined action. 'One of the great wants of India', wrote the *Native Opinion*, 'is national unity'.[24] Even at the height of Indian optimism following the Liberal success in 1880, the *Opinion* had warned that it would be 'foolish to look either to Liberals or Conservatives for what India wants — a good and constitutional government.' Self-reliance alone could help: 'It is the native energy, and native talent that will have to work out the salvation of India.'[25] The 'increasing wants' of India had rendered obsolete the pattern of 'concession on the one part and slight effort on the other'. A 'central unity' was instead required that would transcend the existing political associations and concentrate their efforts.[26] An annual convention of public spirited people drawn from different parts of the country seemed 'a great political desideratum'. Representations on matters affecting Indian interests had been more or less re-

21. *Third Annual Report of the Indian Association*, pp. 22-3.
22. *Proceedings of the First Indian National Congress*, pp. 33, 37.
23. Parekh, ed., *op. cit.*, p. 324.
24. *Native Opinion*, 3 Nov. 1872.
25. *Ibid.*, 18 Apr. 1880.
26. *Ibid.*, 6 Sep. 1885.

gularly made; 'being characteristically sectional', they had lacked 'what such a vastly united assemblage would gain in effectiveness'.[27]

The lead in this respect was taken by the Indian Association which had, 'since its inception', 'aimed at the creation of an active political life in the country'.[28] In 1883 it succeeded in organising a national conference with a view to providing 'a much-desired opportunity for the interchange of views on the many questions which are now agitating the national mind, and for the settlement of a common programme of action in relation thereto.'[29] Despite the presence of persons from different parts of the country, it was predominantly a gathering of Bengalis.[30] But it did discuss questions agitating the national mind. It was hoped that the conference, 'the beginning of a great experiment', would become an annual institution, and pave 'the way for that thorough concert in our political programme and that perfect union in the execution of that programme, upon which alone must rest the hopes of our political advancement.'[31]

The idea of a national body remained unrealised. The national conference neither became an annual convention nor could it attract the foremost public men of the country. The quest continued. In 1885 it stood on the threshold of realisation. The fact that the second national conference, convened in 1885 by the Indian Association, and the first Indian National Congress separately discussed the same issues and arrived at similar conclusions showed the unity of views among sections of educated Indians. But the fact that two such gatherings were simultaneously organized emphasised the lack of unity of action among them. As the *Native Opinion* suggested, 'a joint conference might as well have been held.'[32]

The Indian self-image in 1858 was that of an assemblage of 'so many nationalities and castes'.[33] By 1885 it had been considerably modified to accommodate the belief that India had 'the makings' of a nation.[34] There did exist 'diverging interests' that rendered 'common action impossible on *all* occasions'. But there also had emerged 'questions of an imperial and national interest' in respect of which Indians could 'throw aside all petty differences', and put their 'shoulders to the wheel as one man.'[35] Increasing awareness of these questions had

27. *Ibid.*, 4 Jun. 1882.
28. *Sixth Annual Report of the Indian Association*, 1882, p. 5.
29. A. M. Bose to Mehta, 15 Dec. 1883, *Mehta Papers*, Reel 1.
30. Memorial of the Committee of the Indian Association to Ripon, Home Department, Judicial Proceedings, A, Jul. 1884, No. 103.
31. *Seventh Annual Report of the Indian Association*, 1883, pp. 12-3.
32. *Native Opinion*, 20 Dec. 1885.
33. *Hindoo Patriot*, 4 Jun. 1857.
34. *Indu Prakash*, 28 Dec. 1885.
35. *Hindoo Patriot*, 11 Jan. 1886.

brought about a new 'political phenomenon'.[36] This was the Indian
National Congress, which had signalled 'the cementing of the people
of India into a national organisation'.[37] Contemporary Indians could
now rejoice that 'at no very distant date the so-called hostile nationalities of India may, their Anglo-Indian friends notwithstanding,
unite for common political good.'[38]

Sanguine contemporary reactions to the new political phenomenon
notwithstanding, the process of unity initiated by the emerging national consciousness was not only still incipient, but also affected adversely by the very forces that had contributed largely towards making the phenomenon possible. Material self-interest certainly had become more of a cohesive force over the years. Yet, fissures
produced by narrow group interests had not disappeared. Unsupported by rapid economic development, the motivation provided
by material self-interest was unable to efface traditional group affiliations and create viable substitutes. National consciousness, in
such a situation, could scarcely produce a strong secular public life.
Indeed, it was itself influenced by the traditional loyalties of different sections of Indians, including their sectional cultural reasser-
tions.

36. *Indian Spectator*, 3 Jan. 1886.
37. *Indian Nation*, 4 Jan. 1886, in *Voice of India*, vol. 4, no. 1, p 49.
38. *Hindoo Patriot*, 11 Jan. 1886.